THE ENGLISH NOVEL

THE
ENGLISH NOVEL

BY

GEORGE SAINTSBURY

PROFESSOR OF ENGLISH LITERATURE IN THE
UNIVERSITY OF EDINBURGH

LONDON: J. M. DENT & SONS LTD.
BEDFORD STREET, STRAND   1913
NEW YORK: E. P. DUTTON & CO.

PREFACE

IT is somewhat curious that there is, so far as I know, no complete handling in English of the subject of this volume, popular and important though that subject has been. Dunlop's *History of Fiction*, an excellent book, dealt with a much wider matter, and perforce ceased its dealing just at the beginning of the most abundant and brilliant development of the English division. Sir Walter Raleigh's *English Novel*, a book of the highest value for acute criticism and grace of style, stops short at Miss Austen, and only glances, by a sort of anticipation, at Scott. The late Mr. Sidney Lanier's *English Novel and the Principle of its Development* is really nothing but a laudatory study of " George Eliot," with glances at other writers, including violent denunciations of the great eighteenth-century men. There are numerous monographs on parts of the subject: but nothing else that I know even attempting the whole. I should, of course, have liked to deal with so large a matter in a larger space: but one may and should "cultivate the garden" even if it is not a garden of many acres in extent. I need only add that I have endeavoured, not so much to give " reviews " of individual books and authors, as to indicate what Mr. Lanier took for the second part of his title, but did not, I think, handle very satisfactorily in his text.

I may perhaps add, without impropriety, that the composition of this book has not been hurried, and that I have taken all the pains I could, by revision and addition as it proceeded, to make it a complete survey of the Novel, as it has come from the hands of all the more important novelists, not now alive, up to the end of the nineteenth century.

GEORGE SAINTSBURY.

Christmas, 1912.

CONTENTS

THE ENGLISH NOVEL

CHAPTER I

THE FOUNDATION IN ROMANCE

ONE of the best known, and one of the least intelligible, facts of literary history is the lateness, in Western European Literature at any rate, of prose fiction, and the comparative absence, in the two great classical languages, of what we call by that name. It might be an accident, though a rather improbable one, that we have no Greek prose fiction till a time long subsequent to the Christian era, and nothing in Latin at all except the fragments of Petronius and the romance of Apuleius. But it can be no accident, and it is a very momentous fact, that, from the foundation of Greek criticism, "Imitation," that is to say "Fiction" (for it is neither more nor less), was regarded as not merely the inseparable but the constituent property of poetry, even though those who held this were doubtful whether poetry must necessarily be in verse. It is another fact of the greatest importance that the ancients who, in other forms than deliberate prose fiction, try to "tell a story," do not seem to know very well how to do it.

The *Odyssey* is, indeed, one of the greatest of all stories, it is the original romance of the West; but the *Iliad*, though a magnificent poem, is not much of a story. Herodotus can tell one, if anybody can, and Plato (or

A

Socrates) evidently could have done so if it had lain in his way: while the *Anabasis*, though hardly the *Cyropædia*, shows glimmerings in Xenophon. But otherwise we must come down to Lucian and the East before we find the faculty. So, too, in Latin before the two late writers named above, Ovid is about the only person who is a real story-teller. Virgil makes very little of his *story* in verse: and it is shocking to think how Livy throws away his chances in prose. No: putting the Petronian fragments aside, Lucian and Apuleius are the only two novelists in the classical languages before about 400 A.D.: and putting aside their odd coincidence of subject, it has to be remembered that Lucian was a Syrian Greek and Apuleius an African Latin. The conquered world was to conquer not only its conqueror, but its conqueror's teacher, in this youngest accomplishment of literary art.

It was probably in all cases, if not certainly, mixed blood that produced the curious development generally called Greek Romance. It is no part of our business to survey, in any detail, the not very numerous but distinctly interesting compositions which range in point of authorship from Longus and Heliodorus, probably at the meeting of the fourth and fifth centuries, to Eustathius in the twelfth. At one time indeed, when we may return to them a little, we shall find them exercising direct and powerful influence on modern European fiction, and so both directly and indirectly on English: but that is a time a good way removed from the actual beginning of our journey. Still, *Apollonius of Tyre*, which is probably the oldest piece of English prose fiction that we have, is beyond all doubt derived ultimately from a Greek original of this very class: and the class itself is an immense advance, in the novel direction, upon anything that we have before. It is on the one hand essentially a " romance of adventure," and on the other essentially a " love-story "—in senses to which we find little in classical literature to correspond in the one case and still less in the other. Instead of being, like *Lucius* and the *Golden Ass*, a tissue of stories essentially unconnected and little more than framed by the main tale, it is, though it may have a few episodes, an example of at least romantic unity throughout, with definite hero and definite heroine, the prominence and importance of the latter being specially noteworthy. It is in fact the first division of literature in which the heroine assumes the position of a protagonist. If it falls short in character, so do even later romances to a great extent: if dialogue is not very accomplished, that also was hardly to be thoroughly developed till the novel proper came into being. In the other two great divisions, incident and description, it is abundantly furnished. And, above all, the two great Romantic motives, Adventure and Love, are quite maturely present in it.

To pass to the deluge, and beyond it, and to come to close quarters with our proper division, the origin of Romance itself is a very debatable subject, or rather it is a subject which the wiser mind will hardly care to debate much. The opinion of the present writer—the result, at least, of many years' reading and thought—is that it is a result of the marriage of the older East and the newer (non-classical) West through the agency of the spread of Christianity and the growth and diffusion of the " Saint's Life." The beginnings of Hagiology itself are very uncertain: but what is certain is that they are very early: and that as the amalgamation or leavening of the Roman world with barbarian material proceeded, the spread of Christianity proceeded likewise. The *Vision of St. Paul*—one of the earliest examples and the starter it would seem, if not of the whole class of sacred Romances, at any rate of the large subsection devoted to Things after Death—has been put as early as " before 400 A.D." It would probably be difficult to date such legends as those of St. Margaret and St. Catherine *too* early, having regard to their intrinsic indications: and the vast cycle of Our Lady, though probably later, must have begun long before the modern languages were ready for it, while that of the Cross should be earlier still. And let it be remembered that these Saints' Lives, which are still infinitely good reading, are not in the least confined to homiletic necessities. The jejuneness and woodenness from which the modern religious story too often suffers are in no way chargeable upon all, or even many, of them. They have the widest range of incident—natural as well as supernatural: their touches of nature are indeed extended far beyond mere incident. Purely comic episodes are by no means wanting: and these, like the parallel passages in the dramatising of these very legends, were sure to lead to isolation of them, and to a secular continuation.

But, once more, we must contract the sweep, and quicken the pace to deal not with possible origins, but with actual results — not with Ancient or Transition literature, but with the literature of English in the department first of fiction generally and then, with a third and last narrowing, to the main subject of English fiction in prose.

The very small surviving amount, and the almost completely second-hand character, of Anglo-Saxon literature have combined to frustrate what might have been expected from another characteristic of it—the unusual equality of its verse and prose departments. We have only one—

not quite entire but substantive—prose tale in Anglo-Saxon, the version of the famous story of *Apollonius of Tyre*, which was to be afterwards declined by Chaucer, but attempted by his friend and contemporary Gower, and to be enshrined in the most certain of the Shakespearean " doubtfuls," *Pericles*. It most honestly gives itself out as a translation (no doubt from the Latin though there was an early Greek original) and it deals briefly with the subject. But as an example of narrative style it is very far indeed from being contemptible: and in passages such as Apollonius' escape from shipwreck, and his wooing of the daughter of Arcestrates, there is something which is different from style, and with which style is not always found in company—that faculty of telling a story which has been already referred to. Nor does this fail in the narrative portions of the prose Saints' Lives and Homilies, especially Aelfric's, which we possess; in fact it is in these last distinctly remarkable—as where Aelfric tells the tale of the monk who spied on St. Cuthbert's seaside devotions. The same faculty is observable in Latin work, not least in Bede's still more famous telling of the Caedmon story, and of the vision of the other world.

But these faculties have better chance of exhibiting themselves in the verse division of our Anglo-Saxon wreckage. *Beowulf* itself consists of one first-rate story and one second-rate but not despicable tale, hitched together more or less anyhow. The second, with good points, is, for us, negligible: the first is a " yarn " of the primest character. One may look back to the *Odyssey* itself without finding anything so good, except the adventures of the Golden Ass which had all the story-work of two mightiest literatures behind them. As literature on the other hand, *Beowulf* may be overpraised: it has been so frequently. But let anybody with the slightest faculty of " conveyance " tell the first part of the story to a tolerably receptive audience, and he will not doubt (unless he is fool enough to set the effect down to his own gifts and graces) about its excellence as such. There is character —not much, but enough to make it more than a *mere* story of adventure—and adventure enough for anything; there is by no means ineffectual speech—even dialogue—of a kind: and there is some effective and picturesque description. The same faculties reappear in such mere fragments as that of *Waldhere* and the " Finnsburgh " fight: but they are shown much more fully in the Saints' Lives— best of all in the *Andreas*, no doubt, but remarkably also (especially considering the slender amount of " happenings ") in the *Guthlac* and the *Juliana*. In fact the very fragments of Anglo-Saxon poetry, by a sort of approximation which they show to dramatic narrative and which with a few exceptions is far less present in the classics, foretell much more clearly and certainly than in the case of some other foretellings which have been detected in them, the future achievements of English literature in the department of fiction. *The Ruin* (the finest thing perhaps in all Anglo-Saxon) is a sort of background study for something that might have been much better than *The Last Days of Pompeii:* and *The Complaint of Deor*, in its allusion to the adventures of the smith Weland and others, makes one sorry that some one more like the historian of a later and decadent though agreeable Wayland the Smith, had not told us the tale that is now left untold. A crowd of fantastic imaginings or additions, to supply the main substance, and a certain common-sense grasp of actual conditions and circumstances to set them upon, and contrast them with— these are the great requirements of Fiction in life and character. You must mix prose and poetry to get a good romance or even novel. The consciences of the ancients revolted from this mixture of kinds; but there was no such revolt in the earlier moderns, and least of all in our own mediæval forefathers.

So few people are really acquainted with the whole range of Romance (even in English), or with any large part of it, that one may without undue presumption set down in part, if not in whole, to ignorance, a doctrine and position which we must now attack. This is that romance and novel are widely separated from each other; and that the historian of the novel is really straying out of his ground if he meddles with Romance. These are they who would make our proper subject begin with Marivaux and Richardson, or at earliest with Madame de La Fayette, who exclude Bunyan altogether, and sometimes go so far as to question the right of entry to Defoe. But the counter-arguments are numerous: and any one of them would almost suffice by itself. In the first place the idea of the novel arising so late is unnatural and unhistorical: these Melchisedecs without father or mother are not known in literature. In the second a pedantic insistence on the exclusive definition of the novel involves one practical inconvenience which no one, even among those who believe in it, has yet dared to face. You must carry your wall of partition along the road as well as across it: and write separate histories of Novel and Romance for the last two centuries. The present writer can only say that, though he has dared some tough adventures in literary history, he would altogether decline this. Without the help of the ants that succoured Psyche against Venus that heap would indeed be ill to sort.

But there is a third argument, less practical in appearance

but bolder and deeper, which is really decisive of the matter, though few seem to have seen it or at least taken it up. The separation of romance and novel—of the story of incident and the story of character and motive—is a mistake logically and psychologically. It is a very old mistake, and it has deceived some of the elect: but a mistake it is. It made even Dr. Johnson think Fielding shallower than Richardson; and it has made people very different from Dr. Johnson think that Count Tolstoi is a greater analyst and master of a more developed humanity than Fielding. As a matter of fact, when you have ex-cogitated two or more human beings out of your own head and have set them to work in the narrative (not the dramatic) way, you have made the novel *in posse*, if not *in esse*, from its apparently simplest development, such as *Daphnis and Chloe*, to its apparently most complex, such as the *Kreutzer Sonata* or the triumphs of Mr. Meredith. You have started the "Imitation"—the "fiction"—and *tout est là*. The ancients could do this in the dramatic way admirably, though on few patterns; in the poetical way as admirably, but again not on many. The Middle Ages lost the dramatic way almost entirely, but they actually improved the poetical on its narrative side, and the result was Romance. In every romance there is the germ of a novel and more; there is at least the suggestion and possibility of romance in every novel that deserves the name. In the Tristram story and the Lancelot cycle there are most of the things that the romancer of incident and the novelist of character and motive can want or can use, till the end of the world; and Malory (that "mere compiler" as some pleasantly call him) has put the possibilities of the latter and greater creation so that no one who has eyes can miss them. Nor *in the beginning* does it much or at all matter whether the vehicle was prose or verse. In fact they mostly wrote in verse because prose was not ready.

In the minor romances and tales (taking English versions only) from *Havelok* to *Beryn* there is a whole universe of situation, scenario, opportunity for " business." That they have the dress and the scene-backing of one particular period can matter to no one who has eyes for anything beyond dress and scene-backing. And when we are told that they are apt to run too much into grooves and families, it is sufficient to answer that it really does not lie in the mouth of an age which produces grime-novels, problem-novels, and so forth, as if they had been struck off on a hectograph, possessing the not very exalted gift of varying names and places—to reproach any other age on this score. But we have only limited room here for generalities and still less for controversy; let us turn to our proper work and survey the actual turn-out in fiction—mostly as a result of mere fashion, verse, but partly prose—which the Middle Ages has left us as a contribution to this department of English literature.

It has been said that few people know the treasures of English romance, yet there is little excuse for ignorance of them. It is some century since Ellis's extremely amusing, if sometimes rather prosaic, book put much of the matter before those who will not read originals; to be followed in the same path by Dunlop later, and much later still by the invaluable and delightful *Catalogue of* [British Museum] *Romances* by Mr. Ward. It is nearly as long since the collections of Ritson and Weber, soon supplemented by others, and enlarged for the last forty years by the publications of the Early English Text Society, put these originals themselves within the reach of everybody who is not so lazy or so timid as to be disgusted or daunted by a very few actually obsolete words and a rather large proportion of obsolete spellings, which will yield to even the minimum of intelligent attention. Only a very small number (not perhaps including a single one of importance) remain unprinted, though no doubt a few are out of print or difficult to obtain. The quality and variety of the stories told in them are both very considerable, even without making allowance for what has been called the stock character of mediæval composition. That almost all are directly imitated from the French is probable enough, that most are is certain: but this matters, for our purpose, nothing at all. That the imitation was not haphazard or indiscriminate is obvious. Thus, though we have some, we have not very many representatives of the class which was the most numerous of all in France—the *chansons de geste* or stories of French legendary history, national or family. Except as far as the Saracens are concerned, they would naturally have less interest for English hearers. The *Matière de Rome*, again—the legends of antiquity— though represented, is not very abundant outside of the universally popular Tale of Troy; and the almost equally popular Alexander legend does not occupy a very large part of them. What is perhaps more remarkable is that until Malory exercised his genius upon " the French book," the more poetical parts of the " matter of Britain " itself do not seem to have been very much written about in English. The preliminary stuff about Merlin and Vortigern exists in several handlings; the foreign campaigns of Arthur seem always (perhaps from national vanity) to have been popular. The " off "-branches of Tristram and Percivale, and not a few of the still more episodic romances of adventures concerning Gawain, Iwain, and other knights, receive

attention. The execrable Lonelich or Lovelich, who preceded Malory a little, had of course predecessors in
handling the other parts of the Graal story. But the
crown and flower of the whole—the inspiration which connected the Round Table and the Graal and the love of
Lancelot and Guinevere—though, so far as the present
writer's reading and opinion are of any weight, the recent
attempts to deprive the Englishman, Walter Map, of the
honour of conceiving it are of no force—seems to have
waited till the fifteenth century—that is to say the last part
of three hundred years—before Englishmen took it up.
Most popular of all perhaps, on the principle that in novels
the flock " likes the savour of fresh grass," seem to have
been the pure *romans d'aventures*—quite unconnected or
nearly so with each other or with any of the larger cycles.
Those adventures of particular heroes have sometimes a
sort of Arthurian link, but they really have no more to do
with the main Arthurian story than if Arthur were not.

For the present purpose, however, filiation, origin, and
such-like things are of much less importance than the
actual stories that get themselves told to satisfy that
demand which in due time is to produce the supply of the
novel. Of these the two oldest, as regards the actual forms
in which we have them, are capital examples of the more
and less original handling of " common-form " stories or
motives. They were not then, be it remembered, quite
such common-form as now—the rightful heir kept out of
his rights, the usurper of them, the princess gracious or
scornful or both by turns, the quest, the adventure, the
revolutions and discoveries and fights, the wedding bells
and the poetical justice on the villain. Let it be remembered, too, if anybody is scornful of these as *vieux jeu,* that
they have never been really improved upon except by the

very obvious and unoriginal method common in clever-silly days, of simply reversing some of them, of "turning platitudes topsy-turvy," as not the least gifted, or most old-fashioned, of novelists, Tourguenief, has it. Perhaps the oldest of all, *Havelok the Dane*—a story the age of which, from evidence both internal and external, is so great that people have not quite gratuitously imagined a still older Danish or even Anglo-Saxon original for the French romance from which our existing one is undoubtedly taken—is one of the most spirited of all. Both hero and heroine—Havelok, who should be King of Denmark, and Goldborough, who should be Queen of England—are ousted by their treacherous guardian-viceroys as infants; and Havelok is doomed to drowning by his tutor, the greater or at least bolder villain of the two. But the fisherman Grim, who is chosen as his murderer, discovers that the child has, at night, a *nimbus* of flame round his head; renounces his crime and escapes by sea with the child and his own family to Grimsby. Havelok, growing up undistinguished from his foster-brethren, takes service as scullion with the English usurper. This usurper is seeking how to rid himself of the princess without violence, but in some way that will make her succession to the crown impossible, and Havelok, having shown prowess in sports, is selected as the maiden's husband. She, too, discovers his royalty at night by the same token; and the pair regain their respec-tive inheritances, and take vengeance on their respective traitors, in a lively and adventurous fashion. There are all the elements of a good story in this: and they are by no means wasted or spoilt in the actual handling. It is not a mere sequence of incident; from the mixture of generosity and canniness in the fisherman who ascertains that he is to have traitor's wages before he finally decides to rescue

Havelok, to the not unnatural repugnance of Goldborough at her forced wedding with a scullion, the points where character comes in are not neglected, though of course the author does not avail himself of them either in Shakespearean or in Richardsonian fashion. They are *there*, ready for development by any person who may take it into his head to develop them.

So too is it in the less powerful and rather more cut and dried *King Horn*. Here the opening is not so very different; the hero's father is murdered by pirate invaders, and he himself set adrift in a boat. But in this the princess (daughter of course of the king who shelters him) herself falls in love with Horn, and there is even a scene of considerable comic capabilities in which she confides this affection by mistake to one of his companions (fortunately a faithful one) instead of to himself. But Horn has a faithless friend also; and rivals, and adventures, and journeys; and returns just in the nick of time, and recognitions by rings, and everything that can properly be desired occur. In these — even more perhaps than in Havelok's more masculine and less sentimental fortunes— there are openings not entirely neglected by the romancer (though, as has been said, he does not seem to have been one of the strongest of his kind) for digression, expatiation, embroidery. Transpose these two stories (as the slow kind years will teach novelists inevitably to do) into slightly different keys, introduce variations and episodes and *codas*, and you have the possibilities of a whole library of fiction, as big and as varied as any that has ever established itself for subscribers, and bigger than any that has ever offered itself as one collection to buyers.

The love-stories of these two tales are what it is the fashion—exceedingly complimentary to the age referred

to if not to the age of the fashion itself—to call " mid-
Victorian " in their complete " propriety." Indeed, it is
a Puritan lie, though it seems to possess the vivaciousness
of its class, that the romances are distinguished by " bold
bawdry." They are on the contrary rather singularly pure,
and contrast, in that respect, remarkably with the more
popular folk-tale. But fiction, no more than drama, could
do without the ἁμαρτία—the human and not unpardonable
frailty. This appears in, and complicates, the famous story
of *Tristram*, which, though its present English form is
probably younger than *Havelok* and *Horn*, is likely to have
existed earlier: indeed must have done so if Thomas of
Erceldoune wrote on the subject. Few can require to be
told that beautiful and tragical history of " inauspicious
stars " which hardly any man, of the many who have
handled it in prose and verse, has been able to spoil. Our
Middle English form is not consummate, and is in some
places crude in manner and in sentiment. But it is
notable that the exaggerated and inartistic repulsiveness
of Mark, resorted to by later writers as a rather rudimentary
means of exciting compassion for the lovers, is not to be
found here; in fact, one of the most poetical touches in
the piece is one of sympathy for the luckless husband,
when he sees the face of his faithless queen slumbering by
her lover's side with the sun on it. " And Mark rewed
therefore." The story, especially in its completion with
the " Iseult of Brittany " part and the death of Tristram,
gives scope for every possible faculty and craftsmanship
of the most analytic as of the most picturesque novelist
of modern times. There is nothing in the least like it in
ancient literature; and to get a single writer who would
do it justice in modern times we should have to take the
best notes of Charles Kingsley, and Mr. Blackmore, and

Mr. Meredith, leaving out all their faults, and combine. It is not surprising that, in the very infancy of the art, nobody in German or French, any more than in English (though the German here is, as it happens, the best), should have done it full justice; but it is a wonder that a story of such capacities should have been sketched, and even worked out in considerable detail, so early.

Of the far greater story of which *Tristram* is a mere episode and hardly even that—a chantry or out-lying chapel of the great cathedral—the Arthurian Legend, the earlier English versions, or rather the earlier versions in English, are, as has been said, not only fragmentary but disappointing. There is nothing in the least strange in this, even though (as the present writer, who can speak with indifferent knowledge, still firmly holds) the conception of the story itself in its greatest and unifying stage is probably if not certainly English. The original sources of the story of Arthur are no doubt Celtic; they give themselves out as being so, and there is absolutely no critical reason for disbelieving them. But in these earlier forms— the authority of the most learned Celticists who have any literary gift and any appreciation of evidence is decisive on this point—not only are the most characteristic unifying features—the Graal story and the love of Lancelot and Guinevere—completely wanting, but *the* great stroke of genius—the connection of these two and the subordination of all minor legends as to the dim national hero, Arthur, with those about him—is more conspicuously wanting still. Whether it was the Englishman Walter Map, the Norman Robert de Borron, or the Frenchman Chrestien de Troyes, to whom this flash of illumination came, has never been proved—will pretty certainly now never be proved. M. Gaston Paris failed to do it; and it is exceedingly unlikely that, where he failed, any one else will succeed, unless the thrice and thirty times sifted libraries of Europe yield some quite unexpected windfall.   In the works commonly attributed to Chrestien, all of which are well known to the present writer, there is no sign of his having been able to conceive this, though he is a delightful romancer.   Robert is a mere shadow; and his attributed works, *as* his works, are shadows too, though they are interesting enough in themselves.   Walter not only has the greatest amount of traditional attribution, but is the undoubted author of *De Nugis Curialium*.   And the author of *De Nugis Curialium*, different as it is from the Arthurian story, *could* have finally divined the latter.

But at the time when he wrote, Englishmen, with the rarest exceptions, wrote only in French or Latin; and when they began to write in English, a man of genius, to interpret and improve on him, was not found for a long time.   And the most interesting parts of the Arthurian story are rarely handled at all in such early vernacular versions of it as we have, whether in verse or prose.   Naturally enough, perhaps, it was the fabulous historic connection with British history, and the story of the great British enchanter Merlin, that attracted most attention.   The *Arthour and Merlin* which is in the Auchinleck MS.; the prose *Merlin*, published by the Early English Text Society; the alliterative Thornton *Morte d'Arthur*, and others, are wont to busy themselves about the antecedents of the real story— about the uninteresting wars of the King himself with Saxons, and Romans, and giants, and rival kings, rather than with the great chivalric triple cord of Round Table, Graal, and Guinevere's fault.   The pure Graal poems, *Joseph of Arimathea*, the work of the abominable Lonelich or Lovelich, etc., deal mainly with another branch of previous questions—things bearable as introductions, fill-ings-up, and so forth, but rather jejune in themselves. The Scots *Lancelot* is later than Malory himself, and of very little interest. Layamon's account, the oldest that we have, adds little (though what little it does add is not unimportant) to Geoffrey of Monmouth and Wace; and tells what it has to tell with nearly as little skill in narrative as in poetry. Only the metrical *Morte*—from which, it would appear, Malory actually transprosed some of his most effective passages in the manner in which genius transproses or transverses—has, for that reason, for its dealings with the catastrophe, and for the further oppor-tunity of comparison with Tennyson, interest of the higher kind. But before we come to Malory himself it is desirable to turn to the branches—the chapels, as we have called them, to the cathedral—which he also, in some cases at least, utilised in the *magnum opus* of English prose romance.

These outliers were rather more fortunate, probably for no more recondite reason than that the French originals (from which they were in almost every instance certainly taken) were finished in themselves. Of the special Gawain cycle or sub-cycle we have two romances in pure metrical form, and more than two in alliterative, which are above the average in interest. *Ywain and Gawain*, one of the former, is derived directly or indirectly from the *Chevalier au Lyon* of Chrestien de Troyes; and both present some remarkable affinities with the unknown original of the "Sir Beaumains" episode of Malory, and, through it, with Tennyson's *Gareth and Lynette*. The other, *Lybius Disconus* (*Le Beau Déconnu*) is also concerned with that courteous nephew of Arthur who, in later versions of the main story, is somewhat sacrificed to Lancelot. For a "*real* romance," as it calls itself (though it is fair to say that in the original the word

B

means "royal"), of the simpler kind but extremely well told, there are not many better metrical specimens than *Ywain and Gawain*, but it has less character-interest, actual or possible, than those which have been commented on. The hero, King Urien's son, accepts an adventure in which another knight of the Table, Sir Colgrevance, has fared ill, after it has been told in a conversation at court which is joined in first by the Queen and afterwards by the King. Sir Kay here shows his usual cross-grainedness; and Guinevere "with milde mood" requests to know "What the devil is thee within?" The adventure is of a class well known in romance. You ride to a certain fountain, pour water from it on a stone, and then, after divers marvels, have to do battle with a redoubtable knight. Colgrevance has fared badly; Kay is as usual quite sure that he would fare better; but Ywain actually undertakes the task. He has a tough battle with the knight who answers the challenge, but wounds him mortally; and when the knight flies to his neighbouring castle, is so hard on his heels that the portcullis actually drops on his horse's haunches just behind the saddle, and cuts the beast in two. Ywain is thus left between the portcullis and the (by this time shut) door—a position all the more awkward that the knight himself expires immediately after he has reached shelter. The situation is saved, however, by the guardian damsel of romance, Lunet (the Linet or Lynette of the Beaumains-Gareth story), who emerges from a postern between gate and portcullis and conveys the intruder safe to her own chamber. Here a magic bed makes him invisible: though the whole castle, including the very room, is ransacked by the dead knight's people and would-be revengers, at the bidding of his widow. This widow, however, is rather an Ephesian matron.

The sagacious Lunet, whose confidante she is, suggests to her that, unless she enlists some doughty knight as her champion, the king will confiscate her fief; and that there is no champion like a husband. A very little more finesse effects the marriage, even though the lady is made aware of the identity of her new lover and her own husband's slayer. (It is of course necessary to remember that the death of a combatant in fairly challenged and fought single contest was not reckoned as any fault to his antagonist.) Ywain actually shows his prowess against the King: and has an opportunity of showing Kay once more that it is one thing to blame other people for failing, and another to succeed yourself. And after this the newly married pair live together happily for a time. But it was reckoned a fault in a knight to take too prolonged a honeymoon: and Ywain, after what the French call *adieux déchirants*, obtains leave for the usual " twelvemonth and a day," at the expiration of which, on St. John's Eve, he is without fail to return, the engagement being sealed by the gift from his lady of a special ring. He forgets his promise of course: and at the stated time a damsel appears, sternly demands the ring, and announces her lady's decision to have nothing further to do with him. There is in such cases only one thing for any true knight, from Sir Lancelot to Sir Amadis, to do: and that is to go mad, divest himself of his garments, and take to the greenwood. This Ywain duly does, supporting himself at first on the raw flesh of game which he kills with a bow and arrows wrested from a chance-comer; and then on less savage but still simple food supplied by a benevolent hermit. As he lies asleep under a tree, a lady rides by with attendants, and one of these (another of the wise damsels of romance) recognises him as Sir Ywain. The lady has at the time sore need of a champion against a hostile earl, and she also fortunately possesses a box of ointment infallible against madness, which Morgane la Faye has given her. With this the damsel is sent back to anoint Ywain. He comes to his senses, is armed and clothed, undertakes the lady's defence, and discomfits the earl: but is as miserable as ever. Resisting the lady's offer of herself and all her possessions, he rides off once more "with heavy heart and dreary cheer."

Soon he hears a hideous noise and, riding in its direction, finds that a dragon has attacked a lion. He succours the holier beast, kills the dragon, and though he has unavoidably wounded the lion in the *mêlée* is thenceforth attended by him not merely as a food-provider, but as the doughtiest of squires and comrades in fight. To aggravate his sorrow he comes to the fountain and thorn-tree of the original adventure, and hears some one complaining in the chapel hard by. They exchange questions. "A man," he said, "some time I was" (which must be one of the earliest occurrences in English of a striking phrase), and the prisoner turns out to be Lunet. She has been accused of treason by the usual steward (it is *very* hard for a steward of romance to be good) and two brothers—of treason to her lady, and is to be burnt, unless she can find a knight who will fight the three. Ywain agrees to defend her: but before he can carry out his promise he has, on the same morning, to meet a terrible giant who is molesting his hosts at a castle where he is guested. Both adventures, however, are achieved on the same day, with very notable aid from the lion: and Ywain undertakes a fresh one, being recruited by the necessary damsel-messenger, against two half-fiend brother knights. They stipulate that the lion is to be forcibly prevented from interfering, and he is locked up in a room; but, hearing the noise of battle, he scratches up the earth under the door, frees himself, and once more succours his master at the nick of time. Even this does not expiate Ywain's fault: and yet another task falls to him—the championship of the rights of the younger of a pair of sisters, the elder of whom has secured no less a representative than Gawain himself. The pair, unknowing and unknown, fight all day long before Arthur's court with no advantage on either side: and when the light fails an interchange of courtesies leads to recognition and the settlement of the dispute. Now the tale is nearly full. Ywain rides yet again to the magic fountain and performs the rite; there is no one to meet him; the castle rocks and the inmates quake. But the crafty Lunet persuades her mistress to swear that if the Knight of the Lion, who has fallen at variance with his lady, will come to the rescue, she will do all she can to reconcile the pair. Which not ill-prepared " curtain " duly falls: leaving us comfortably assured that Ywain and his Lady and Lunet and the Lion (one wishes that these two could have made a match of it, and he must surely have been a bewitched knight) lived happily

> "Until that death had driven them down."

This, it has been said, is a specimen of the pure romance; with little except incident in it, and a touch or two of manners. It does not, as the others noticed above do, lend itself much to character-drawing. But it is spiritedly told; though rougher, it is much more vigorous than the French original; and the mere expletives and stock phrases, which are the curse of these romances, do not obtrude themselves too much. In this respect, and some others, it is the superior of the one coupled above with it, *Lybius Disconus*, which is closer, except in names, to the Beaumains story. Still, this also is not a bad specimen of the same class. The hero of it is a son, not a brother, of Gawain, comes nameless or nicknamed, but as " Beaufils," not " Beaumains," to Arthur's court, and is knighted at once, not made to go through the " kitchen-knave " stage. Accordingly, the damsel Elene (not Lunet), to whom he is assigned as champion in the adventure of the Lady of Sinadowne, objects only to his novelty of knighthood and is converted by his first victory. The course of the adventures is, however, different from that which some people know from Malory, and many from Tennyson. One of them is farcical: the Fair Unknown rescues a damsel at her utmost need from two giants, a red and a black, one of whom is roasting a wild boar and uses the animal as a weapon, with the spit in it, for the combat. Moreover, he falls a victim to the wiles of a sorceress-chatelaine whom he has also succoured: and it is only after the year and day that Elene goads him on to his proper quest. But this also is no bad story.

The limits of this volume admit of not much farther " argument " (though the writer would very gladly give it) of these minor romances of adventure, Arthurian and other. Ellis's easily accessible book supplies abstracts of the main Arthurian story before Malory; of the two most famous, though by no means best, of all the non-Arthurian romances, *Guy of Warwick* and *Bevis of Hampton* (the former of which was handled and rehandled from age to age, moralised, curtailed, lengthened, and hashed up in every form); of the brilliant and vigorous *Richard Cœur-de-Lion ;* of the less racy Charlemagne romances in English; of the *Seven Wise Masters*, brought from the East and naturalised all over Europe; of the delightful love story of *Florice and Blancheflour ;* of that powerful and pathetic

legend of the *Proud King* (Robert of Sicily), which Long-
fellow and Mr. William Morris both modernised, each in
his way; of those other legends, *Sir Isumbras* and *Amis and
Amillion*, which are so beautiful to those who can appreciate
the mediæval mind, and to the beauty of which others
seem insensible; of *Sir Triamond* and *Sir Eglamour*
(examples of the romance at its weakest); of the exceedingly spirited and interesting *Ipomydon*, and of some others,
including the best of Scotch romances, *Sir Eger, Sir Grame,
and Sir Graysteel*. But Ellis could not know others, and
he left alone yet others that he might have known—the
exquisite *Sir Launfal* of Thomas Chester at the beginning
of the fifteenth century, where an unworthy presentment
of Guinevere is compensated by the gracious image of
Launfal's fairy love; the lively adventures of *William
of Palerne*, who had a werewolf for his friend and an em-
peror's daughter for his love, eloping with her in white
bear-skins, the unusual meat of which was being cooked
in her father's kitchen; *Sir Orfeo*—Orpheus and Eurydice,
with a happy ending; *Emarè*, one of the tales of innocent
but persecuted heroines of which Chaucer's Constance is
the best known; *Florence of Rome ;* the rather famous
Squire of Low Degree ; Sir Amadas, not a very good
handling of a fine motive, charity to a corpse; many others.

Nor does he seem to have known one of the finest of all
—the alliterative romance of *Gawain and the Green Knight*
which, since Dr. Morris published it some forty years ago
for the Early English Text Society, has made its way
through text - books into more general knowledge than
most of its fellows enjoy. In this the hero is tempted
repeatedly, elaborately, and with great knowledge of nature
and no small command of art on the teller's part, by the
wife of his host and destined antagonist. He resists in the

main, but succumbs in the point of accepting a magic
preservative as a gift: and is discovered and lectured
accordingly. It is curious that this, which is far above the
usual mere adventure-story and is novel of a high kind
as well as romance, has no known French original; and is
strongly English in many characteristics besides its verse-
form.

On the whole, however, one need have no difficulty in
admitting that the majority of these romances *do* somewhat
content themselves with incident, incident only, and
incident not merely of a naïf but of a stock kind, for their
staple. There are striking situations, even striking phrases,
here and there; there is plenty of variety in scene, and
more than is sometimes thought in detail; but the motive-
and-character-interest is rarely utilised as it might be, and
very generally is not even suggested. There is seldom any
real plot or " fable "—only a chain of events: and though
no one but a very dull person will object to the supernatural
element, or to the exaggerated feats of professedly natural
prowess and endurance, it cannot be said that on the whole
they are artistically managed. You feel, not merely that
the picture would have been better if the painter had taken
more pains, but that the reason why he did not is that he
did not know how.

Sir Thomas Malory, himself most unknown perhaps of
all great writers, did know how; and a cynical person
might echo the *I nunc* of the Roman satirist, and dwell on
the futility of doing great things, in reference to the fact
that it used to be fashionable, and is still not uncommon,
to call Malory a " mere compiler." Indeed from the
direction which modern study so often takes, of putting
inquiry into origins above everything, and neglecting the
consideration of the work as work, this practice is not

likely soon to cease.   But no mistake about the mysterious Englishman (the place-names with which the designation is connected are all pure English) is possible to any one who has read his book, and who knows what prose fiction is.   *The Noble Histories of King Arthur, La Morte d'Arthur, The Story of the most Noble and Worthy King Arthur, The Most Ancient and Famous History of the Renowned Prince Arthur, The Birth, Life, and Acts of King Arthur*—call it by whichever name anybody likes of those which various printers and reprinters have given it—is one of the great books of the world.   If they can give us any single " French book "—the reference to which is a commonplace of the subject—from which it was taken, let them; they have not yet.   If they point out (as they can) French and English books from which parts of it were taken, similar things may be done with Dante and Chaucer, with Shakespeare and Milton, and very probably could have been done with Homer.   It is what the artist does with his materials, not where he gets them, that is the question. And Malory has done, with *his* materials, a very great thing indeed.   He is working no doubt to a certain extent blindly; working much better than he knows, and sometimes as he would not work if he knew better; though whether he would work as well if he knew better is quite a different point.   Sometimes he may not take the best available version of a story; but we must ask ourselves whether he knew it.   Sometimes he may put in what we do not want: but we must ask ourselves whether there was not a reason for doing so, to him if not to us.   What is certain is that he, and he only in any language, makes of this vast assemblage of stories one story, and one book.

He does it (much more than half unconsciously no doubt) by following the lines of, as I suppose, Walter Map, and fusing the different motives, holding to this method even in parts of the legend with which, so far as one knows, Map cannot have meddled. Before him this legend consisted of half a dozen great divisions—a word which may be used of malice prepense. These were the story of Merlin, that of Arthur's own origin, and that of the previous history of the Graal for introduction; the story of Arthur's winning the throne, of the Round Table, and of the marriage with Guinevere, also endless branchings of special knights' adventures, and of the wars with the Saxons and the Romans, and the episode of the False Guinevere—with whom for a time Arthur lives as with his queen—for middle; and the story of the Graal-quest, the love of Lancelot for the Queen, and the rebellion of Mordred with its fatal consequences, for close. Exactly how much of this Malory personally had before him we cannot of course say: but of any working up of the whole that would have spared him trouble, and robbed him of credit, we do not know. In fact the favourite term "compiler" gives up the only dangerous point. Now in what way did Malory *compile?* In the way in which the ordinary compiler proceeds he most emphatically does not. He cuts down the preliminaries mercilessly: but they can be perfectly well spared. He misses almost all the wars with the Saxons, which are the most tedious parts of the originals. He adopts, most happily, the early, not the late, placing of those with the Romans. He drops the false Guinevere altogether, which is imperative, that the true one may have no right to plead the incident—though he does not represent Arthur as "blameless." He gives the *roman d'aventures* side of the Round Table stories, from the great Tristram and Palomides romances through the Beaumains episode downwards, because they are interesting in themselves and lead up to the Graal quest. He gives that Quest as plentifully because it leads up to the " dolorous death and departing out of this world of them all." How he gives the Lancelot and Guinevere tragedy we shall see presently. And the catastrophe of the actual " departing " he gives perfectly; with the magnificent final scenes which he has converted, sometimes in almost Shakespearean fashion, by the slightest verbal touches from mediocre verse to splendid prose. A very remarkable compiler! It is a pity that they did not take him and cut him up in little stars for a light to all his brethren in compiling thereafter.

For he has what no compiler as such can have—because the moment he has it he ceases to be a compiler, and becomes an artist—the sense of *grasp*, the power to put his finger, and to keep it, on the central pulse and nerve of the story. That he did this deliberately is so unlikely as to be practically impossible: that he did it is certain. The Arthurian Legend is the greatest of mediæval creations as a subject—a " fable "—just as the *Divina Commedia* is the greatest of mediæval " imitations " and works of art. And as such it is inevitable that it should carry with it the sense of the greatest mediæval *differences*, Chivalry and Romance. The strong point of these differences is the way in which they combine the three great motives, as Dante isolates them, of Valour, Love, and Religion. The ancients never realised this combination at all; the moderns have merely struggled after it, or blasphemed it in fox-and-grapes fashion: the mediævals *had* it—in theory at any rate. The Round Table stories, merely as such, illustrate Valour; the Graal stories, Religion; the passion of Lancelot and Guinevere with the minor instances, Love. All these have their ἁμαρτία—their tragic and tragedy-causing fault and flaw. The knight wastes his valour in idle bickerings;

he forgets law in his love; and though there is no actual degradation of religion, he fails to live up to the ideal that he does not actually forswear. To throw the presentation —the *mimesis*—of all this into perfectly worthy form would probably have been too much for any single genius of that curious time (when genius was so widely spread and so little concentrated) except Dante himself, whose hand found other work to do. To colour and shape the various fragments of the mosaic was the work of scores. To put them together, if not in absolutely perfect yet in more than sufficient shape, was, so far as we know, the luck of Malory only: though some one (Map or another) had done a mighty day's work long before in creating the figure and the adventures of Lancelot and imagining the later quest of the Graal with the figure of Galahad—that "improved Percivale," as the seedsmen say.

But besides this power of shaping (or even of merely combining) scattered elements into a story, Malory has another—*the* other of the first importance to the novelist proper—in his attraction to character, if not exactly in his making up of it. It has been said above that the defect of the pure romances—especially those of continental origin—is the absence of this. What the Greeks called διάνοια—"sentiment," "thought," "cast of thought," as it has been variously rendered—is even more absent from them than plot or character itself: and of its almost necessary connection with this latter they often seem to have no idea. Very rare is such a touch as that of Sir Amadas being unable at the feast to get rid of the memory of the unburied corse, kept by enemies from the kindly earth that would hide it, and the rites that would help it to peace: still rarer that in *Guy of Warwick* when the hero, at the height of his fame and in the full enjoyment of his

desires, looks from the tower and is struck by the selfishness
and earthliness of his career. The first notion is not
"improved" in the original at all, and the second very
badly; but in most of the others such things do not even
exist. Now the greater Legend is full of situations which
encourage such thoughts, and even of expressed thoughts
that only need craftsmanship to turn them into the corner-
stones of character-building, and the jewels, five or fifty
words long, of literature. The fate and metaphysical aid
that determine the relations of Tristram and Iseult; the
unconscious incest of Arthur and Margause with its Greek-
tragic consequence; the unrewarded fidelity of Palomides,
and (an early instance of the soon to be triumphant
allegory) his fruitless chase of the Beast Glatissant; all
these are matters in point. But of course the main nursery
of such things is the Lancelot-and-Guinevere story itself.
Nobody has yet made Guinevere a person—nobody but
Shakespeare could have done so perhaps, though Shakespeare's Guinevere would probably have been the greatest
woman in all art. But Malory has not been the least
successful with her: and of Lancelot he has made, if only in
study, one of the great characters of that fictitious world
which is so much truer than the real. And let no one say
that we are reading Tennyson or any one else into Malory.
There are yet persons, at least at the time this was written
not quite Methusalahs, who read the *Morte d'Arthur* before
the *Idylls* appeared and who have never allowed even the
Idylls to overlay their original idea of the most perfect and
most gentle of knights.

It is probable indeed that Malory invented little or
nothing in the various situations, by which the character of
Lancelot, and the history of his fatal love, are evolved. We
know in most cases that this is so. It is possible, too,

that at first (probably because the possibilities had not dawned on him, as it has been admitted they never did very consciously) he has not made the most of the introduction of lover and lady. But when the interest becomes concentrated, as in the various passages of Guinevere's wrath with her lover and their consequences, or in the final series of catastrophes, he is fully equal to the occasion. We *know*—this time to his credit—how he has improved, in the act of borrowing them, the earlier verse-pictures of the final parting of the lovers, and there are many other episodes and juxtapositions of which as much may be said. That except as to Lancelot's remorse (which after all is the great point) there is not much actual talk about motive and sentiment is nothing; or nothing but the condition of the time. The important point is that, as the electricians say, "the house is wired" for the actual installation of character-novelling. There is here the complete scenario, and a good deal more, for a novel as long as *Clarissa* and much more interesting, capable of being worked out in the manner, not merely of Richardson himself, but of Mr. Meredith or Mr. Hardy. It *is* a great romance, if not the greatest of romances: it has a great novel, if not the greatest of novels, written in sympathetic ink between the lines, and with more than a little of the writing sometimes emerging to view.

Little in the restricted space here available can be, though much might be in a larger, said about the remaining attempts in English fiction before the middle of the sixteenth century. The later romances, down to those of Lord Berners, show the character of the older with a certain addition of the "conjuror's supernatural" of the *Amadis* school. But the short verse-tales, especially those of the Robin Hood cycle, and some of the purely comic kind,

introduce an important variation of interest: and even
some of the longer, such as that *Tale of Beryn*, which used to
be included in Chaucer's works, vary the chivalrous model
in a useful way.   Still more important is the influence of
the short *prose* tale:—first Latin, as in the *Gesta Romanorum*
(which of course had older and positively mediæval forerunners), then Italian and French.   The prose saved the
writer from verbiage and stock phrase; the shortness from
the tendency to " watering out " which is the curse of the
long verse or prose romance.   Moreover, to get point and
appeal, it was especially necessary to *throw up* the subject—
incident, emotion, or whatever it was—to bring it out; not
merely to meander and palaver about it.   But language
and literature were both too much in a state of transition
to admit of anything capital being done at this time.   It
was the great good fortune of England, corresponding to
that experienced with Chaucer in poetry three quarters of
a century earlier, that Malory came to give the sum and
substance of what mediæval fiction could do in prose.   For
more, the times and the men had to come.

CHAPTER II

DURING the dying-off of romance proper, or its transference from verse to prose in the late fifteenth and earlier sixteenth century, there is not very much to note about prose fiction in England. But, as the conditions of modern literature fashioned themselves, a very great influence in this as in other departments was no doubt exercised with us by Italian, as well as some by Spanish in a way which may be postponed for a little. The Italian prose tale had begun to exercise that influence as early as Chaucer's time: but circumstances and atmosphere were as yet unfavourable for its growth. It is a hackneyed truism that Italian society was very much more modern than any other in Europe at this time—in fact it would not be a mere paradox to say that it was, and continued to be till the later sixteenth, much more modern than it has ever been since—or till very recently. By " modern " is here meant the kind of society which is fairly cultivated, fairly comfortable, fairly complicated with classes not very sharply separated from each other, not dominated by any very high ideals, tolerably corrupt, and sufficiently business-like. The Italian *novella*, of course, admits wild passions and extravagant crimes: but the general tone of it is *bourgeois* —at any rate domestic. With its great number of situations and motives, presented in miniature, careful work is necessary to bring out the effect: and, above all, there is abundant room for study of manners, for proverbial and popular wisdom and witticism, for " furniture "—to use

32

that word in a wide sense.   Above all, the Italian mind,
like the Greek, had an ethical twist—twist in more senses
than one, some would say, but that does not matter.
Manners, morals, motives—these three could not but dis-
place, to some extent, mere incident: though there was
generally incident of a poignant or piquant kind as well.
In other words the *novella* was actually (though still in
miniature) a novel in nature as well as in name.   And
these *novelle* became, as is generally known, common in
English translations after the middle of the sixteenth
century.   Painter's huge *Palace of Pleasure* (1566) is only
the largest and best known of many translations, single
and collected, of the Italian *novellieri* and the French
tale-tellers, contemporary, or of times more or less earlier.

For some time, as almost everybody knows, these collections of translated matter served a purpose—great indeed,
but somewhat outside their proper department—by furnishing the Elizabethan dramatists with a large part—
perhaps the larger part—of their subjects.   But they very
soon began to exercise it directly by suggesting the fictitious
part of the prose pamphlet—a department which, though
infinitely less well known than the plays, and still not very
easy to know, holds almost the second position as representing the popular literature of the Elizabethan time.
And they also had—in one case certainly, in the other
probably—no little influence upon the two great Elizabethan works which in a manner founded the modern
novel and the modern romance in English—the *Euphues* of
Lyly and the *Arcadia* of Sir Philip Sidney.

The pamphlet stories (which are themselves often play-
connected, as in the case of Lodge's *Rosalynde* and Greene's
Pandosto) do not require much notice, with one exception—
Nash's *Jack Wilton or the Unfortunate Traveller*, to which

some have assigned a position equal, or perhaps superior in our particular subject, to that of the *Arcadia* or that of *Euphues*. This seems to the present writer a mistake: but as to appear important is (in a not wholly unreal sense) to be so, the piece shall be separately considered. The rest are mostly marred by a superabundance of rather rudimentary art, and a very poor allowance of matter. There is hardly any character, and except in a few pieces, such as Lodge's *Margarite of America*, there is little attempt to utilise new scenes and conditions. But the whole class has special interest for us in one peculiarity which makes it perhaps unreadable to any but students, and that is its saturation with the Elizabethan conceit and word-play which is sometimes called Euphuism. Nor is this wonderful, considering that more than one of these " pamphlets " is directly connected with the matter and the personages of *Euphues* itself. To this famous book, therefore, we had better turn.

Some people, it is believed, have denied that *Euphues* is a novel at all; and some of these some have been almost indignant at its being called one. It is certainly, with *Rasselas*, the most remarkable example, in English, of a novel which is to a great extent deprived of the *agrémens* to which we have for some two centuries been accustomed in the kind, and, to a still greater, loaded with others which do not appeal to us. To put aside altogether its extraordinary and in a way epoch-making style, which gives it its main actual place in the history of English literature, it is further loaded with didactic digressions which, though certain later novelists have been somewhat peccant in the kind, have never been quite equalled—no, not in *Rasselas* itself or the *Fool of Quality*. But if anybody, who has the necessary knowledge to understand, and therefore the

necessary patience to tolerate, these knotty knarry enve-
lopes, insertions, and excrescences, will for the moment
pay no attention to them, but merely strip them off, he
will find the carcass of a very tolerable novel left behind.
The first plot of Philautus - Euphues - Lucilla, and the
successive jilting of the two friends for each other and for
Curio, is no mean novel-substance. Not Balzac himself,
certainly no one of his successors, need disdain it: and
more than one of them has taken up something like it.
The journey from Naples to London, and the episode of
Fidus and Iffida, could have been worked up, in the good
old three-volume days, to a most effective second volume.
And the picture of the court, with the further loves of
Philautus, Camilla, and the " violet " Frances, would supply
a third of themselves even if Euphues were left out, though
some livelier presentation of his character (which Lyly
himself was obviously too much personally interested to
make at all clear) would improve the whole immensely.
But it was still too early: the thing was not yet to be
done. Only, I do not know any book in which the possibilities, and even the outlines, of this thing were indicated
and vaguely sketched earlier in any European language,
unless it be the *Lucretia and Euryalus* of Æneas Silvius,
which is much more confined in its scope.

The fact is that the very confusedness, the many un-
developed sides, of *Euphues*, make it much more of an
ancestor of the modern novel than if it were more of a
piece. The *quicquid agunt homines* is as much the province
of the novel as of the satire; and there is more than something of this as it affected Elizabethan times in *Euphues*.
Men's interest in morals, politics, and education; their
development of the modern idea of society; their taste for
letters; their conceits and fancies—all these appear in it.

The *Arcadia* stands in a different compartment. *Euphues* is very much *sui generis :* failure as it may be from some points of view, it deserves the highest respect for this, and like most other things *sui generis* it was destined to propagate the genus, if only after many days. The *Arcadia* was in intention certainly, and to great extent in actual fact, merely a carrying out of the attempt, common all over Europe (as a result of the critical searchings of heart of the Italians), to practise a new kind—the Heroic Romance of the sub-variety called pastoral. The " heroic " idea generally was (as ought to be, but perhaps is not, well known) to blend, after a fashion, classical and romantic characteristics—to substitute something like the classic unity of fable or plot for the mere " meandering " of romantic story, and to pay at least as much attention to character as the classics had paid, instead of neglecting it altogether, as had recently though not always been the case in Romance. But the scheme retained on the other hand the variety of incident and appeal of this latter: and especially assigned to Love the high place which Romance had given it. As for the Pastoral—that is almost a story to itself, and a story which has been only once (by Mr. W. W. Greg) satisfactorily, and then not quite completely, told. It is enough to say here, and as affecting our own subject, that it supplied a new opportunity of gratifying the passion of the Renaissance for imitating antiquity, at the same time permitting to no small extent the introduction of things that were really romantic, and above all providing a convention. The Heroic romance generally and the Pastoral in particular went directly back to the Greek romances of Heliodorus and Longus: but they admitted many new and foreign elements.

At the same time, bastard as the heroic romance was, it

could not but exercise an important influence on the
future of fiction, inasmuch as it combined, or attempted
to combine, with classical unity and mediæval variety
the more modern interest of manners and (sometimes)
personality. Sidney's attempt (which, it must be remembered, is not certainly known to be wholly his as it
stands, and *is* certainly known not to have been revised
by him for publication) exercised a very great influence in
English. For its popularity was enormous, and it doubtless
served as shoehorn to draw on that of the English translations of French and Spanish romance which supplied,
during the greater part of the seventeenth century, the
want of original composition of the kind. The uncon-
scionable amount of talk and of writing " about it and
about it " which *Euphues* and the minor Euphuist romances
display is at least as prominent in the *Arcadia:* and this
talk rarely takes a form congenial to the modern novel-
reader's demands. Moreover, though there really is a
plot, and a sufficient amount of incident, this reader undoubtedly, and to no small extent justly, demands that
both incident and plot shall be more disengaged from their
framework—that they should be brought into higher
relief, should stand out more than is the case. Yet further,
the pure character - interest is small — is almost non-
existent: and the rococo-mosaic of manners and sentiment which was to prove the curse of the heroic romance
generally prevents much interest being felt in that direction.[1]
It would also be impossible to devise a style less suited to
prose narrative, except of a very peculiar kind and on a
small scale, than that either of *Euphues* or of the *Arcadia,*

---

[1] As a work of general literature, the attraction of the *Arcadia* is of course
much enhanced by, if it does not chiefly depend upon, its abundant,
varied, and sometimes charming verse-insets. But, as a novel, it cannot
count these.

which, though an uncritical tradition credits it with driving out Lyly's, is practically only a whelp of the same litter. Embarrassed, heavy, rhetorical, it has its place in the general evolution of English prose, and a proper and valuable place too. But it is bad even for pure romance purposes: and nearly hopeless for the panoramic and kaleidoscopic variety which should characterise the novel. To the actual successors of the *Arcadia* in English we shall come presently.

The Unfortunate Traveller is of much less importance than the other two. It has obtained such reputation as it possesses, partly because of its invention or improvement of the fable of " Surrey and Geraldine "; more, and more justly, because it does work up a certain amount of historical material—the wars of Henry VIII. in French Flanders—into something premonitory (with a little kindness on the part of the premonished) of the great and long missed historical novel; still more for something else. Nash, with his quick wit, seems to have been really the first to perceive the capabilities of that foreign travel and observation of manners which was becoming common, stripped of the special atmosphere of pilgrimage which had formerly enveloped it. Even here, he had had the " notion of the notion " supplied to him by Lyly in *Euphues :* and a tolerably skilful advocate would not have so very much difficulty in claiming the book as one of the tribe of Euphuist pamphlets. But Jack Wilton the " traveller " is a little more of a person than the pedagogic Euphues and the shadowy Philautus. At any rate he has a very strong anticipation of Defoe, whose " Cavalier " was not improbably suggested by him. But Nash has neither the patience of Defoe, nor that singular originality, which accompanies in the author of *Moll Flanders* a

certain inability to make the most of it. *The Unfortunate
Traveller* is a sort of compilation or congeries of current
fabliaux, *novelle*, and *facetiæ*, with the introduction of
famous actual persons of the time, from the crowned heads
of the period, through Luther and Aretine downwards, to
give bait and attraction. Sometimes it reminds one of
a working up of the *Colloquies* of Erasmus: three centuries
earlier than *The Cloister and the Hearth*, with much less
genius than Charles Reade's, and still more without his
illegitimate advantage of actual novels behind him for
nearly half the time. But it gives us " disjectæ membra
novellæ " rather than a novel itself: and the oftener one
reads it the more clear one is that the time for writing novels
had not yet come. The materials are there; the desire
to utilise—and even a faint vague idea of *how* to utilise—
them is there; but the art is almost completely absent.
Even regarded as an early attempt in the " picaresque "
manner, it is abortive and only half organised.

The subject of the English " Heroic " Romance, in the
wide sense, is one which has been very little dealt with.
Dunlop neglected it rather surprisingly, and until Professor Raleigh's chapter on the subject there was little of
a satisfactory kind to be found about it anywhere. It
must, however, be admitted that the abstainers from it
have been to some extent justified in their abstention.
The subject is a curious one: and it has an important place
in the history of the Novel, because it shows at once how
strong was the *nisus* towards prose fiction and how surprisingly difficult writers seem, nevertheless, to have
found it to hit upon anything really good, much more anything really original in kind. For it is hardly too much
to say that this century of attempt—we cannot call it a
century of invention—from Ford to Congreve, does not

add a single piece of any considerable merit to the roll of English books. As for a masterpiece, there is nothing in respect of which the use of such a word would not be purely ridiculous. And yet the attempts are interesting to the historian, and should not be uninteresting to the historical student of literature. One or two of them have a sort of shadowy name and place in literary history already.

In tracing their progress and character, we must allow for two native models: and for three foreign sources, one ancient, two modern, of influence. *The Arcadia* and *Euphues*, the former continuously, the latter by revival after an interval, exercised very great effect in the first half of the seventeenth century, during at least the earlier part of which the vogue of *Amadis* and its successors, as Englished by Anthony Munday and others, likewise continued. The Greek romances also had much to do with the matter: for the Elizabethan translators had introduced them to the vulgar, and the seventeenth century paid a good deal of attention to Greek. Then, when that century itself was on its way, the pastoral romance of D'Urfé first, and the Calprenède-Scudéry productions in the second place, came to give a fresh impulse, and something of a new turn. The actual translations of French and Spanish romance, shorter and longer, good, bad, and indifferent, are of immense bulk and doubtless excited imitation: but we cannot possibly deal with them here. A bare list would fill a chapter. But some work of more or less (generally less) originality, in at least adaptation, calls for a little individual notice: and some general characterisation may be added.

It may be desirable to prelude the story by a reminder to the reader that the *general* characteristics of these various sources were "harlequin" in their diversity of apparent colour. The *Amadis* romances and, indeed, all the later examples of that great kind, such as *Arthur of Little Britain*, which Berners translated, were distinguished on the one side by a curious convention of unsmooth running of the course of love, on the other sometimes by a much greater licence of morality than their predecessors, and always by a prodigality of the " conjuror's supernatural "— witches and giants and magic black and white. The Spanish " picaresque " story was pretty real but even less decent: and its French imitations (though not usually reaching the licence of the short tale, which clung to *fabliau* ways in this respect) imitated it here also. The French heroic romance, on the other hand, observed the most scrupulous propriety in language and situation: but aggravated the Amadisian troubling of the course of true love, and complicated everything, very frequently if not invariably, by an insinuated " key " interest of identification of the ancient personages selected as heroes and heroines with modern personages of quality and distinction.

Emanuel Ford (whom the British Museum catalogue insists on spelling Ford*e* and of whom very little seems to be known) published *Parismus, Prince of Bohemia*, as early as 1598. In less than a hundred years (1696) it had reached its fourteenth edition, and it continued to be popular in abridged and chap-booked form [1] far into the eighteenth century. (It is sometimes called *Parismus and Parismenus :* the second part being, as very commonly in romances of the class after the *Amadis* pattern, occupied largely with the adventures of the son of the hero of the first.) On the whole, *Parismus*, though it has few pretensions to elegance of style, and though some delicate tastes have been shocked at certain licences of incident, descrip-

---

[1] It is pleasant to remember that one of the chief publishers of these things in the late seventeenth century was *W. Thackeray*.

tion, and phrase in it, is quite the best of our bunch in this kind. It is, in general conception, pure *Amadis* of the later and slightly degraded type. Laurana, the heroine (of whom a peculiarly hideous portrait adorns the black-letter editions side by side with Parismus himself, who is rather a " jolly gentleman ") is won with much less difficulty and in much less time than Oriana—but separations and difficulties duly follow in " desolate isles " and the like. And though Parismus himself is less of an Amadis than Amadis, the " contrast of friends," founded by that hero and Galaor, is kept up by his association with a certain Pollipus—" a man of his hands " if ever there was one, for with them he literally wrings the neck of the enchantress Bellona, who has enticed him to embrace her. There is plenty of the book, as there always should be in its kind (between 400 and 500 very closely printed quarto pages), and its bulk is composed of proportionately plentiful fighting and love-making and of a very much smaller proportion of what schoolboys irreverently call " jaw " than is usual in the class. If it were not for the black letter (which is trying to the eyes) I should not myself object to have no other reading than *Parismus* for some holiday evenings, or even after pretty tough days of literary and professional work. *The Famous History of Montelion, the Knight of the Oracle* (1633?) proclaims its Amadisian type even more clearly: but I have only read it in an abridged edition of the close of the century. I should imagine that *in extenso* it was a good deal duller than *Parismus*. And of course the comparative praise which has been given to that book must be subject to the reminder that it is what it is—a romance of disorderly and what some people call childish adventure, and of the above-ticketed " conjuror's supernatural." If anybody cannot read *Amadis* itself, he

certainly will not read *Parismus :* and perhaps not everybody who can manage the original—perhaps not even
everybody who can manage *Palmerin*—could put up with
Ford's copy. I can take this Ford as I find him: but I
am not sure that I would go much lower.

Ornatus and Artesia (1607 ?), on the other hand—his
second or third book—strikes me as owing more to Heliodorus than to Montalvo, or Lobeira, or whoever was the
author of the great romance of the last chivalric type.
There are more intricacies in it; the heroine plays a rather
more important part; there is even something of a nearer
approach to modern novel-ways in this production, which
reappeared at " Grub Street near the Upper Pump " in
the year 1650. Ornatus sees his mistress asleep and in a
kind of deshabille, employs a noble go-between, Adellena
(a queer spelling of " Adelina " which may be intentional),
is rejected with apparent indignation, of course; writes
elaborate letters in vain, but overhears Artesia soliloquising
confession of her love for him and disguises himself as a
girl, Silvia. Then the villain of the piece, Floretus, to
obtain the love of this supposed Silvia, murders a person
of distinction and plots to poison Artesia herself. Ornatus-
Silvia is banished: and all sorts of adventures and disguises follow, entirely in the Greek style. The book is not
very long, extending only to signature R in a very small
quarto. Except that it is much less lively and considerably less " free," it reminds one rather in type of
Kynaston's verse *Leoline and Sydanis*. In fact the verse
and prose romances of the time are very closely connected:
and Chamberlayne's *Pharonnida*—far the finest production
of the English " heroic " school in prose, verse, or drama—
was, when the fancy for abridging set in, condensed into a
tiny prose *Eromena*. But *Ornatus and Artesia*, if more

modern, more decent, and less extravagant than *Parismus*, is nothing like so interesting to read. It is indeed quite possible that there is, if not in it, in its popularity, a set-back to the *Arcadia* itself, which had been directly followed in Lady Mary Wroth's *Urania* (1621), and to which (by the time of the edition noted) Charles I.'s admiration—so indecently and ignobly referred to by Milton—had given a fresh attraction for all good anti-Puritans. That an anti-Puritan should be a romance-lover was almost a necessity.

When the French "heroics" began to appear it was only natural that they should be translated, and scarcely less so that they should be imitated in England. For they were not far off the *Arcadia* pattern: and they were a distinct and considerable effort to supply the appetite for fiction which has been dwelt upon. But except for this, and for fashion's sake, they did not contain much that would appeal to an English taste: and it is a little significant that one great reader of them who is known to us —Mrs. Pepys—was a Frenchwoman. Indeed, save for the very considerable "pastime" of a kind that they gave to a time, much of which required passing, it is difficult to understand their attraction for English readers. Their interminable talk never (till perhaps very recently) was a thing to suit our nation: and the "key" interest strikes us at any rate as of the most languid kind. But they *were* imitated as well as translated: and the three most famous of the imitations are the work of men of mark in their different ways. These are the *Parthenissa* (1654) of Roger Boyle, Lord Broghill and Earl of Orrery; the *Aretina* (1661) of Sir George Mackenzie; and the *Pandion and Amphigeneia* (1665) of "starch Johnny" Crowne.

Boyle was a strong Francophile in literature, and his not inconsiderable influence on the development of the heroic *play* showed it only less decidedly than his imitation of the Scudéry romance. I cannot say that I have read *Parthenissa* through: and I can say that I do not intend to do so. It is enough to have read Sainte Madeleine of the Ink-Desert herself, without reading bad imitations of her. But I have read enough to know that *Parthenissa* would never give me anything like the modified satisfaction that is given by *Parismus :* and after all, if a man will not take the trouble to finish writing his book (which Orrery never did) why should his readers take the trouble even to finish reading what he has written? The scene is Parthia, with alternation to Syria, and diversions and episodes elsewhere: and though there is a certain amount of fighting, the staple is quite decorous but exceedingly dull love-making, conducted partly in the endless dialogue (or rather automatic monologue) already referred to, and partly in letters more " handsome " even than Mr. Frank Churchill's, and probably a good deal more sincere in their conventional way, but pretty certainly less amusing. The original attraction indeed of this class of novel consisted, and, in so far as it still exists, may be said to consist, in noble sentiment, elegantly expressed. It deserved, and in a manner deserves, the commendatory part of Aramis's rebuke to Porthos for expressing impatience with the compliments between Athos and D'Artagnan at their first and hostile rencounter.[1] Otherwise there is not much to be said for it. It does not indeed deserve Johnson's often quoted remark as to Richardson (on whom when we come to him we shall have something more to say in connection with these heroic romances), If any one were to read *Parthenissa* for the story he would

[1] " Quant à moi, je trouve les choses que ces messieurs se disent fort bien dites et tout à fait dignes de deux gentilhommes."

not, unless he were a very impulsive person, "hang himself."
He would simply, after a number of pages varying with the
individual, cease to read it.

The work of the great Lord Advocate who was traduced
by Covenanting malice is in a certain sense more interesting: and that not merely because it is much shorter.
Aretina or *The Serious Romance*, opens with an
" apology for Romances " generally, which goes far to
justify Dryden's high opinion of Mackenzie as a critic.
But it cannot be said to be much—it is a little—more
interesting as a story than *Parthenissa*, and it is written in
a most singular lingo—not displaying the racy quaintness
of Mackenzie's elder contemporary and fellow-loyalist
Urquhart, but a sort of Scotified and modernised
Euphuism rather terrible to peruse. A library is " a
bibliotheck richly tapestried with books." Somebody
possesses, or is compared to " a cacochymick stomach,
which transubstantiates the best of meats in its own
malignant humour." And when the hero meets a pair of
cannibal ruffians he confronts one and " pulling out a pistol,
sends from its barrel two balls clothed in Death's livery,
and by them opens a sallyport to his soul to fly out of that
nasty prison." A certain zest may be given by these
oddities, but it hardly lasts out more than 400 pages: and
though the lives of Aretina and Philaretes are more simply
and straightforwardly told than might be thought likely—
though there are ingenious disguises of contemporary
politics, and though Mackenzie was both a wise man and
a wit—it is more certain than ever, when we close his book,
that this is not the way of the world, nor the man to walk
in that way.

Pandion and Amphigeneia is the inferior in importance
of both these books. Crowne had perhaps rather more

talent than it is usual to credit him with, but he does not show it here. I think Sir Walter Raleigh is quite right in regarding the book as more or less traced over the *Arcadia:* and it may be said to have all the defects of Sidney's scheme—which, it is fair once more to observe, we do not possess in any form definitely settled by its author—with none of the merits of his ornament, his execution, and his atmosphere of poetic fancy.

The fact is that this heroic romance was foredoomed to inefficiency. It was not a genuine *kind* at all: but a sort of patchwork of imitations of imitations—a mule which, unlike the natural animal, was itself bred, and bred in and in, of mules for generations back. It was true to no time, to no country, to no system of manners, life, or thought. Its oldest ancestor in one sense, though not in another— the Greek romance—was itself the growth of the latest and most artificial period of the literature to which it belonged. The pure mediæval romance of chivalry was another, but of this it had practically nothing left. The *Amadis* class, the late Renaissance pastorals, the immediately preceding or accompanying French romances of the Scudéry type, were, in increasing degree, hybrid, artificial, and dead-alive. Impotence and sterility in every sense could but be its portion. Of the two great qualities of the novel— Variety and Life—it had never succeeded in attaining any considerable share, and it had now the merest show of variety and no life at all. There is hardly anything to be said in its favour, except that its vogue, as has been observed, testified to the craving for prose fiction, and kept at least a simulacrum of that fiction before the public. How far there may be any real, though metaphysical, connection between the great dramatic output of this seventeenth century in England and its small production in novel is a question not to be discussed here. But undoubtedly the fact of the contrast is a " document in the case," and one of the most important in its own direction; completing the testimony of the mediæval period in the other (that as romance dwindled, drama grew) and leading up to that of the eighteenth century when drama dwindled and the novel grew. The practice of Afra Behn in both, and the fact that Congreve, the greatest English dramatist of the close of the century, began with a novel and deserted the style for drama, are also interesting, and combine themselves very apparently with the considerations just glanced at. But Congreve and Afra must be postponed for a moment.

The two last discussed books, with *Eromena* and some others, are posterior to the Restoration in date, but somewhat earlier in type. The reign of Charles II., besides the " heroic " romances and Bunyan, and one most curious little production to be noticed presently, is properly represented in fiction by two writers, to whom, by those who like to make discoveries, considerable importance has sometimes been assigned in the history of the English Novel. These are Richard Head and Afra Behn, otherwise " the divine Astræa." It is, however, something of an injustice to class them together: for Afra was a woman of very great ability, with a suspicion of genius, while Head was at the very best a bookmaker of not quite the lowest order, though pretty near it. Of *The English Rogue* (1665-1680), which earns him his place here, only the first part, and a certain section of the fourth, are even attributed to him by Francis Kirkman, the Curll of his generation, who published the thing at intervals and admittedly wrote parts of it himself. It is quite openly a picaresque novel: and imitated not merely from the Spanish originals but from Sorel's

Francion, which had appeared in France some forty years before. Yet, if we compare this latter curious book with Head's we shall see how very far behind, even with forty years' advantage in time, was the country which, in the next century, was practically to create the modern novel. *Francion* is not a work of genius: and it does not pretend to much more than the usual picaresque farrago of adventure, unmoral and sometimes rather cruel, but comic of a kind, strung together with little art in fable, and less in character. But the author is to some extent " cumbered about serving." He names his characters, tries to give them some vague personality, furnishes them with some roughly and sketchily painted scenery, and gives us not merely told tales, but occasionally something distantly resembling conversation. Head takes no trouble of this kind: and Kirkman does not seem to think that any such thing is required of him. Very few of the characters of *The English Rogue* have so much as a name to their backs: they are " a prentice," " a master," " a mistress," " a servant," " a daughter," " a tapster," etc. They are invested with hardly the slightest individuality: the very hero is a scoundrel as characterless as he is nameless: [1] he is the mere thread which keeps the beads of the story together after a fashion. These beads themselves, moreover, are only the old anecdotes of " coney-catching," over-reaching, and worse, which had separately filled a thousand *fabliaux, novelle,* " jests," and so forth: and which are now flung together in gross, chiefly by the excessively clumsy and unimaginative expedient of making the personages tell long strings of them as their own experience. When anything more is wanted, accounts of the manners of foreign countries, taken from " voyage-

---

[1] He *has* a name, Meriton Latroon, but it is practically never used in the actual story.

and-travel " books; of the tricks of particular trades (as here of piratical book-selling); of anything and everything that the writer's dull fancy can think of, are foisted in. The thing is in four volumes, and it seems that a fifth was intended as a close: but there is no particular reason why it should not have extended to forty or fifty, nay to four or five hundred. It could have had no real end, just as it has no real beginning or middle.

One other point deserves notice. The tone of the Spanish and French picaresque novel had never been high: but it is curiously degraded in this English example. Furetière honestly called his book *Roman Bourgeois*. Head might have called his, if he had written in French, *Roman Canaille*. Not merely the sentiments but the very outward trappings and accidents of gentility are banished from the book. Yet we do not get any real reality in compensation. Head is no Defoe: he can give us the company that Colonel Jack kept in his youth and Moll Flanders in her middle age: but he makes not the slightest attempt to give us Moll or Jack, or even Moll's or Jack's habit, environment, novel-furniture of any kind whatsoever. The receipt to make *The English Rogue* is simply this: " Take from two to three dozen Elizabethan pamphlets of different kinds, but principally of the ' coney-catching ' variety, and string them together by making a batch of shadowy personages tell them to each other when they are not acting in them." Except in a dim sort of idea that a novel should have some bulk and substance, it is difficult to see any advance whatever in this muck-heap—which the present writer, having had to read it a second time for the present purpose, most heartily hopes to be able to leave henceforth undisturbed on his shelves.

Not in this fashion must the illustrious Afra be spoken of.

It is true that—since it ceased to be the fashion merely to dismiss her with a " fie-fie! " which her prose work, at any rate, by no means merits—there has sometimes been a tendency rather to overdo praise of her, not merely in reference to her lyrics, some of which can never be praised too highly, but in reference to these novels. *Oroonoko* or *The Royal Slave*, with its celebration of the virtues of a noble negro and his love for his Imoinda, and his brutal ill-treatment and death by torture at the hands of white murderers, undoubtedly took the fancy of the public. But to see at once Rousseau and Byron in it, Chateaubriand and Wilberforce and I know not what else, is rather in the " lunatic, lover, and poet " order of vision. Even Head and Kirkman, as we have observed, had perceived the advantage of foreign scenery and travel to vary their matter; Afra had herself been in Guiana; and, as she was of a very inflammable disposition, it is quite possible that some Indian Othello had caught her fresh imagination. On the other hand, there was the heroic romance, with all its sighs and flames, still the rage: and a much less nimble intellect than Afra's, with a much less cosmopolitan experience, might easily see the use of transposing it into a new key. Still, there is no doubt that *The Royal Slave* and even its companions are far above the dull, dirty, and never more than half alive stuff of *The English Rogue*. *Oroonoko* is a story, not a pamphlet or a mere " coney-catching " jest. To say that it wants either contraction or expansion; less " talk about it " and more actual conversation; a stronger projection of character and other things; is merely to say that it is an experiment in the infancy of the novel, not a following out of secrets already divulged. It certainly is the first prose story in English which can be ranked with things that already existed in

foreign literatures.   Nor is it the only one of the batch in
which advance is seen. "The King of Bantam," for
instance, is the account of an "extravagant," though not
quite a fool, who is "coney-catched" in the old manner.
But it opens in a fashion very different indeed from the
old manner. "This money is certainly a most devilish
thing! I'm sure the want of it had been like to ruin my
dear Philibella!" and the succeeding adventures are pretty
freshly told. The trick of headlong overture was a
favourite with Afra.   "The Adventure of the Black Lady"
begins, "About the beginning of last June, as near as I
can remember, Bellamira came to town from Hampshire."
It is a trick of course: and here probably borrowed from
the French: but the line which separates trick from
artistic device is an exceedingly narrow and winding one.
At any rate, this plunging into the middle of things wakes
up the reader's attention, and does not permit him to
doze. "The Lucky Mistake," on the other hand, opens
with a little landscape, "The river Loire has on its delightful banks, etc." "The Fair Jilt," a Bandello-like story,
begins with an exaltation of Love: and so on. Now these
things, though they may seem matters of course to the
mere modern reader, were not matters of course then.
Afra very likely imitated; her works have never been
critically edited; and have not served as field for much origin-
hunting. But whether she followed others or not, she led
her own division. All these things and others are signs of
an awakened conscience—of a sense of the fact that fiction,
to be literature, must be something more than the relation
of a bare fact, tragic, comic, or neutral—that the novelist
is a cook, and must prepare and serve his materials with a
sauce as much his own as possible, of plot, arrangement,
character-drawing, scenery, conversation, reflection, and

what not. That conversation itself—the subtlest instrument of all and the most effective for constructing character —is so little developed, can only, I think, be accounted for by supposing Afra and others to be under the not unnatural mistake that conversation especially belonged to the drama, which was still the most popular form of literature, and in which she herself was a copious practitioner. But this mistake was not long to prevail: and it had no effect on that great contemporary of hers who would, it is to be feared, have used the harshest language respecting her, and to whom we now come.

It is impossible to share, and not very easy even to understand, the scruples of those who would not admit John Bunyan to a place in the hierarchy and the pedigree of the English novel, or would at best grant him an outside position in relation to it. Their exquisite reasons, so far as one can discern them, appear to be (or to concern) the facts that *The Pilgrim's Progress* and *The Holy War* are religious, and that they are allegories.[1] It may be humbly suggested that by applying the double rule to verse we can exclude *Paradise Lost* and the *Faerie Queene* from the

[1] The heroic kind had lent itself very easily and obviously to allegory. Not very long before Bunyan English literature had been enriched with a specimen of this double variety which for Sir W. Raleigh " marks the lowest depth to which English romance writing sank." I do not know that I could go quite so far as this in regard to the book—*Bentivolio and Urania* by Nathaniel Ingelo. The first edition of this appeared in 1660: the second (there seem to have been at least four) lies before me at this moment dated 1669, or nine years before the *Progress* itself. You require a deep-sea-lead of uncommonly cunning construction to sound, register, and compare the profundities of the bathos in novels. The book has about 400 folio pages very closely packed with type, besides an alphabetical index full of Hebrew and Greek derivations of its names—" Gnothisauton," " Achamoth," " Ametameletus," " Dogmapernes," and so forth. Its principles are inexorably virtuous; there is occasional action interspersed among its innumerable discourses, and I think it not improbable that if it were only possible to read it, it might do one some good. But it would not be the good of the novel.

succession of English Poetry, whereby no doubt we shall be finely holpen in understanding the same: while it is by no means certain that, if the exclusion of allegory be pushed home, we must not cancel *Don Quixote* from the list of the world's novels. Even in prose, to speak plainly, the hesitation—unless it comes from the foolish dislike to things religious, as such, which has been the bigotry of the last generation or two—comes from the almost equally foolish determination to draw up arbitrary laws of literary kind. Discarding prejudice and punctilio, every one must surely see that, in diminishing measure, even *The Holy War* is a novel, and that *The Pilgrim's Progress* has every one of the four requisites—plot, character, description, and dialogue—while one of these requisites—character with its accessory manners—is further developed in the *History of Mr. Badman* after a fashion for which we shall look vainly in any division of European literature (except drama) before it. This latter fact has indeed obtained a fair amount of recognition since Mr. Froude drew the attention of the general reader to it in his book on Bunyan, in the " English Men of Letters " series, five-and-twenty years ago: but it must have struck careful readers of the great tinker's minor works long before. Indeed there are very good internal reasons for thinking that no less a person than Thackeray must have known *Mr. Badman*. This wonderful little sketch, however—the related history of a man who is an utter rascal both in family and commercial relations, but preserves his reputation intact and does not even experience any deathbed repentance — is rather an unconscious study for a character in a novel—a sketch of a *bourgeois* Barnes Newcome—than anything more. It has the old drawback of being narrated, not acted or spoken at first hand: and so, though it is in a sense Fielding at nearly his best, more than half a century before Fielding attempted *Joseph Andrews*, no more need be said of it. So, too, the religious element and the allegory *are* too prominent in *The Holy War*—the novelist's desk is made too much of a pulpit in large parts of it. Other parts, concerning the inhabitants of Mansoul and their private affairs, are domestic novel-writing of nearly the pure kind: and if *The Pilgrim's Progress* did not exist, it would be worth while to pick them out and discuss them. But, as it most fortunately does exist, this is not needful.

The only fault with the novel-character of the greater book which might possibly be found by a critic who did not let the allegory bite him, and was not frightened by the religion, is that there is next to no love element in it, though there are wedding bells. Mercy is indeed quite nice enough for a heroine: but Bunyan might have bestowed her better than on a young gentleman so very young that he had not long before made himself (no doubt allegorically) ill with unripe and unwholesome fruit. But if he had done so, the suspicions of his brethren—*they* were acute enough as it was not to mistake the character of the book, whatever modern critics may do—would have been even more unallayable. And, as it is, the " alluring countenance " does shed not a little grace upon the story, or at least upon the Second Part: while the intenser character of the First hardly requires this. Any other lack is, to the present writer, imperceptible. The romance interest of quest, adventure, achievement, is present to the fullest degree: and what is sometimes called the pure novel interest of character and conversation is present in a degree not lower. It must be accepted as a great blessing, even by those who regard Puritanism as an almost unmitigated curse, that its principles forbade Bunyan to think of choosing the profane and abominable stage-play as the form of his creation. We had had our fill of good plays, and were beginning to drink of that which was worse: while we had no good novels and wanted them. Of course the large amount of actual " Tig and Tirry " dialogue (as Dr. Johnson would say) is probably one of the things which have made precisians shy of accepting the *Progress* for what it really is. But we must remember that this encroachment on the dramatic province was exactly what was wanted to remove the reproach of fiction. The inability to put actual conversation of a lively kind in the mouths of personages has been indicated as one of the great defects of the novel up to this time. Except Cervantes, it is difficult to think of any novelist who had shown himself able to supply the want. Bunyan can do it as few have done it even since his time. The famous dialogue of Christian and By-ends is only the best—if it is the best—of scores nearly or quite as good. The curious intellectual flaccidity of the present day seems to be " put off " by the " ticket " names; but no one who has the true literary sense cares for these one way or another, or is more disturbed by them than if they were Wilkins and Jones. Just as Coleridge observed that to enjoy some kinds of poetry you must suspend disbelief, so, with mere literary fashions, you must suspend disagreement. We should not call By-ends By-ends now: and whether we should do better or worse nobody, as Plato says, knows but the Deity. But the best of us would be hard put to it to make By-ends reveal his By-endishness more perfectly than he does by his conversation, and without any ticket-name at all.

Not less remarkable, and only a little less new, is the vividness and sufficiency of the scene painting and setting.

It has been said that the great novelists not only provide us with a world of friends more real and enjoyable than the actual folk we know, but also with a world for those friends to live in, more real and far more enjoyable than the world in which we ourselves sojourn. And this is well seen of Christian. The Slough of Despond and the terrible overhanging hill; the gateway and the Interpreter's House and the House Beautiful; the ups and downs of the road, and the arbours and the giants' dens: Beulah and the Delectable Mountains:—one knows them as one knows the country that one has walked over, and perhaps even better. There is no description for description's sake: yet nothing is wanting of the descriptive kind.

Yet all these things are—as they should be—only subsidiary to the main interest of the Pilgrimage itself. Once more, one may fear that it is no good sign of the wits of the age that readers should be unable to discard familiarity with the argument of the story. It is the way in which that argument is worked out and illustrated that is the thing. I have never myself, since I became thoroughly acquainted with Lydgate's Englishing of Deguilevile's *Pilgrimage of the Soul of Man,* had any doubt that—in some way or other, direct or indirect, at tenth or twentieth hand perhaps—Bunyan was acquainted with it: but this is of no importance. He might undoubtedly have got all his materials straight out of the Bible. But his working of them up is all his own, and is wonderful. Here, to begin with, is the marvel not merely of a continuation which is not a falling off, but of a repetition of the same general scheme with different but closely connected personages, which is entirely free from monotony. One is so accustomed to the facts that perhaps it hardly strikes one at first how extraordinarily audacious the attempt is: nay, the very success of it may blind all but critics to the difficulty. It is no wonder that people tried further continuations and further complications: still less wonder that they utterly failed. Probably even Bunyan himself could not have " done it a third time." But he did it these twice with such vividness of figure and action; such completeness of fable; such sufficiency of behaviour and of speech as have scarcely ever been equalled. As ideal as Spenser, as real as Defoe: such is Bunyan. And he shows this realism and this idealism in a prose narrative, bringing the thoughts and actions and characters and speech of fictitious human beings before his readers—for their inspection perhaps; for their delight certainly. If this is not the being and the doing of a novelist this deponent very humbly declareth that he knoweth not what the being and the doing of a novelist are.

We must now turn to two small but noteworthy attempts at the kind, which have been referred to above.

In 1668 there appeared a very curious little book (entitled at great length after the manner of the times, but more shortly called *The Isle of Pines*), which is important in the literary ancestry of Defoe and Swift and not unimportant in itself. Its author was Henry Neville, of the Nevilles of Billingbeare, son of one Sir Henry and grandson of another, the grandfather having been of some mark in diplomacy and courtiership in late Elizabethan and early Jacobean times. The grandson had had a life of some stir earlier. Born in 1620, and educated at Merton and University Colleges, he had left Oxford without a degree, had taken the Parliamentary side, but as a rigid Republican and anti-Cromwellite; had been a member of the Rota, and after the Restoration had been arrested in 1663 for supposed treasonable practices, but escaped serious punishment. He lived quietly for more than thirty years longer and died in 1694. Besides *The Isle of Pines* he wrote satirical tracts (the *Parliament of Ladies* being the best known), translated Machiavelli, and was evidently a man of parts, though, like his friend Harrington, something of a " crank." He seems also to have been, as some others of the extremer Puritans certainly were, pretty loose in his construction of moral laws.

The Isle is a very short book of thirty-one quarto pages: but there is a good deal in it, and it must have been very carefully written. A certain Cornelius van Sloetten writes, " supported by letters from Amsterdam," how a Dutch ship, driven far out of reckoning in the Southern Ocean, comes to a " fourth island, near Terra Australis Incognita," which is inhabited by white people, speaking English, but mostly naked. The headman is a certain William Pine, whose grandfather, George, has left a written account of the origin of the community. This relates how George was wrecked on the island, the ship perishing " with man and mouse," except himself, his master's daughter, two white maidservants, and a negro girl. The island proves pleasant and habitable: and George, to prevent unfairness and ill-feeling, unites himself to all his female companions, the quintet living in perfect harmony. Thirty-seven children result: and these at first necessarily intermarry; but after this first generation, a rule is made that brothers and sisters may not unite—the descendants of the four original wives forming clans who may marry into the others but not into their own. A wider legal code of fair stringency is arranged, with the sanction of capital and other punishments: and things go so well that the patriarch musters a tribe of 565 persons by the time he is sixty, and of 1789 twenty years later, when he departs this life,

piously praying God " to multiply them and send them
the true report of the gospel." The multiplication has
duly taken place, and there is something like a civil war
while the Dutch are there; but they interfere with fire-
arms to restore order, and leave all well. The writer's
cunning is shown by the fact that he does not stop abruptly:
but finishes off with some subsequent and quite *verisimilar*
experiences of the Dutch ship. The book does not appear
to have had a very great popularity in England, though it
was reprinted and abridged at least once, pretty shortly.
But it was very popular abroad, was translated into three
or four languages, and was apparently taken as a genuine
account.

Neville's art is in fact not inconsiderable. Earlier
voyages and travels of course supplied him with his
technical and geographical details: and the codification of
the Isle of Pines suggests the Bacon-Harrington tradition.
But he has got the vividness and realism which have
usually been lacking before: and though some of his
details are pretty " free " it is by no means only through
such things that these qualities are secured. To Cyrano
de Bergerac he bears no likeness at all. In fact, though
Neville *was* a satirist, satire does not seem to have been
in any way his object here. Whatever that object may
have been, he has certainly struck, by accident or not, on
the secret of producing an interesting account by in-
geniously multiplied and adjusted detail. Moreover, as
there is no conversation, the book stands—accidentally this
time almost without doubt—at the opposite pole from the
talk-deluged romances of the Scudéry type. Whether
Defoe actually knew it or not matters exceedingly little:
that something of his method, and in a manner the subject
of his first and most famous novel, are here before him,

seems quite indisputable. Perhaps not the least piquant
thing to do with *The Isle of Pines* is to contrast it with
Oceana. Of course the contrast is unfair: nearly all
contrasts are. But there is actually, as has been pointed
out, a slight contact between the work of the two friends:
and their complete difference in every other respect makes
this more curiously apparent. And another odd thing is
that Neville—" Rota "-republican as he was—should have
adopted patriarchal (one can hardly say *legitimate*) government here.

Congreve's *Incognita* (1692), the last seventeenth-century
novel that requires special notice, belongs much more
to the class of Afra's tales than to that of the heroic
romances. It is a short story of seventy-five small pages only
and of the Italian-Spanish imbroglio type. The friends
Aurelian and Hippolito take each other's names for certain
purposes, and their beloveds, " Incognita," Juliana and
Leonora, are perplexed accordingly: while family feuds,
letter assignations at a convent where the name of
the convent unluckily happens to be torn off, and other
stock ingredients of the kind are freely used. Most
writers have either said nothing about the book or have
given it scanty praise; with the exception, Sir Walter
Raleigh, I confess that I cannot here agree. Being
Congreve's it could not be quite without flashes of wit,
but they do not appear to me to be either very numerous
or very brilliant; the plot, such as it is, is a plot of drama
rather than of fiction; and there is no character that I can
see. It is in fact only one of a vast multitude of
similar stories, not merely in the two languages just referred
to, but in French, which were but to show that the time
of the novel was not yet come, even when the time of this
century was all but over.

It was quite over, and the first two decades of the next were all but over too, before the way was, to any important extent, further explored: but important assistance in the exploration was given at the beginning of the second of these decades. The history of the question of the relations of the Addison-Steele periodical, and especially of the " Coverley Papers," to the novel is both instructive and amusing to those who have come to appreciate the humours of literary things. It would probably have shocked the more orthodox admirers of the *Spectator*, during the eighteenth century, to have any such connection or relation so much as hinted. But when people began to consider literature and literary history in a better arranged perspective, the fact that there *is* such a connection or relation must have been soon perceived. It has become comparatively a commonplace: and now the third stage—that in which people become uneasy and suspicious of the commonplace and obvious and try to turn it topsy-turvy—has begun.

It is of course undeniable that the " Coverley Papers," as they stand, are not a novel, even on the loosest conception and construction of the term. There is no plot; some of what should be the most important characters are merely heard of, not seen; and the various scenes have no sort of connection, except that the same persons figure in them. But these undeniable facts do not interfere with two other facts, equally undeniable and much more important. The first is that the papers could be turned into a novel with hardly any important alteration, and with only *quantum suff.* of addition and completion. " The widow " is there in the background ready to be produced and made a heroine; many of the incidents are told novel-fashion already, and more could be translated into that

fashion by the veriest tyro at novel writing who has
written at any time during the last one hundred and fifty
years. The personages of the club have merely to step
down and out; the scenes to be connected, amplified, and
multiplied; the conversation to undergo the same process.

But the second point is of greater importance still.
Not only could the "Coverley Papers," be made into a novel
without the slightest difficulty, and by a process much of
which would be simple enlargement of material; but they
already possess, in a fashion which requires no alteration
at all, many of the features of the novel, far more successfully hit off than had ever been done before in the novel
itself. This is true of the dialogue to no small extent, and
of the description even more: but it is truest of all of the
characters. Except Bunyan, nobody in prose fiction had
ever made personages so thoroughly spirited as Sir Roger
and even the two Wills, Honeycomb and Wimble; while
here there was " no allaying Thames " in the shape of
allegory, little moralising and that of a kind quite human,
a plentiful setting of ordinary and familiar scene, and a
more plentiful and exact adjustment of ordinary and
familiar manners. It is true that Addison, partly owing
to the undercurrent of his satirical humour (Steele succeeds
rather better here), has not attained the astonishing
verisimilitude of the writer to whom we shall come next
and last but one in this chapter. His characters are
perfectly natural, but we know, all the while, that they are
works of art. But in most of the points just mentioned
he has exactly the tricks of the novelist's art that Defoe
has not. The smaller tales in the *Tatler* and its followers
undoubtedly did something to remove the reproach from
prose fiction, and more to sharpen the appetite for it.
But they were nothing new: the short tale being of un-

known antiquity. The "Coverley Papers" *were* new and did much more. This new kind of treatment may not have suggested beforehand (it is not certain that it did not) the extensive novel of character and manners—the play lengthened, bodied more strongly, and turned into narrative form. But the process was *there;* the instances of it were highly reputed and widely known. It must in almost any case have gone hard but a further step still would be taken. It was actually taken by the person who had suggested the periodical essay itself.

Much has been written about Defoe, but, curiously enough, the least part of what has been written about him has concerned the very part of him that is read—his novels. Nay, occasional eccentrics, and not only these, have shown a sort of disposition to belittle him as a novelist: indeed the stock description of Richardson as the Father of the English Novel almost pointedly rules Defoe out. Yet further, the most adequate and intelligent appreciation of his novel work itself has too often been mainly confined to what is no doubt a subject of exceeding interest —the special means by which he secures the attention, and procures the delight, of his readers. We shall have to deal with this too. But the point to which it is wished to draw special attention now is different, and we may reach it best by the ordinary " statement of case."

Almost everybody who knows any literary history, knows that the book by which, after thirty or forty years of restless publication in all sorts of prose and rhyme, Defoe niched himself immovably in English literature, was a new departure by almost an old man. He was all but, if not quite, sixty when *Robinson Crusoe* appeared: and a very few following years saw the appearance of his pretty voluminous " minor " novels. The subject of the first every one knows without limitation: it is not so certain, though vigorous efforts have been made to popularise the others, that even their subjects are clearly known to many people. *Captain Singleton* (1720), *Moll Flanders*, and *Colonel Jack* (both 1722) are picaresque romances with tolerably sordid heroes and heroines, but with the style entirely rejuvenated by Defoe's secret. *Roxana* (1724), a very puzzling book which is perhaps not entirely his writing, is of the same general class: the *Voyage round the World* (1725), the least interesting, but not *un*interesting, is exactly what its title imports,—in other words, the " stuffing " of the *Robinson* pie without the game. The *Memoirs of a Cavalier* (1720) approach the historical novel (or at least the similar " stuffing " of that) and have raised curious and probably insoluble questions as to whether they are inventions at all—questions intimately connected with that general one referred to above. One or two minor things are sometimes added to the list: but they require no special notice. The seven books just mentioned are Defoe's contribution to the English novel. Let us consider the quality of this contribution first—and then the means used to attain it.

Their novel-quality (which, as has been hinted, has not been claimed so loudly or so steadily as it should have been for Defoe) is the quality of Story-Interest—and this, one dares say, he not only infused for the first time in full dose, but practically introduced into the English novel, putting the best of the old mediæval romances aside and also putting aside *The Pilgrim's Progress*, which is not likely to have been without influence on himself. It may be said, " Oh! but the *Amadis* romances, and the Elizabethan novels, and the ' heroics ' must have interested or they would not have been read." This looks plausible,

E

but is a mistake. Few people who have not studied the
history of criticism know the respectable reluctance to be
pleased with literature which distinguished mankind till
very recent times; and which in fact kept the novel back
or was itself maintained by the absence of the novel. In
life people pleased themselves irregularly enough: in literature they could not get out of the idea that they ought to
be instructed, that it was enough to be instructed, and that
it was discreditable to ask for more. Even the poet was
allowed to delight grudgingly and at his peril; was suspected because he did delight, and had to pay a sort of
heavy licence-duty for it, in the shape of concomitant
instruction to others and good behaviour in himself. In
fact he was a publican who was bound to serve stodgy
food as well as exhilarating drink.

It is impossible to doubt that people were similarly
affected to the fiction of the Renaissance and the seventeenth century, at least in its longer examples—for the
smaller *novelle* could amuse in their own way sometimes,
though they could hardly absorb. It is equally impossible
to imagine any one being " enthralled " by *Euphues*.
Admiration, of a kind, must have been the only passion
excited by it. In the *Arcadia* there is a certain charm,
but it belongs to the inset verse—to the almost Spenserian
visionariness of parts—to the gracious lulling atmosphere
of the whole. If it had been published in three volumes,
one cannot imagine the most enthusiastic novel-reader
knocking up a friend late at night for volume two or
volume three. I have said that I can read *Parismus* for
pastime: but the pastime that it provides is certainly not
over-stimulating, and the mild stimulant becomes un-
sweetened and unlemoned barley-water in books of the
Parthenissa class. If with them conversing one forgets all

time, it must be by the influence of the kind go-between Sleep. We know, of course, that their contemporaries did not go to sleep over them: but it was because they felt that they were being done good to—that they were in the height of polite society—that their manners were being softened and not allowed to be gross. The time, in its blunt way, was fond of contrasting the attractions of a mistress on one side and " a friend and a bottle " on the other. That a novel could enter into competition with either or both, as an interesting and even exciting means of passing the time, would have entered very few heads at all and have been contemptuously dismissed from most of those that it did enter.

Addison and Steele in the " Coverley Papers " had shown the way to construct this new spell: Defoe actually constructed it. It may be that some may question whether the word " exciting " applies exactly to his stories. But this is logomachy: and in fact a well-willing reader *can* get very fairly excited while the Cavalier is escaping after Marston Moor; while it is doubtful whether the savages have really come and what will be the event; while it is again doubtful whether Moll is caught or not; or what has become of those gains of the boy Jack, which can hardly be called ill-gotten because there is such a perfect unconsciousness of ill on the part of the getter. At any rate, if such a reader cannot feel excitement here, he would utterly stagnate in any previous novel.

In presence of this superior—this emphatically and doubly " novel "—interest, all other things become comparatively unimportant. The relations of *Robinson Crusoe* to Selkirk's experiences and to one or two other books (especially the already mentioned *Isle of Pines*) may not unfitly employ the literary historian who chooses to occupy himself with them. The allegory which Defoe alleges in it, and which some biographers have endeavoured to work out, cannot, I suppose, be absolutely pooh-poohed, but presents no attractions whatever to the present writer. Whether the *Cavalier* is pure fiction, or partly embroidered fact, *is* a somewhat interesting question, if only because it seems to be impossible to find out the answer: and the same may be said of the not impossible (indeed almost more than probable) Portuguese maps and documents at the back of *Captain Singleton*. To disembroil the chronological muddle of *Roxana*, and follow out the tangles of the hide-and-seek of that most unpleasant " lady of pleasure " and her daughter, may suit some. But, apart from all these things, there abides the fact that you can *read* the books—read them again and again—enjoy them most keenly at first and hardly less keenly afterwards, however often you repeat the reading.

As has been partly said, the means by which this effect is achieved, and also the means by which it is not, are almost equally remarkable. The Four Elements of the novel are sometimes, and not incorrectly, said to be Plot, Character, Description, and Dialogue—Style, which some would make a fifth, being rather a characteristic in another order of division. It is curious that Defoe is rebellious or evasive under any analysis of this kind. His plots are of the " strong " order—the events succeed each other and are fairly connected, but do not compose a history so much as a chronicle. In character, despite his intense verisimilitude, he is not very individual. Robinson himself, Moll, Jack, William the Quaker in *Singleton*, even Roxana the cold-blooded and covetous courtesan, cannot be said not to be real—they and almost every one of the minorities are an immense advance on the colourless and bloodless ticketed puppets of the Middle Fiction. But they still want *something*—the snap of the fingers of the artist. Moll is perhaps the most real of all of them and yet one has no flash-sights of her being—never sees her standing out against soft blue sky or thunder-cloud as one sees the great characters of fiction; never hears her steps winding and recognises her gesture as one does theirs.

So again his description is sufficient: and the enumerative particularity of it is even great part of the *secret de Polichinelle* to which we are coming. But it is far from elaborate in any other way and has hardly the least decoration or poetical quality. Well as we know Crusoe's Island the actual scenery of it is not half so much impressed as that even, for instance, of Masterman Ready's— it is either of the human figures—Crusoe's own grotesque bedizenment, the savages, Friday, the Spaniards, Will Atkins—or of the works of man—the stockade, the boat, and the rest—that we think. A little play is made with Jack's glass-house squalor and Roxana's magnificence *de mauvais lieu,* but not much: the gold-dust and deserts of *Singleton* are a necessary part of the " business," but nothing more. *Moll Flanders* — in some respects the greatest of all his books—has the bareness of an Elizabethan stage in scenery and properties—it is much if Greenfield spares us a table or a bed to furnish it.

Of Dialogue Defoe is specially fond—even making his personages soliloquise in this after a fashion—and it plays a very important part in " the secret: " yet it can hardly be classed very high *as* dialogue. And this is at least partly due to the strange *drab* shapelessness of his style, which never takes on any brilliant colour, or quaint individual form.

Yet it is very questionable whether any other style would have suited the method so well, or would even have suited it at all. For this method—to leave off hinting at it and playing round it—is one of almost endless accumulation of individually trivial incident, detail, and sometimes observation, the combined effect of which is to produce an insensible but undoubting acceptance, on the reader's part, of the facts presented to him. The process has been more than once analysed in that curious and convenient miniature example of it, the " Mrs. Veal " *supercherie :* but you may open the novels proper almost anywhere and discover it in full operation. Like most great processes of art, this is an adoption and perfecting of habits usual with the most inartistic people—a turning to good account of the interminably circumstantial superfluities of the common gossip and newsmonger. Very often Defoe actually does not go beyond this—just as in *The Shortest Way with the Dissenters* he had simply reproduced the actual thoughts and wishes of those who disliked dissent. But sometimes he got the better of this also, as in the elaborate building up of Robinson's surroundings and not a little in the other books. And there the effect is not only verisimilar but wonderful in its verisimilitude. At any rate, in him, and for English prose and secular fiction, we have first that mysterious charm of the *real that is not real* —of the " human creation "—which constitutes the appeal of the novel. In some of the books there is hardly any appeal of any other sort. Moll Flanders, though not unkindly, and " improper " rather from the force of circumstances than from any specially vicious inclination, is certainly not a person for whom one has much liking. Colonel Jack, after his youthful experiences in pocket-picking, is rather a nonentity, something of a coward, a fellow of no particular wits, parts, or definite qualities of any kind. Singleton is a rascal who " plays Charlemagne," as the French gambling term has it, and endows his repentance with the profits of his sin. As for Roxana there are few more repulsive heroines in fiction—while the Cavalier and the chief figure in the *Voyage Round the World* are simply threads on which their respective adventures are strung. Even Robinson himself enlists no particular sympathy except of the " put-yourself-in-his-place " kind. Yet these sorry or negative personages, of whom, in the actual creation of God, we should be content to know nothing except from paragraphs in the newspaper (and generally in the police-reports thereof), content us perfectly well with their company through hundreds and thousands of solid pages, and leave us perfectly ready to enjoy it again after a reasonable interval.

This, as has been said, is the mystery of fiction—a mystery partly set a-working in the mediæval romance, then mostly lost, and now recovered—in his own way and according to his own capacity — by Defoe. It was to escape others for a little longer and then to be yet again rediscovered by the great quartette of the mid-eighteenth century—to slip in and out of hands during the later part of that century, and then to be all but finally established, in patterns for everlasting pursuance, by Miss Austen and by Scott. But Defoe is really (unless we put Bunyan before him) the first of the magicians—not the greatest by any means, but great and almost alone in the peculiar talent of making uninteresting things interesting—not by burlesquing them or satirising them; not by suffusing or inflaming them with passion; not by giving them the amber of style; but by serving them " simple of themselves " as though they actually existed.

The position of Defoe in novel history is so great that there is a temptation to end this chapter with him. But to do so would cause an inconvenience greater than any resulting advantages. For the greatest of Defoe's contemporaries in English letters also comes into our division, and comes best here. One cannot conveniently rank Swift with the great quartette of the next chapter, because he is a novelist " by interim " and incompletely: to rank him among the minor and later novelists of the eighteenth century would be as to the first part of the classification absurd and as to the last false. And he comes, not merely in time, pretty close to Defoe, incommensurable as is the genius of the two. It has even been thought (plausibly enough, though the matter is of no great importance) that the form of *Gulliver* may have been to some extent determined by *Robinson Crusoe* and Defoe's other novels of travel. And there is a subtler reason for taking the pair together and both close to Addison and Steele.

Swift had shown the general set towards prose fiction, and his own bent in the same direction, long before Defoe's novel-period and as early as the *Tale of a Tub* and the *Battle of the Books* (*published* 1704 but certainly earlier in part). The easy flow of the narrative, and the vivid dialogue of the Spider and the Bee in the latter, rank high among those premonitions of novel with which, in this place, we should be specially busied. In the former Peter, Martin, and Jack want but a little more of the alchemist's furnace to accomplish their projection into real characters, and not merely allegorical figure-heads. But, of course, in both books, the satiric purpose dominates too much to allow them to be really ranked among novels, even if they had taken the trouble to clothe themselves with more of the novel-garb.

With *Gulliver* it is different. It is a commonplace on its subject (but like many other commonplaces a thing ill to forget or ignore) that natural and unsophisticated children always *do*, and that almost anybody who has a certain power of turning blind eyes when and where he chooses *can*, read it simply as a story of adventure and enjoy it hugely. It would be a most preternatural child or a most singularly constituted adult who could read *Utopia* or *Oceana*, or even Cyrano's *Voyages*, " for the story " and enjoy them hugely. This means that Swift had either learnt from Defoe or—and considering those earlier productions of his own much more probably—had independently developed the knack of *absorbing* the reader— the knack of telling a story. But of course there is in one sense much more, and in another much less, than a story in *Gulliver :* and the finest things in it are independent of story, though (and this once more comes in for our present purpose) they are quite capable of adaptation to story-purposes, and have been so adapted ever since by the greatest masters of the art. These are strokes of satire, turns of phrase, little illuminations of character, and seasonings of description. But the great point of *Gulliver* is that, like Defoe's work, though in not quite the same way, it is *interesting*—that it takes hold of its reader and gives him its " peculiar pleasure." When a work of art does this, it is pretty near perfection.

There is, however, another book of Swift's which, though perhaps seldom mentioned or even thought of in connection with the novel, is of real importance in that connection, and comes specially in with our present main consideration —the way in which the several parts of the completed novel were being, as it were, separately got ready and set apart for the use of the accomplished novelist. This is the very curious and agreeable piece called *Polite Conversation* (1738), on which, though it was not printed till late in his life and close on *Pamela* itself, there is good reason for thinking that he had been for many years engaged. The importance of dialogue in the novel has been often mentioned and will scarcely be contested: while frequent occasion has been taken to point out that it had hitherto been very ill-achieved. Swift's " conversation " though designedly *underlined*, as it were, to show up current follies and extravagances of phrase and of fashion generally, is yet pretty certainly in the main the real average conversation of the society of his time, which he knew well and thoroughly. Further, there is a distinct, though it may be almost impalpable, difference between it and the conversation of the stage, though it is naturally connected therewith. Non-poetical stage dialogue in capable hands is either deliberate talking for display of " wit," like that of Congreve, or is conditioned and directed by the necessities of action and character. Of course, novel conversation may diverge in the first direction, and cannot properly neglect the second altogether. But, as there is room for very much more of it, it may and should allow itself a considerably wider range and imitate, on proper occasions, the desultory gossip and small talk of people who live on the " boards " of a room-floor and not of a stage.

This is just what Swift's does, and just what there is very little of in Defoe; almost necessarily less in Addison and his group because of their essay form; and hardly anything elsewhere and earlier. Just as the Coverley Papers could, by one process and no difficult one, have been thrown into a novel; so by another, a not much more difficult and a much less complicated one, could the *Polite Conversation* be thrown into part of a novel—while in each case the incomplete and unintentional draft itself supplies patterns for the complete work in new kind such as had never been given before. Indeed the *Conversation* may almost be said to *be* part of a novel—and no small part—as it stands, and of such a novel as had never been written before.

But there was something still further all but absolutely necessary to the novel, though not necessary to it alone, which Defoe, Addison, and Swift, each in his several way, worked mightily to supply: and that was a flexible business-like "workaday" prose style. Not merely so long as men aimed at the eccentric and contorted styles of *Euphues* and the *Arcadia*, but so long as the old splendid and gorgeous, but cumbrous and complicated pre-Restoration style lasted, romances were possible, but novels were not. You might indeed pick out of Shakespeare—especially from such parts as those of Beatrice, Rosalind, and some of the fools—a capital novel-style: but then you can pick almost anything out of Shakespeare. Elsewhere the constant presence either of semi-poetic phraseology or of some kind of "lingo" was almost fatal. You want what Sprat calls a more "natural way of speaking" (though not necessarily a "naked" one) for novel purposes— a certain absence of ceremony and parade of phrase: though the presence of slang and some other things, the rebuking of which was partly Swift's object in the *Conversation*, is *not* fatal, and so he, in a manner, blessed and prescribed what he meant to ban.

Thus, by the early years of the reign of George II., or a little later, we find, on the one side, an evident, and variously though inarticulately proclaimed, desire for novels; on the other, the accumulation, in haphazard and desultory way, of almost all the methods, the processes, the "plant," necessary to turn novels out; but hardly anything except the considered work of Bunyan, Defoe, and Swift which really deserves the name of novel. A similar process had been going on in France; and, in the different work of Le Sage and Marivaux, had actually produced work in the kind more advanced than anything in English. But the tables were soon to be turned: and during the rest of the century the English Novel was at last to assert itself as a distinct, an increasingly popular, and a widely cultivated kind. That this was due to the work of the four great novelists who fill its central third and will fill our next chapter cannot perhaps be said: that their work was the first great desertion of it may be said safely.

CHAPTER III

THE FOUR WHEELS OF THE NOVEL WAIN

IT does not enter into the plan, because it would be entirely inconsistent with the scale, of the present book to give details of the lives of the novelists, except when they have something special to do with the subject, or when (as in the case of a few minorities who happen to be of some importance) even well-informed readers are likely to be quite ignorant about them. Accounts, in all degrees of scale and competence, of the lives of Richardson, Fielding, Smollett, and Sterne abound. It is sufficient—but in the special circumstances at this point perhaps necessary— here to sum the facts very briefly in so far as they bear on the main issue. Richardson (1689-1761), not merely the first to write, but the eldest by much more than his priority in writing, was the son of a Derbyshire tradesman, was educated for some time at Charterhouse, but apprenticed early to a printer—which trade he pursued with diligence and profit for the rest of his life in London and its immediate neighbourhood. After his literary success, he gathered round him a circle of ladies and gentlemen interested in literature: but he never had any first-hand acquaintance with general society of the " gentle " kind, much less with that of the upper classes. Fielding (1707-1754), on the contrary, was a member (though only as the son of a younger son of a younger son) of a family of great antiquity and distinction, which held an earldom in England and another in Ireland, and was connected as well as

77

it was derived, Lady Mary Wortley Montagu, for instance, being the novelist's cousin. He was educated at Eton and Leyden: but his branch of the family being decidedly impecunious, was thrown very much on his own resources. These were mainly drawn from literature, first as a playwright then as a novelist, journalism and miscellanies coming in. But he was called to the Bar: and though he probably did not make much money there, he obtained the poorly paid and hard-worked but rather important position of " Bow Street Magistrate," which meant that he was head, directly of the London police such as it was, and indirectly of that of the whole kingdom. His temper was in some ways as aristocratic as his birth: but though Horace Walpole's accounts of his fancy for low company are obviously exaggerated, there is no doubt that he was a good deal of what has since been called a " Bohemian." His experience of variety in scene was much wider than Richardson's, although after he came home from Leyden (where he went to study law) it was chiefly confined to London and the south of England (especially Bath, Dorsetshire, where he lived for a time, and the Western Circuit), till his last voyage, in hopeless quest of health, to Lisbon, where he died. His knowledge of literature, and even what may be called his scholarship, were considerable, and did credit to the public school education of those days.

Smollett (1721-1771) differed from his two predecessors in being a Scotsman: but in family was very much nearer to Fielding than to Richardson, being the grandson of a judge who was a Commissioner of the Union, and a gentleman of birth and property—which last would, had he lived long enough, have come to Smollett himself. But he suffered in his youth from some indistinctly known family jars, was apprenticed to a Glasgow surgeon, and escaping thence to London with a tragedy in his pocket, was in undoubted difficulties till (and after) he obtained the post of surgeon's mate on board a man-of-war, and took part in the Carthagena expedition. After coming home he made at least some attempts to practise: but was once more drawn off to literature, though fortunately not to tragedy. For the rest of his life he was a hard-worked but by no means ill-paid journalist, novelist, and miscellanist, making as much as £2000 by his *History of England*, not ill-written, though now never read. Like Fielding (though, unlike him, more than once) he went abroad in search of health and died in the quest at Leghorn. Smollett was not ignorant, but he seems to have known modern languages better than ancient: though there is doubt about his direct share in the translations to which he gave his name. Moreover he had some though no great skill in verse.

Lastly Sterne (1713-1768), though hardly, as it is the custom to call him, "an Irishman," yet vindicated the claims of the third constituent of the United Kingdom by being born in Ireland, from which country his mother came. But the Sternes were pure English, of a gentle family which had migrated from East Anglia through Nottingham to Yorkshire, and was much connected with Cambridge. Thither Laurence, the novelist, after a very roving childhood (his father was a soldier), and a rather irregular education, duly went: and, receiving preferment in the Church from his Yorkshire relations, lived for more than twenty years in that county without a history, till he took the literary world—hardly by storm, but by a sort of fantastic capful of wind—with *Tristram Shandy* in 1760. Seven or eight years of fame, some profit, not hard work (for his books shrink into no great solid bulk), and constant travelling, ended by a sudden death at his

Bond Street lodgings, after a long course of ill-health very carelessly attended to.

One or two more traits are relevant. All the four were married, and married pretty early; two of them married twice. Richardson's first wife was, in orthodox fashion, his master's daughter: of his second little is known. Fielding's first (he had made a vain attempt earlier to abduct an heiress who was a relation) was, by universal consent, the model both of Sophia and Amelia, almost as charming as either, and as amiable; his second was her maid. Of Mrs. Smollett, who was a Miss Lascelles and a West Indian heiress in a small way, we know very little—the habit of identifying her with the " Narcissa " of *Roderick Random* is natural, inconclusive, but not ridiculous. Sterne's matrimonial relations are the most famous of all: and though posterity has, with its usual charity, constructed a legend for the pair which is probably much worse than the reality, that reality is more than a little awkward. Mrs. Sterne was a Miss Lumley, of a good Yorkshire family, some, though small, fortune, and more friends who exerted themselves for her husband. By inexcusable levity, ignorance, misjudgment, or heartless cupidity their daughter Lydia published, after the death of both, letters some of which contain courtship of the most lackadaisical sentimentality and others later expressions (which occasionally reach the scandalous) of weariness and disgust on Sterne's part. Other evidence of an indisputable character shows that he was, at least and best, an extravagant and mawkish philanderer with any girl or woman who would join in a flirtation: and while there is no evidence against Mrs. Sterne's character in the ordinary sense, and hardly any of value against her temper, she seems (which is perhaps not wonderful) to have latterly preferred to live apart from her husband, and to have put him to considerable, if not unreasonable, expenses by her fancy for wandering about France with the daughter.

Finally, in general character, Richardson seems to have been a respectable person of rather feminine temperament and, though good-natured to his friends, endowed with a feminine spitefulness. Fielding, though by no means answering to the standard of minor and even major morals demanded

> "by the wise ones,
> By the grave and the precise ones,"

though reckless and disorderly in his ways and habits, appears to have been in the main a thorough gentleman, faithful to truth and honour, fearless, compassionate, intolerant of meanness and brutality and of treachery most of all—a man of many faults perhaps, but of no really bad or disgusting ones. Concerning Smollett's person- ality we know least of all the four. It was certainly dis- figured by an almost savage pugnacity of temper; by a strange indifference to what ought to be at the lowest the conduct of a gentleman, and by a most repulsive inclination —perhaps natural, but developed by training—to the merely foul and nasty. But he seems to have been brave, charitable though not in the most gracious way, honest, and on the whole a much better fellow than he might generally seem. Sterne is the most difficult of the four to characterise fairly, because of the unlucky revelations to which we possess no parallel in the case of the other three, and which, if we had them, might probably alter our estimates of a good many now well reputed people. It is perhaps enough to say that his letters contain many good traits as well as some bad ones; that his unlucky

F

portrait, with its combination of leer and sneer, is probably responsible for much; and that the parts which, as we shall see further, he chose to play, of extravagant humorist and extravagant sentimentalist, not only almost necessitate attitudes which may easily become offensive in the playing, but are very likely, in practice, to communicate something apparently not natural and unattractive to the player.

But enough of the workers, though not too much in the case of such remarkable contemporary exponents of a new kind of Human Comedy: let us go to the work.

In the long " History of the Unexpected," thick-strewn as it is with curiosities, there are few things odder than the appearance and the sequels of *Pamela : or Virtue Rewarded*, which, in circumstances to be noted presently, is said to have been begun on November 12, 1739, was finished (as far as the first part goes) exactly two months later, and (there being, in the case of the author's business, no obstacle of the kind that has frequently beset the appearance of greater works) was published later in the year 1740. That author was over fifty years old: though he had had much to do with ushering literature into the world, he had never attempted to produce it; he belonged to a class which was apt to regard *belles lettres* with profound suspicion; and his experiences, both in literature itself and in life, had been necessarily of the most limited kind. But there were certain counterbalancing facts to be taken into considera-tion which, though they can hardly be said to be *causes* of the marvel—the cause was the Hour, which hit, as it listed, on the Man—were a little more than accidental occasions of it. Richardson, as we see from his work, must have been a rather careful student of such novels as there were. The name of his first heroine, with the essen-tially English throwing back of the accent added, is the same as that of one of Sidney's heroines in the *Arcadia*, which had been not long before modernised for eighteenth-century reading by a certain Mrs. Stanley. The not very usual form " Laurana," which is the name of a character in his latest novel, is that of the heroine of *Parismus*. Further, he had had curious early experiences (which we know from his own meticulous revelations) of writing love-letters, when he was a mere boy, for girl-friends of his to adapt in writing to their lovers. " His eye," he says, " had been always on the ladies," though no doubt always also in the most honourable way. And, quite recently, the crystallisation had been precipitated by a commission from two of his bookseller (*i.e.* publisher) patrons—the founder of the House of Rivington and the unlucky Osborne who was knocked down by Johnson and picked up (not quite as one would wish to be) by Pope. They asked him to prepare a series of " Familiar Letters on the useful concerns of common life." Five-and-twenty years before, he had heard in outline something like the story of *Pamela*. In shaping this into letters he thought it might be a " new species of writing that might possibly turn young people into a course of reading different from the pomp and parade of romance-writing, and dismissing the improbable and marvellous with which novels generally abound, might tend to promote the cause of religion and virtue." His wife and " a young lady living with them," to whom he had read some of it, used to come into his little closet every night with, " Have you any more of *Pamela*, Mr. R. ?" Two other female friends joined in the interest and eulogy. He finished it (that is, the first two volumes which contain the whole of the original idea) and published it, though at first with the business-like precaution of appearing to " edit " only, and the more business-like liberty of liberal praise of what he edited. It became at once popular: and received the often repeated, but to the author very annoying, compliment of piratical continuation. So he set to work and continued it himself: as usually (though by no means invariably) with rather diminished success. On such points as the suggestion that he may have owed a debt to Marivaux (in *Marianne*) and others, little need be said here. I have never had much doubt myself that the indebtedness existed: though it would be rash, and is unnecessary, to attempt to determine to what extent and in what particular form.

It is by no means so difficult as it may at first sight appear to put oneself very much in the situation of a contemporary reader of *Pamela*, even if one has read it three or four times, provided that a fairly long period has elapsed since the last reading, and that the novels of the preceding age are fairly—and freshly—familiar. The thing has been in fact done—with unexpected but not in the least deliberate or suspicious success—by the present writer, who has read the book after an interval of some fifteen years and just after reading (in some cases again, in some for the first time) most of the works noticed in the preceding chapter. The difference of " the new species of writing " (one is reminded of the description of Spenser as " the new poet ") is almost startling: and of a kind which Richardson pretty certainly did not fully apprehend when he used the phrase. In order to appreciate it, one must not only leave out the two last volumes (which, as has been said, the first readers had not before them at all, and had better never have had) but also the second, or great part of it, which they would only have reached after they had been half whetted, half satiated, and wholly bribed, by the first. The defects of this later part and indeed of the first itself will be duly noticed presently. Let it be to us, for the moment, the story of Pamela up to and including " Mr. B.'s " repentance and amendment of mind: and the " difference " of this story, which fills some hundred and twenty or thirty closely printed, double columned, royal octavo pages in the " Ballantyne Novels," is (despite the awkwardness of such a form for the enjoyment of a novel) almost astounding.

To begin with, the novel-attractions are presented with a completeness which, as has been pointed out in the last chapter, is almost entirely lacking before. There is, of course, not very much plot, in the martinet sense of that word: there never was in Richardson, despite his immense apparatus and elaboration. The story is not knotted and unknotted; the wheel does not come full circle on itself; it merely runs along pleasantly till it is time for it to stop, and it stops rather abruptly. The siege of Pamela's virtue ends merely because the besieger is tired of assaults which fail, and of offering dishonourable terms of capitulation which are rejected: because he prefers peace and alliance. But such as it is, it is told with a spirit which must have been surprising enough to its readers, and which makes it, I confess, seem to me now much the best *story* in Richardson. The various alarums and excursions of the siege itself go off smartly and briskly: there may be more sequence than connection—there is *some* connection, as in the case of that most unlucky and ill-treated person the Rev. Mr. Williams—but the sequence is rapid and unbroken, and the constituents of it as it were jostle each other—not in any unfavourable sense, but in a sort of rapid dance, " cross hands and down the middle," which is inspiriting and contagious. He lost this faculty later: or rather he allowed it to be diluted and slackened into the interminable episodes of the not dissimilar though worse-starred plot against Clarissa, and the *massacrant* trivialities of the Italian part of *Grandison*.   But he had it here: and it is not a fair argument to say (as even in these days I have known it said) that Pamela's honour is a commodity of too little importance to justify such a pother about it.

This may bring us to the characters.   They also are not of the absolutely first class—excepting, as to be discussed later, the great attempt of Lovelace, Richardson's never are.   But they are an immense advance on the personages that did duty as persons in preceding novels, even in Defoe. " Mr. B. " himself is indeed not very capital.   One does not quite see why a man who went on as long as he did and used the means which he permitted himself to use, did not go on longer or use them more thoroughly.   But Richardson has at least vindicated his much-praised " knowledge of the human heart " by recognising two truths: first, that there are many natures (perhaps most) who are constantly tempted to " over-bid "—to give more and more for something that they want and cannot get; and, secondly, that there are others (again, perhaps, the majority, if not always the same individuals) who, when they are peremptorily told *not* to do a thing, at once determine to do it.   It was to Lady Davers mainly that Pamela owed her escape from the fate of Clarissa, though she would hardly have taken, or had the chance of taking, that fate in the same way. As for the minor characters, at least the lower examples are more than sufficient: and Mrs. Jewkes wants very little of being a masterpiece.   But of course Pamela herself is the cynosure, such as there is.   She has had rather hard measure with critics for the last century and a little more. The questions to ask now are, " Is she a probable human being? " and then, " Where are we to find a probable human being, worked out to the same degree, before? "

I say unhesitatingly that the answer to the first is " Yes,"
and the answer to the second " Nowhere." The last
triumph of originality and individuality she does not
indeed reach. Richardson had, even more than other
men of his century in England, a strong Gallic touch: and
he always tends to the type rather than the individual.
Beatrix Esmond is a coquette of the highest—almost of the
heroic-poetic—class, but she is first of all Beatrix Esmond.
Blanche Amory is a middle-class minx, hardly heroic at all,
but she is first of all Blanche Amory. Becky Sharp is an
adventuress who would go pretty close to, and perhaps not
stop at, positive crime, but she is first of all Becky Sharp.
Pamela Andrews is not first of all—perhaps she is hardly
at all—Pamela Andrews. There might be fifty or five
hundred Pamelas, while there could be only one of each
of the others. She is the pretty, good-natured, well-
principled, and rather well-educated menial, whose prudence
comes to the aid of her principles, whose pride does not
interfere with either, and who has a certain—it is hardly
unfair to call it—slyness which is of the sex rather than
of the individual. But, as such, she is quite admirably
worked out — a heroine of Racine in more detail and
different circumstances, a triumph of art, and at the same
time with so much nature that it is impossible to dismiss
her as merely artificial. The nearest thing to her in English
prose fiction before (Marianne, of course, is closer in French)
is Moll Flanders: and good as Moll is, she is flat and lifeless
in comparison with Pamela. You may call " my master's "
mistress (actually in the honourable sense, but never in the
dishonourable) again a minx, though a better minx than
Blanche, if you like. But there is no animal more alive
than a minx: and you will certainly not find a specimen of
the species in any English novel before.

As for description and dialogue, there is not very much of the former in *Pamela*, though it might not be unfair to include under the head those details, after the manner of Defoe (such as Pamela's list of purchases when she thinks she is going home), which supply their own measure of verisimilitude to the story. But there are some things of the kind which Defoe never would have thought of—such as the touches of the " tufts of grass " and the " pretty sort of wildflower that grows yonder near the elm, the fifth from us on the left," which occur in the gipsy scene. The dialogue plays a much more important part: and may be brought into parallel with that in the *Polite Conversation*, referred to above and published just before *Pamela*. It is " reported " of course, instead of being directly delivered, in accordance with the letter-scheme of which more presently, but that makes very little difference; to the first readers it probably made no difference at all. Here again that process of " vivification," which has been so often dwelt on, makes an astonishing progress—the blood and colour of the novel, which distinguish it from the more statuesque narrative, are supplied, if indirectly yet sufficiently and, in comparison with previous examples, amply. Here you get, almost or quite for the first time in the English novel, those spurts and sparks of animation which only the living voice can supply. Richardson is a humorist but indirectly; yet only the greatest humorists have strokes much better than that admirable touch in which, when the " reconciliations and forgivenesses of injuries " are being arranged, and Mr. B. (quite in the manner of the time) suggests marrying Mrs. Jewkes to the treacherous footman John and giving them an inn to keep—Pamela, the mild and semi-angelic but exceedingly feminine Pamela, timidly inquires whether, " This would not look like very heavy punishment to poor John?" She forgives Mrs. Jewkes of course, but only "as a Christian"—as a greater than Richardson put it afterwards and commented on it in the mouth of a personage whom Richardson could never have drawn, though Fielding most certainly could.

The original admirers of *Pamela*, then, were certainly justified: and even the rather fatuous eulogies which the author prefixed to it from his own and (let us hope) other pens (and which probably provoked Fielding himself more than even the substance of the piece) could be transposed into a reasonable key. But we ought nowadays to consider this first complete English novel from a rather higher point of view, and ask ourselves, not merely what its comparative merits were in regard to its predecessors, and as presented to its first readers, but what its positive character is and what, as far as it goes, are the positive merits or defects which it shows in its author.

The first thing to strike one in this connection is, almost of course, the letter-form. More agreement has been reached about this, perhaps, than about some other points in the inquiry. The initial difficulty of fiction which does not borrow the glamour of verse or of the stage is the question, "What does all this mean?" "What is the authority?" "How does the author know it all?" And a hundred critics have pointed out that there are practically only three ways of meeting this. The boldest and the best by far is to follow the poet and the dramatist themselves; to treat it like one of the magic lions of romance, ignore it, and pass on, secure of safety, to tell your story "from the blue," as if it were an actual history or revelation, or something passing before the eyes of the reader. But at that time few novelists had the courage to do this, daunted as they were by the absence of the sword and shield of

verse, of the vantage-room of the stage. Then there is
the alternative of recounting it by the mouth of one of the
actors in, or spectators of, the events—a plan obvious,
early, presenting some advantages, still very commonly
followed, but always full of little traps and pits of improbability, and peculiarly trying in respect to the character (if he is made to have any) of the narrator himself.
Thirdly, there is the again easy resource of the " document "
in its various forms. Of these, letters and diaries possess
some prerogative advantages; and were likely to suggest
themselves very particularly at this time when the actual
letter and diary (long rather strangely rare in English)
had for some generations appeared, and were beginning
to be common. In the first place the information thus
obtained looks natural and plausible: and there is a subsidiary advantage—on which Richardson does not draw
very much in *Pamela*, but which he employs to the full
later—that by varying your correspondents you can get
different views of the same event, and first-hand manifestations of extremely different characters.

Its disadvantages, on the other hand, are equally
obvious: but there are two or three of them of especial
importance. In the first place, it is essentially an artificial
rather than an artful plan—its want of verisimilitude, as
soon as you begin to think of it, is as great as that of either
of the others if not greater. In the second, without
immense pains, it must be " gappy and scrappy," while
the more these pains are taken the more artificial it will
become. In the third, the book is extremely likely, in the
taking of these pains and even without them, to become
intolerably lengthy and verbose. In the first part at
least of the first part of *Pamela*, Richardson avoided these
dangers fairly if not fully; in the second part he succumbed

to them; in his two later novels, though more elaborate and important plots to some extent bore up the expansion, he succumbed to them almost more. Pains have been taken above to show how the first readers of *Pamela* might rejoice in it, because of its contrast with the character of the seventeenth-century novel which was most read—the Scudéry or " heroic " romance. It is not, I think, too severe to say that nothing but the parallel with that romance, and the tolerance induced by familiarity with it, could make any one put up with the second part of *Pamela* itself, or with the inhumanly prolonged divagation of *Clarissa* and *Grandison*. Nor, as has been hinted, is the solace of the letters—in the opportunity of setting forth different tempers and styles—here much taken.

There is no doubt that one main attraction of this letter-plan (whether consciously experienced or not does not matter) was its ready adaptation to Richardson's own special and peculiar gift of minute analysis of mood, temper, and motive. The diary avowedly, and the letter in reality, even though it may be addressed to somebody else, is a continuous soliloquy: and the novelist can use it with a frequency and to a length which would be intolerable and impossible on the stage. Now soliloquy is the great engine for self-revelation and analysis. It is of course to a great extent in consequence of this analysis that Richardson owes his pride of place in the general judgment. It is quite possible to lay too much stress on it, as distinguishing the novel from the romance: and the present writer is of opinion that too much stress has actually been laid. The real difference between romance *per se* and novel *per se* (so far as they are capable of distinct existence) is that the romance depends more on incident and the novel more on character. Now this minute

analysis and exhibition, though it is one way of drawing
or constructing character, is not the only, nor even a
necessary, one.   It can be done without: but it has impressed the vulgar, and even some who are not the vulgar,
from Dr. Johnson to persons whom it is unnecessary to
mention.   They cannot believe that there is " no decep-
tion "—that the time is correctly told—unless the works
of the watch are bared to them: and this Richardson most
undoubtedly does.   Even in his 'prentice work, every
flutter of Pamela's little heart is registered, and registered
probably enough: nor could the registry have been effected,
perhaps, in any other way that should be in the least
probable so well as by the letter and journal method.   Of
course this analysis was not quite new; it had existed in
a sort of way in the heroic novel: and it had been eminently
present in the famous *Princesse de Clèves* of Madame de la
Fayette as well as in her French successors.   But these
stories had generally been as short as the heroics had been
long: and no one had risen (or descended) to anything
like the minuteness and fullness of Richardson.   As was
before pointed out in regard to the letter-system generally,
this method of treatment is exposed to special dangers,
particularly those of verbosity and " overdoing "—not to
mention the greater one of missing the mark.   Richardson
can hardly be charged with error, though he may be with
excess, in regard to Pamela herself in the earlier part of the
book—perhaps even not in regard to Mr. B.'s intricacies
of courtship, matrimonial compliment, and arbitrary
temper later.   But he certainly succumbs to them in the
long and monstrous scene in which Lady Davers bullies,
storms at, and positively assaults her unfortunate sister-in-
law before she is forced to allow that she *is* her sister-in-
law.   Part of course of his error here comes from the

mistake with which Lady Mary afterwards most justly reproached him—that he talked about fine ladies and gentlemen without knowing anything about them. It was quite natural for Lady Davers to be disgusted, to be incredulous, to be tyrannical, to be in a certain sense violent. But it is improbable that she would in any case have spoken and behaved like a drunken fishfag quarrelling with another in the street: and the extreme prolongation of the scene brings its impropriety more forcibly into view. Here, as elsewhere (a point of great importance to which I may invite attention), Richardson follows out, with extraordinary minuteness and confidence, a wrong course: and his very expertness in the process betrays him and brings him to grief. If he had run the false scent for a few yards only it would not matter: in a chase prolonged to something like " Hartleap Well " extension there is less excuse for his not finding it out. Nevertheless it would of course be absurd not to rank this " knowledge of the human heart " among the claims which not only gave him but have kept his reputation. I do not know that he shows it much less in the later part of the first two volumes (Pamela's recurrent tortures of jealous curiosity about Sally Godfrey are admirable) or even in the dreary sequel. But analysis for analysis' sake can have few real, though it may have some pretended, devotees.

The foregoing remarks have been designed, less as a criticism of *Pamela* (which would be unnecessary here), or even of Richardson (which would be more in place, but shall be given in brief presently), than as an account and justification of the book's position in the real subject of this volume—the History of the English Novel. And this account will dispense us from dealing, at corresponding length, with the individually more important but historically subordinate books which followed. Of these *Clarissa*, as few people can be ignorant, is a sort of enlarged, diversified, and transposed *Pamela*, in which the attempts of a libertine of more resolution and higher gifts than Mr. B. upon a young lady of much more than proportionately higher station and qualities than Pamela's, are—as such success goes—successful at last: but only to result in the death of the victim and the punishment of the criminal. The book is far longer than even the extended *Pamela ;* has a much wider range; admits of episodes and minor plots, and is altogether much more ambitious; but still—though the part of the seducer Lovelace is much more important than that of Mr. B.—it is chiefly occupied with the heroine. In *Sir Charles Grandison*, on the contrary, though no less than three heroines exist after a fashion and are carefully treated, the author's principal object is to depict—in direct contrast to Mr. B. and Lovelace—a " Good Man "—the actual first title of the book, which he wisely altered. This faultless and insufferable monster is frantically beloved by, and hesitates long between, two beauties, the Italian Clementina della Porretta and the English Harriet Byron. The latter of these carries him off (rather because of religious difficulties than of any great predilection on his own part) and the piece ends with a repetition, extension, and intensification of the bounties showered upon Pamela by her husband, and her almost abject gratitude for them. Only of course " the good man " could never be guilty of Mr. B.'s meditated relapse from the path of rectitude, nor (one may perhaps add) does Miss Byron seem to possess the insinuating astuteness by which Pamela once more

" Reconciles the new perverted man,"

to adapt the last line of *A Lover's Complaint* to the situation.

Grandison, like *Clarissa,* has a much wider range of personage and incident than *Pamela,* and is again double the length of it. No detailed criticism of these enormous books (both of which are conducted in the letter-form, though, in the latter case especially, with long retrospects and narratives which rather strain the style) is possible here. But a few remarks on the characters of Lovelace and Clarissa, which have usually been regarded as Richardson's greatest triumphs, may fitly precede some on his whole character as a novelist.

Admiration and sympathy, tempered with a few reserves, have been the general notes of comment on Clarissa: and —as she goes through the long martyrdom of persecution by her family for not marrying the man she does not love; of worse persecution from the man whom she does love, but who will not marry her, at least until he has conquered her virtue; and of perhaps worst when she feels it her duty to resist his repentant and (as such things go) honourable proffers after he has treacherously deprived her of technical honour—compassion at least is impossible to refuse. But " compassion," though it literally translates " sympathy " from Greek into Latin, is not its synonym in English. It is a disagreeable thing to have to say: but Clarissa's purity strikes one as having at once too much questionable prudery in it and too little honest prudence: while her later resolution has as much false pride as real principle. Even some of her admirers admit a want of straightforwardness in her; she has no passion, which rather derogates from the merit of her conduct in any case; and though she is abominably ill-treated by almost everybody, one's pity for her never comes very near to love.

Towards Lovelace, on the other hand, the orthodox attitude, with even greater uniformity, has been shocked, or sometimes even unshocked, admiration. Hazlitt went into frequently quoted raptures over the " regality " of his character: and though to approve of him as a man would only be the pretence of a cheap paradoxer, general opinion seems to have gone various lengths in the same direction. There have, however, been a few dissenters: and I venture to join myself to them in the very dissidence of their dissent. Lovelace, it is true, is a most astonishingly " succeeded " blend of a snob's fine gentleman and of the fine gentleman of a silly and rather unhealthy-minded schoolgirl. He is—it is difficult to resist the temptation of dropping and inserting the h's—handsome, haughty, arbitrary, as well as rich, generous after a fashion, well descended, well dressed, well mannered—except when he is insolent. He is also—which certainly stands to his credit in the bank which is not that of the snob or the schoolgirl—no fool in a general way. But he is not in the least a gentleman except in externals: and there is nothing really " great " about him at all. Even his scoundrelism is mostly, if not wholly, *pose*—which abominable thing indeed distinguishes him throughout, in every speech and every act, from the time when he sighs as he kisses Miss Arabella Harlowe's hand to the time when he says, " Let this expiate! " as that hallowed sword of Colonel Morden's passes through his rotten heart. Now if Richardson had *meant* this, it might be granted at once that Lovelace is one of the greatest characters of fiction: and I do not deny that *taken as this*, meant or not meant, he is great. But Richardson obviously did *not* mean it; and Hazlitt did not mean it; and none of the admirers mean it. *They* all thought and think that Lovelace is something like what Milton's Satan was, and what my Lord Byron would have liked to be. This is very unfair to the Prince of

Darkness: and it is even not quite just to " the noble poet."

At the same time, the acute reader will have noticed, the acknowledgment that the fact that Richardson—even not knowing it and intending to do something else—did hit off perfectly and consummately the ideal of such a " prevailing party " (to quote Lord Foppington) as snobs and schoolgirls, is a serious and splendid tribute to his merits: as is also the fact that his two chief characters are characters still interesting and worth arguing about. Those merits, indeed, are absolutely incontestable. His immediate and immense popularity, abroad as well as at home, would not necessarily prove much, though it must not be neglected, and historically, at least, is of the first importance. But he does not need it.

For, as should have been sufficiently shown, he did very great things—first by gathering up the scattered means and methods which had been half ignorantly hit on by others, and co-ordinating them into the production of the finished and complete novel; secondly (though less) by that infusion of elaborate " minor psychology " as it may be called, which is his great characteristic; and, thirdly, by means of it and of other things, in raising the pitch of interest in his readers to an infinitely higher degree than had ever been known before. The dithyrambs of Diderot are, though not ridiculously, amusingly excessive: but they are only an exaggeration of the truth. On the comic side he was weak: and he made a most unfortunate mistake by throwing this part of the business on young ladies of position and (as he thought) of charm—Miss Darnford, Miss Howe, Charlotte Grandison—who are by no means particularly comic and who are sometimes very particularly vulgar. But of tragedy positive, in the *bourgeois* kind, he

G

had no small command, and in the middle business—in affairs neither definitely comic nor definitely tragic—he was wonderfully prolific and facile. His immense and heart-breaking lengthiness is not *mere* verbosity: it comes partly from the artist's natural delight in a true and newly found method, partly from a still more respectably artistic desire not to do the work negligently. As for the un-healthiness of atmosphere which has been generally and not unjustly charged upon him, it is, in part, no doubt the result of imperfect temperament and breeding: but it is also as closely connected with his very method as are the merits thereof. You cannot "consider so curiously" without considering too curiously. The drawbacks of his work are obvious, and they were likely to be, and were, exaggerated. But they might be avoided and the merits kept: nor is it too much to say that the triumphs of the English novel in the last century have been not a little due to the avoidance of the one and the keeping of the other.

It would be, in the circumstances, peculiarly uncivil and disobliging to lay very much stress on the fact that, after all, the greatest of Richardson's works is his successor, caricaturist, and superior—Fielding. When the memoirs of Miss Pamela Andrews appeared, the future biographer of her doubly supposititious brother was a not very young man of thirty-three, who had written a good many not very good plays, had contributed to periodicals, and had done a little work at the Bar, besides living, at least till his marriage and it may be feared later, an exceedingly "rackety" life. It is not improbable, though it is not certain, that he had already turned his attention to prose fiction of a kind. For, though the *Miscellanies* which followed *Joseph Andrews* were three years later than

Pamela in appearance, the *Journey from this World to the Next* which they contain has the immaturity of earliness; and we can hardly conceive it as written after the adventures and character of Mr. Abraham Adams. It is unequal, rather tedious in parts, and in conception merely a *pastiche* of Lucian and Fontenelle: but it contains some remarkable things in the way of shrewd satirical observation of human nature. And the very fact that it is a following of something else is interesting, in connection with the infinitely more important work that preceded it in publication, *The Adventures of Joseph Andrews and his Friend Mr. Abraham Adams* (1742).

Nobody has ever had much difficulty in accounting for the way in which Fielding availed himself of the appearance and popularity of *Pamela*. And though Richardson would have been superhuman instead of very human indeed (with an ordinary British middle-class humanity, and an extraordinary vein of genius) if he had done otherwise, few have joined him in thinking *Joseph* a "lewd and ungenerous engraftment." We have not ourselves been very severe on the faults of *Pamela*, the reason of lenity being, among other things, that it in a manner produced Fielding, and all the fair herd of his successors down to the present day. But those faults are glaring: and they were of a kind specially likely to attract the notice and the censure of a genial, wholesome, and, above all, masculine taste and intellect like Fielding's. Even at that time, libertine as it was in some ways, and sentimental as it was in others, people had not failed to notice that Pamela's virtue is not quite what was then called "neat" wine— the pure and unadulterated juice of the grape. The *longueurs* and the fiddle-faddle, the shameless and fulsome preface-advertisements and the rest lay open enough to

censure. So Fielding saw the handles, and gripped them
at once by starting a *male* Pamela—a situation not only
offering " most excellent differences," but in itself possessing, to graceless humanity at all times it may be feared,
and at that time perhaps specially, something essentially
ludicrous in minor points. At first he kept the parody
very close: though the necessary transposition of the
parts afforded opportunity (amply taken) for display of
character and knowledge of nature superior to Richardson's own. Later the general opinion is that he, especially
inspirited by his *trouvaille* of Adams, almost forgot the
parody, and only furbished up the *Pamela*-connection at
the end to make a formal correspondence with the beginning, and to get a convenient and conventional " curtain."
I am not so sure of this. Even Adams is to a certain
extent suggested by Williams, though they turn out such
very different persons. Mrs. Slipslop, a character, as Gray
saw, not so very far inferior to Adams, is not only a parallel
to Mrs. Jewkes, but also, and much more, a contrast to
the respectable Mrs. Jervis and Mrs. Warden. All sorts
of fantastic and not-fantastic doublets may be traced
throughout: and I am not certain that Parson Trulliber's
majestic doctrine that no man, even in his own house, shall
drink when he " caaled vurst " is not a demoniacally
ingenious travesty of Pamela's characteristic casuistry,
when she says that she will do anything to propitiate Lady
Davers, but she will not " fill wine " to her in her own
husband's house.

But this matters little: and we have no room for it.
Suffice it as agreed and out of controversy that *Joseph
Andrews* started as a parody of *Pamela* and that, whether
in addition or in substitution, it turned to something very
different. It is not quite so uncontroversial, but will be

asserted here as capable of all but demonstration, that the
" something different " is also something much greater.
There is still not very much plot—the parody did not
necessitate and indeed rather discouraged that, and what
there is is arrived at chiefly by the old and seldom very
satisfactory system of *anagnorisis*—the long-lost-child
business. But, under the three other heads, Joseph
distances his sister hopelessly and can afford her much
more than weight for sex. It has been said that there are
doubtfully in Richardson anywhere, and certainly not in
Pamela, those startling creations of personality which are
almost more real to us than the persons we know in the
flesh. It is not that Pamela and her meyney are *un*real;
for they are not: but that they are not personal. The
Reverend Abraham Adams is a good deal more real than
half the parsons who preached last Sunday, and a good
deal more personal: and the quality is not confined to him,
though he has most of it. So, too, with the description.
The time was not yet for any minute or elaborate picture-
setting. But here again also that extra dose of life and
action—almost of bustle—which Fielding knows how to
instil is present. In *Pamela* the settings are frequent, but
they are " still life " and rather shadowy: we do not *see*
the Bedfordshire and Lincolnshire mansions, the summer
houses where (as she observes with demure relish when the
danger is over) Mr. B. was " very naughty; " even the
pond where, if she had been another sort of girl, the *drame*
might have become real tragedy. Fielding does not take
very much more trouble and yet somehow we *do* see it all,
with a little help from our own imaginations perhaps, but
on his suggestion and start. Especially the outdoor life
and scenes—the inn-yards and the high roads and the
downs by night or day; the pig-sty where poor Adams is

the victim of live pigs and the public-house kitchen where he succumbs to a by-product of dead ones—these are all real for us.

But most of all is the regular progress of vivification visible in the dialogue. This, as we have seen, had been the very weakest point of the weakness of almost all (we might say of all) English novels up to the close of the first quarter of the eighteenth century. Richardson had done a great deal for it: but it was impossible that, on his method, it should not, for the most part, be languid, or at any rate long-winded. Here again Fielding spirits the thing up—oxygenates and ozonises the atmosphere: while, in even fuller measure than his predecessor and victim, he recognises the efficacy of dialogue as the revealer of character. He has, assisted no doubt by Shakespeare and his own dramatic practice, discovered that you do not want volumes of it to do the business—that single moments and single sentences will do that business at times, if they are used in the proper way.

In short, Fielding here used his reluctant and indignant forerunner as a spring-board, whence to attain heights which that forerunner could never have reached: he " stood upon his shoulders " in the most cavalier but also the most successful fashion. In the novel as Richardson knew it and was thinking of it, when he began *Pamela*, you were, as a rule, in an artificial world altogether—a world artificial with an artificiality only faintly and occasionally touched with any reality at all. In *Pamela* itself there is perhaps nothing, and certainly not much, that is *wholly* unreal: but the reality is treated and rendered in an artificial way. In *Joseph Andrews*, though its professed genesis and procedure are artificial too, you break away at once from serious artifice. These are all real people who do real things in a real way now, as they did nearly two hundred years ago: however much dress, and speech, and manners may have changed. And we are told of their doings in a real way, too. Exactly how the teller knew it we do not know: but we do not think of this at all. And on the other hand there is no perpetual reminder of art, like the letter-ending and beginning, to disturb or alloy the once and gladly accepted " suspension of disbelief."

A slight digression may not be improper here. Even in their own days, when the *gros mot* was much less shocking than it is now, there was a general notion—which has more or less persisted, in spite of all changes of fashion in this respect, and exists even now when licence of subject as distinguished from phrase has to a great extent returned—that Fielding is more " coarse," more " improper," and so forth than Richardson. As a matter of fact, neither admits positively indecent language—that had gone out, except in the outskirts and fringes of English literature, generations earlier. But I am much mistaken if there are not in Richardson more than a few scenes and situations the " impropriety " of which positively exceeds anything in Fielding. Naturally one does not give indications: but readers may be pretty confident about the fact. The comparative " bloodlessness," however—the absence of life and colour in the earlier and older writer—acts as a sort of veil to them.

Yet (to return to larger and purer air), however much one may admire *Joseph Andrews*, the kind of *parasitic* representation which it allows itself, and the absence of any attempt to give an original story tells against it. And it may, in any case, be regarded as showing that the novelist, even yet, was hugging the shore or allowing himself to be taken in tow—that he did not dare to launch out

into the deep and trust to his own sails and the wind of
nature to propel him—to his own wits and soul to guide.
Even Fielding's next venture—the wonderful and almost
unique venture of *Jonathan Wild*—leaves some objection
of this sort possible, though, for myself, I should never
dream of admitting it.   Jonathan was (so much the worse
for human nature) a real person: and the outlines of his
story—if not the actual details—are given partly by his
actual life, partly by Gay's *Beggar's Opera* and its sequel.
Moreover, the whole marvellous little book has a purpose—
the purpose of satire on false ideas of greatness, historical
and political.   The invention and the art of the writer are
not even yet allowed frank and free course.

But though criticism will allow this, it will, if it be competent and courageous, allow no deduction to be made from
the other greatness of this little masterpiece.   It has never
been popular; it is never likely to be popular; and one
may almost say that it is sincerely to be hoped that it
never will be popular.   For if it were, either all the world
would be scoundrels, which would be a pity: or all the
world would be philosophers and persons of taste, in which
case it would be impossible, as the famous story has it, to
"look down on one's fellow-creatures from a proper
elevation."   It really is a novel and a remarkable one—
superior even to *Vanity Fair*, according to Thackeray's
own definition, as a delineation of " a set of people living
without God in the world."   But it is even more (and here
its only parallel is *A Tale of a Tub*, which is more desultory
and much more of a *fatrasie* or salmagundy of odds and
ends) a masterpiece and quintessential example of irony.
Irony had come in with the plain prose style, without
which it is almost impossible: and not merely Swift but
others had done great things with it.   It is, however, only

here that it reaches the quintessence just spoken of with
a coherent and substantive purpose to serve as vehicle
for it. It is possibly too strong for most people's taste:
and one may admit that, for anything like frequent enjoyment, it wants a certain admixture of the fantastic in its
various senses—after the method of Voltaire in one way,
of Beckford in another, of Peacock in a third, of Disraeli
in a fourth—to make it acceptable to more than a very
few. But it shows, even from our present limited point
of view, of what immense and exalted application the
novel-method was capable: and it shows also the astonishing powers of its author. " Genial," in the usual sense, it
certainly cannot be called; in the proper sense as equalling
" what is the production of genius " there are few books
which deserve the term better. But it is an exercise in
a by-way of the novel road-system, though an early proof
of the fact that such by-ways are endlessly open.

But the time was coming, though it did not (and could
hardly) come very quickly, when Fielding was to discard
all kinds of adventitious aids and suggestions—all crutches,
spring-boards, go-carts, tugs, patterns, tracings—and go
his own way—and the Way of the Novel—with no guidance
but something of the example of Cervantes directly and
Shakespeare indirectly among the moderns, and of the
poetic fiction-writers of old. It is perfectly clear that he
had thought widely (and perhaps had read not a little)
on the subject of literary criticism, in a sense not common
in his day, and that the thinking had led him to a conception of the " prose epic " which, though it might have
been partly (not wholly by any means) pieced out of the
Italian and Spanish critics of the late sixteenth and early
seventeenth centuries, had never been worked out as a
complete theory, much less applied in practice and to

prose. The Prose Epic aims at—and in Fielding's case
has been generally admitted to have hit—something like
the classical unity of main action. But it borrows from
the romance - idea the liberty of a large accretion and
divagation of minor and accessory plot:—not the mere
" episode " of the ancients, but the true minor plot of
Shakespeare. It assumes, necessarily and once for all,
the licence of tragi-comedy, in that sense of the term in
which *Much Ado About Nothing* and *A Winter's Tale* are
tragi-comedies, and in which *Othello* itself might have been
made one. And it follows further in the wake of the
Shakespearean drama by insisting far more largely than
ancient literature of any kind, and far more than any
modern up to its date except drama had done, on the
importance of Character. Description and dialogue are
rather subordinate to these things than on a level with them
—but they are still further worked out than before. And
there is a new element—perhaps suggested by the *parabasis*
of ancient comedy, but, it may be, more directly by the
peculiar method of Swift in *A Tale of a Tub*. At various
places in his narrative, but especially at the beginnings of
books and chapters, Fielding as it were " calls a halt " and
addresses his readers on matters more or less relevant to
the story, but rather in the manner of a commentator and
scholiast upon it than as actual parts of it. Of this more
later : for the immediate purpose is to survey and not to
criticise.

The result of all this was *Tom Jones* — by practically
universal consent one of the capital books of English
literature. It is unnecessary to recapitulate the famous
praises of Gibbon, of Coleridge, of Byron, and of others: and
it is only necessary to deal briefly with the complaints
which, if they have never found such monumental expres-

sion as the praises, have been sometimes widely entertained.
These objections—as regards interest—fasten partly on
the address-digressions, partly on the great inset-episode
of " The Man of the Hill: " as regards morality on a certain
alleged looseness of principle in that respect throughout,
and especially on the licence of conduct accorded to the
hero himself and the almost entire absence of punishment
for it. As for the first, " The Man of the Hill " was partly
a concession to the fancy of the time for such things, partly
a following of such actual examples as Fielding admitted—
for it need hardly be said that the inset-episode, of no or
very slight connection with the story, is common both in
the ancients and in Cervantes, while it is to be found as
long after Fielding as in the early novel-work of Dickens.
The digression-openings are at least as satisfactory to
some as they are unsatisfactory to others; it is even
doubtful whether they annoy anybody half so much as
they have delighted some excellent judges. The other
point is well worn: but the wearing has not taken off its
awkwardness and unsavouriness. Difference of habit and
manners at the time will account for much: but the wiser
apologists will simply say that Fielding's attitude to certain
deviations from the strict moral law was undoubtedly very
indulgent, provided that such deviations were unaccom-
panied by the graver and more detestable vices of cruelty,
treachery, and fraud—that to vice which was accompanied
by these blacker crimes he was utterly merciless; and
that if he is thus rather exposed to the charge of " com-
pounding by damning "—in the famous phrase—the things
that he damned admit of no excuse and those that he
compounded for have been leniently dealt with by all
but the sternest moralists.

Such things are, however (in the admirable French sense),

misères—wretched petty cavils and shallows of criticism. The only sensible thing to do is to launch out with Fielding into that deep and open sea of human character and fate which he dared so gloriously. During the curious phase of literary opinion which the last twenty years or so have seen, it has apparently been discovered by some people that his scheme of human thought and feeling is too simple —" toylike " I think they call it—in comparison with that, say, of Count Tolstoi or of Mr. Meredith, that modern practice has reached a finer technique than his or even than that of his greatest follower, Thackeray. Far be it from the present writer to say, or to insinuate, anything disrespectful of the great moderns who have lately left us. Yet it may be said without the slightest disrespect to them that the unfavourable comparison is mainly a revival of Johnson's mistake as to Fielding and Richardson. It is, however, something more—for it comes also from a failure to estimate aright the *parabasis*-openings which have been more than once referred to. These passages do not perhaps exhibit the by-work and the process in the conspicuous skeleton-clock fashion which their critics admire and desire, but they contain an amount of acute and profound exploration of human nature which it would be difficult to match and impossible to surpass elsewhere: while the results of Fielding's working, of his " toylike " scheme, are remarkable toys indeed—toys which, if we regard them as such, must surely strike us as rather uncanny. One is sometimes constrained to think that it is perhaps not much more difficult to make than to recognise a thoroughly live character. It certainly must be very difficult to do the latter if there is any considerable number of persons who are unable to do it in the case of almost every one of the personages of *Tom Jones*. With one possible exception they are all alive—even more so than those of *Joseph Andrews* and with a less peculiar and limited liveliness than those of *Jonathan Wild*. But it certainly is curious that as the one good man of *Jonathan*, Heartfree, is the least alive of its personages, so the one bad man of *Tom*, Blifil, occupies the same position.

The result of this variety and abundance of life is an even more than corresponding opportunity for enjoyment. This enjoyment may arise in different persons from different sources. The much praised and seldom cavilled at unity and completeness of the story may appeal to some. There are others who are inclined towards elaborate plots as Sam Weller was to the "'rig'nal" of his subpœna. It was a "gratifyin' sort o' thing, and eased his mind" to be aware of its existence, and that was all. These latter find *their* sources of enjoyment elsewhere, but everywhere else. The abundance and the vividness of character-presentation; the liveliness and the abundance of the staging of that character; the variety of scene and incident—all most properly connected with the plot, but capable of existing and of being felt without it; the human dialogue; the admirable phrase in that dialogue and out of it, in the digressions, in the narrative, above, and through, and about, and below it all—these things and others (for it is practically impossible to exhaust the catalogue) fill up the cup to the brim, and keep it full, for the born lover of the special novel-pleasure.

In one point only was Fielding a little unfortunate perhaps: and even here the "perhaps" has to be underlined. He came just before the end of a series of almost imperceptible changes in ordinary English speech which brought about something like a stationary state. His maligner and only slightly younger contemporary, Horace Walpole, in some of his letters, writes in a fashion which, putting mere slang aside, has hardly any difference from that of to-day.   Fielding still uses " hath " for " has " and a few other things which seem archaic, not to students of literature but to the general.   In the same way dress, manners, etc., though much more picturesque, were by that fact distinguished from those of almost the whole nineteenth century and the twentieth as far as it has gone: while incidents were, even in ordinary life, still usual which have long ceased to be so.   In this way the immense advance— greater than was made by any one else till Miss Austen— that he made in the pure novel of this ordinary life may be missed.   But the intrinsic magnificence, interest, nature, abundance of *Tom Jones* can only be missed by those who were predestined to miss them.   It is tempting—but the temptation must be resisted—to enliven these pages with an abstract of its astonishing " biograph-panorama."   But nothing save itself can do it justice.   " Take and read " is the only wise advice.

No such general agreement has been reached in respect of Fielding's last novel, *Amelia*.   The author's great adversary, Johnson—an adversary whose hostility was due partly to generous and grateful personal relations with Richardson, partly to political disagreement (for Fielding was certainly " a vile Whig "), but most of all perhaps to a sort of horrified recoil from the novelist's easy handling of temptations which were no easy matter to his critic— was nearly if not quite propitiated by it: and the enthusiasm for it of such a " cynic " as Thackeray is well known. Of the very few persons whom it would not be ridiculous to name with these, Scott—whose competence in criticising his own art is one of the most wonderful though the least generally recognised things about him — inclines, in the interesting Introduction-Dialogue to *The Fortunes of Nigel*, to put it on a level with *Tom Jones* itself as a perfectly constructed novel. But modern criticism has, rightly or wrongly, been more dubious. Amelia is almost too perfect: her very forgiveness (it has been suggested) would be more interesting if she had not almost completely shut her eyes to there being anything to forgive. Her husband seems to us to prolong the irresponsibility of youth, which was pardonable in Tom, to a period of life and to circumstances of enforced responsibility which make us rather decline to honour the drafts he draws; and he is also a little bit of a fool, which Tom, to do him justice, is not, though he is something of a scatterbrain. Dr. Harrison, whose alternate wrath and reconciliation supply the most important springs of the plot, is, though a natural, a rather unreasonable person. The " total impression " has even been pronounced by some people to be a little dull. What there is of truth in these criticisms and others (which it would be long even to summarise) may perhaps be put briefly under two heads. It is never so easy to arouse interest in virtue as it is in vice: or in weak and watered vice as in vice rectified (or *un*rectified) to full strength. And the old requirement of " the quest " is one which will hardly be dispensed with. Here (for we know perfectly well that Amelia's virtue is in no danger) there is no quest, except that of the fortune which ought to be hers, which at last comes to her husband, and which we are told (and hope rather doubtfully) that husband had at last been taught—by the Fool's Tutor, Experience—not utterly to throw away. But this fortune drops in half casually at the last by a series of stage accidents, not ill-machined by any means, but not very particularly interesting.

Such, however, are the criticisms which Fielding himself

has taught people to make, by the very excellence of his
success in the earlier novels: and there is a certain comparative and relative validity in them. But consider
Amelia in itself, and they begin to look, if not positively
unfounded, rather unimportant.   Once more, the astonishing truth and variety of scene and character make themselves felt—even more felt—even felt in new directions.
The opening prison scenes exceed anything earlier even in
Fielding himself, much more in any one else, as examples
of the presentation of the unfamiliar. Miss Matthews—
whom Fielding has probably abstained from working out
as much as he might lest she should, from the literary
point of view, obscure Amelia—is a marvellous outline;
Colonels James and Bath are perfectly finished studies of
ordinary and extraordinary " character " in the stage
sense. No novel even of the author's is fuller of *vignettes*
—little pictures of action and behaviour, of manners and
society, which are not in the least irrelevant to the general
story, but on the contrary extra - illustrate and carry
it out.

While, therefore, we must in no way recede from the
position above adopted in regard to Richardson, we may
quite consistently accord an even higher place to Fielding.
He relieved the novel of the tyranny and constraint of the
Letter; he took it out of the rut of confinement to a single
or a very limited class of subjects—for the themes of
Pamela and *Clarissa* to a very large extent, of *Pamela* and
Grandison to a considerable one, and of all three to an
extent not small, are practically the same. He gave it
altogether a larger, wider, higher, deeper range. He
infused in it (or restored to it) the refreshing and preserving
element of humour. He peopled it with a great crowd of
lively and interesting characters—endowed, almost without

regard to their technical " position *in* life," with unlimited
possession *of* life. He shook up its pillows, and bustled
its business arrangements. He first gave it—for in matter
of prose style Richardson has few resources, and those
rather respectable than transporting, and decidedly
monotonous—the attractions of pure literature in form,
and in pretty various form. He also gave it the attraction
of pure comedy, only legitimately salted with farce, in
such personages as Adams and Partridge; of lower and
more farcical, but still admirable comedy in Slipslop and
Trulliber and Squire Western; of comedy almost romantic
and certainly charming in Sophia; of domestic drama in
Amelia; of satiric portraiture in a hundred figures from
the cousins (respectable and disreputable), Miss Western and
Lady Bellaston, downwards. He stocked it with infinite
miscellanies of personage, and scene, and picture, and
phrase. As has happened in one or two other cases, he
carried, at least in the opinion of the present writer, the
particular art as far as it will go. He did not indeed leave
nothing for his successors to do—on the contrary he left
them in a sense everything—for he showed how everything
could be done. But if he has sometimes been equalled,
he has never been surpassed: and it is not easy to see even
how he can be surpassed. For as his greatest follower
has it somewhere, though not of him, " You cannot beat
the best, you know."

One point only remains, the handling of which may
complete a treatment which is designedly kept down in
detail. It has been hinted at already, perhaps more than
once, but has not been brought out. This is the enormous
range of suggestion in Fielding—the innumerable doors
which stand open in his ample room, and lead from it to
other chambers and corridors of the endless palace of

H

Novel-Romance. This had most emphatically not been the case with his predecessor: for Richardson, except in point of mere length, showed little power of expatiation, kept himself very much to the same ground and round, and was not likely to teach anybody else to make excursions. Indeed Fielding's breaking away in *Joseph Andrews* is an allegory in itself. But, at least with pupils and followers of any wits, there was not even any need of such breaking away from himself, though no doubt there are in existence many dull and slavish attempts to follow his work, especially *Tom Jones*. " Find it out for yourself " —the great English motto which in the day of England's glory was the motto of her men of learning as well as of her men of business, of her artists as well as of her craftsmen—might have been Fielding's: but he supplemented it with infinite finger-pointings towards the various things that might be found out. Almost every kind of novel exists—potentially—in his Four (the custom of leaving out *Jonathan Wild* should be wholly abrogated), though of course they do not themselves illustrate or carry out at length many of the kinds that they thus suggest.

And in fact it could not be otherwise: because, as has been pointed out, while Fielding had no inconsiderable command of the Book of Literature, he turned over by day and night the larger, the more difficult, but still the greater Book of Life. Not merely *quicquid agunt homines*, but *quicquid sentiunt, quicquid cogitant*, whatever they love and hate, whatever they desire or decline—all these things are the subjects of his own books: and the range of subject which they suggest to others is thus of necessity inexhaustible.

If there have been some who denied or failed to recognise his greatness, it must be because he has played on these unwary ones the same trick that Garrick, in an immortal scene, played on his own Partridge. There is so little parade about Fielding (for even the opening addresses are not parade to these good people: they may disconcert or even disgust, but they do not dazzle them), that his characters and his scenes look commonplace. They feel sure that " if they had seen a ghost they would have looked in the very same manner and done just as he does." They are sure that, in the scene with Gertrude, " Lord, help them! any man—that is any good man—that had such a mother would have done exactly the same."

Well! in a way no doubt they are right; and one may imitate the wisdom of Mr. Jones on the original occasion in not saying much more to them. To others, of course, this is the very miracle of art—a miracle, as far as the art of prose fiction is concerned, achieved in its fullness for practically the first time. This is the true *mimesis*—the re-creation or fresh creation of fictitious reality. There were in Fielding's time, and probably ever since have been, those who thought him " low; " there were, even in his own time, and have been in varying, but on the whole rather increased, degree since, those who thought him immoral: there appear to be some who think (or would like it to be thought that they think) him commonplace and obvious. Now, as it happens, all these charges have been brought against Nature too. To embellish, and correct, and heighten, and extra-decorate her was not Fielding's way: but to follow, and to interpret, and to take up her own processes with results uncommonly like her own. That is his immense glory to all those who can realise and understand it: and as for the others we must let them alone, joined to their own idols.

In passing to the third of this great quartette, we make

a little descent, but not much of one, while the new peak
to which we come is well defined and separated, with
characters and outlines all its own.   It may be doubted
whether any competent critic not, like Scott, bribed by
compatriotism, ever put Smollett above Fielding, or even on
a level with him.   Thackeray, in one of the most inspired
moments of his rather irregularly - inspired criticism,
remarks, " I fancy he did not invent much," and this of
itself would refer him to a lower class.   The writer of
fiction is not to refuse suggestion from his experience; on
the contrary, he will do so at his peril, and will hardly by
any possibility escape shipwreck unless his line is the
purely fantastic.   But if he relies solely, or too much, on
such experience, though he may be quite successful, his
success will be subject to discount, bound to pay royalty
to experience itself.   It is pretty certain that most of
Smollett's most successful things, from *Roderick Random*
to *Humphry Clinker*, and in those two capital books,
perhaps, most of all, kept very close to actual experience,
and sometimes merely reported it.

This, however, is only a comparative drawback; it is in
a sense a positive merit; and it is connected, in a very
intimate way, with the general character of Smollett's
novel-method.   This is, to a great extent, a reaction or
relapse towards the picaresque style.   Smollett may
have translated both Cervantes and Le Sage; he certainly
translated the latter: and it was Le Sage who in any case
had the greatest influence over him.   Now the picaresque
method is not exactly untrue to ordinary life: on the
contrary, as we have seen, it was a powerful schoolmaster
to bring the novel thereto.   But it subjects the scenes of
ordinary life to a peculiar process of sifting: and when it
has got what it wants, it proceeds to heighten them and

" touch them up " in its own peculiar manner of decoration. This is Smollett's method throughout, even in that singular *pastiche* of *Don Quixote* itself, *Sir Launcelot Greaves*, which certainly was not his happiest conception, but which has had rather hard measure.

As used by him it has singular merits, and communicates to at least three of his five books (*The Adventures of an Atom* is deliberately excluded as not really a novel at all) a certain " liveliness " which, though it is not the life*like*-ness of Fielding, is a great attraction. He showed it first in *Roderick Random* (1748), which appeared a little before *Tom Jones*, and was actually taken by some as the work of the same author. It would be not much more just to take Roderick as Smollett's deliberate presentment of himself than to apply the same construction to Marryat's not very dissimilar, but more unlucky, *coup d'essai* of *Frank Mildmay*. But it is certain that there was some-thing, though exactly how much has never been determined, of the author's family history in the earliest part, a great deal of his experiences on board ship in the middle, and probably not a little, though less, of his fortunes in Bath and London towards the end. As a single source of interest and popularity, no doubt, the principal place must be given to the naval part of the book. Important as the English navy had been, for nearly two centuries if not for much longer, it had never played any great part in litera-ture, though it had furnished some caricatured and rather conventional sketches. There is something more in a play, *The Fair Quaker of Deal*, by Charles Shadwell, nephew or son of Dryden's victim, but this was only of third or fourth rate literary value, and an isolated example to boot. The causes of the neglect have been set forth by many writers from Macaulay downwards, and need not be discussed here;

the fact is certain. Smollett's employment of " the service" as a subject may have been, consciously and intentionally, only one of those utilisings of personal experience of which we have spoken. But really it was an instance of the great fact that the novelist, on the instigation mainly of Fielding himself, was beginning to take all actual life to be his province.

Smollett brought to his work peculiar powers, the chief of which was a very remarkable one, and almost as much " improved on " Fielding as Fielding's exercise of it was improved on Richardson—that of providing his characters and scenes with accessories. Roderick is not only a much more disagreeable person than Tom, but he is much *less* of a person: and Strap, though (*vice versâ*) rather a better fellow than Partridge, is a much fainter and more washed-out character. But in mere interest of story and accessories the journey of Roderick and Strap to London is quite the equal, and perhaps the superior, of that of Tom and his hanger-on after we once leave Upton, where the interest is of a kind that Smollett could not reach. It is probable that Fielding might, if he had chosen, have made the prison in *Amelia* as horribly and disgustingly realistic (to use a horrible and disgusting word) as the ship in *Roderick*, but he at any rate did not choose. Moreover Smollett, himself a member of one of the less predominant partners of the British and Irish partnership, perhaps for that reason hit on utilising the difference of these partners (after a fashion which had never been seen since Shakespeare) in the Welshman Morgan. As far as mere plot goes, he enters into no competition whatever with either Fielding or Richardson: the picaresque model did not require that he should. When Roderick has made use of his friends, knocked down his enemies, and generally elbowed and shoved his way through the crowd of adventures long enough, Narcissa and her fortune are not so much the reward of his exertions as a stock and convenient method of putting an end to the account of them. The customer has been served with a sufficient amount of the commodity he demands: and the scissors are applied, the canister shut up, the tap turned off. It almost results—it certainly coincides—that some of the minor characters, and some of the minor scenes, are much more vivid than the hero (the heroine is almost an absolute nonentity) and the whole story. The curate and the exciseman in the ninth chapter are, by common consent, among Smollett's greatest triumphs; but the curate might be excommunicated and the exciseman excised without anybody who read the book perceiving the slightest gap or missing link, as far as the story is concerned.

Smollett's second venture, *Peregrine Pickle* (1751), was more ambitious, perhaps rose higher in parts, but undoubtedly contained even more doubtful and inferior matter. No one can justly blame him, though any one may most justly refrain from praising, from the general point of view, as regards the " insets " of Miss Williams's story in *Roderick* and of that of Lady Vane here. From that point of view they range with the " Man of the Hill " in *Tom Jones*, and in the first case at least, though most certainly not in the second, have more justification of connection with the central story. He may so far underlie the charge of error of judgment, but nothing worse. Unluckily the " Lady Vane " insertion was, to a practical certainty, a commercial not an artistic transaction: and both here and elsewhere Smollett carried his already large licence to the extent of something like positive pornography. He is in fact one of the few writers of real eminence who have been forced to Bowdlerise themselves. Further, there would be more excuse for the most offensive part of *Peregrine* if it were not half plagiarism of the main situations of *Pamela* and *Clarissa*: if Smollett had not deprived his hero of all the excuses which, even in the view of some of the most respectable characters of *Pamela*, attached to the conduct of Mr. B.; and if he had not vulgarised Lovelace out of any possible attribution of " regality," except of being what the time would have called King of the Black Guard. As for Tom Jones, he does not come into comparison with " Perry " at all, and he would doubtless have been most willing and able—competent physically as well as morally—to administer the proper punishment to that young ruffian by drubbing him within an inch of his life.

These, no doubt, are grave drawbacks: but the racy fun of the book almost atones for them: and the exaltation of the naval element of *Roderick* which one finds here in Trunnion and Hatchway and Pipes carries the balance quite to the other side. This is the case even without, but much more with, the taking into account of Smollett's usual irregular and almost irrelevant *bonuses*, such as the dinner after the fashion of the ancients and the rest. No: *Peregrine Pickle* can never be thrown to the wolves, even to the most respectable and moral of these animals in the most imposing as well as ravening of attitudes. English Literature cannot do without it.

Without *Ferdinand Count Fathom* (1753) many people have thought that English Literature could do perfectly well: and without going quite so far, one may acknowledge that perhaps a shift could be made. The idea of re-transferring the method (in the first place at any rate) to foreign parts was not a bad one, and it may be observed that by

far the best portion of *Fathom* is thus occupied. Not a
few of these opening passages are excellent: and Fathom's
mother, if not a person, is an excellent type: it is probable
that the writer knew the kind well. But his unhappy
tendency to enter for the same stakes as his great forerunners makes it almost impossible not to compare
Ferdinand Fathom with *Jonathan Wild*: and the effect is
very damaging to the Count. Much of the book is dull:
and Fathom's conversation is (to adopt a cant word)
extremely unconvincing. The fact seems to be that
Smollett had run his picaresque vein dry, as far as it connected itself with mere rascality of various kinds, and he
did well to close it. He had published three novels in five
years: he waited seven before his next, and then eleven
more before his last.

A qualified apology has been hinted above for *Sir
Launcelot Greaves*. It is undoubtedly evidence of the
greatness of *Don Quixote* that there should have been so
many direct imitations of it by persons of genius and talent:
but this particular instance is unfortunate to the verge
of the preposterous, if not over it. The eighteenth century
was indeed almost the capital time of English eccentricity:
and it was also a time of licence which sometimes looked
very like lawlessness. But its eccentricities were not at
this special period romantic: and its lawlessness was
rather abuse of law than wholesale neglect of it. A rascally
attorney or a stony-hearted creditor might inflict great
hardship under the laws affecting money: and a brutal
or tyrannical squire might do the same under those affecting
the tenure or the enjoyment of house or land. " Persons
of quality " might go very far. But even a person of
quality, if he took to riding about the country in complete
steel, assaulting the lieges, and setting up a sort of cadi-

justice of his own in opposition to the king's, would probably have been brought pretty rapidly, if not to the recovery of his senses, to the loss of his liberty. Nor, with rare exceptions, are the subordinate or incidental humours of the first class. But I have always thought that the opening passage more than entitles the book to an honourable place in the history of English fiction. I do not know where to look, before it, for such an " interior " —such a complete Dutch picture of room and furniture and accessories generally. Even so learned a critic as the late M. Brunetière thought that things of the kind were not older than Balzac. I have known English readers, not ignorant, who thought they were scarcely older than Dickens. Dickens, however, undoubtedly took them from Smollett, of whom we know that he was an early and enthusiastic admirer: and Scott, who has them much earlier than Dickens, not improbably was in some degree indebted for them to his countryman. At any rate in that countryman they are: and you will not find a much better example of them anywhere than this of the inn-kitchen. But apart from it, and from a few other things of the same or similar kinds, there is little to be said for the book. The divine Aurelia especially is almost more shadowy than the divine Narcissa and the divine Emilia: and can claim no sort of sistership in personality with Amelia or Sophia, even with Clarissa or Pamela. In fact, up to this time Smollett's women—save in the case of Fathom's hell-cat of a mother, and one or two more who are " minors "—have done absolutely nothing for his books. It was to be quite otherwise in the last and best, though even here the heroine *en titre* is hardly, even though we have her own letters to body her out, more substantial than her elder sisters. But Lydia, though the *ingénue*, is not the real heroine of this book: her aunt and her aunt's maid divide that position between them.

A sufficiently ungracious critic may, if he chooses, see in Smollett's falling back on the letter-plan for *Humphry Clinker* (1771) an additional proof of that deficiency in strictly inventive faculty which has been noticed. The more generous " judge by results " will hardly care to consider so curiously in the case of such a masterpiece. For a masterpiece it really is. The comparative absence of " character " in the higher and literary sense as contrasted with " character-*parts* " in the technical meaning of the theatre has been admitted in the other books. Here, with the aid of the letters, it is amply supplied, or perhaps (to speak with extreme critical closeness) the character-parts are turned into characters by this means. There is no stint, because of the provision of this higher interest, of the miscellaneous fun and " business " which Smollett had always supplied so lavishly out of his experience, his observation, and, if not his invention, his combining faculty. And there is the setting of interior and exterior " furniture " which has been also referred to. Abundant as is the information which the eighteenth century has given us as to its justly beloved place of pilgrimage, Bath, there is nothing livelier than the Bath scenes here, from Chesterfield to Miss Austen, and few things, if any, so vivid and detailed. So it is with Clifton earlier, with London later, with Scotland last of all, and with the journeys connecting them. Yet these things are mere *hors d'œuvre*, pickles, sauces, condiments, beside the solid character-food of the Brambles and Melfords, of Winifred Jenkins and of the redoubtable Lismahago. That there is no exaggeration or caricature cannot, of course, be said. It was not Smollett's notion of art to present the elaborate academies of Richardson, or the almost uncanny duplications of Nature which Fielding could achieve. He must embolden, in fact grotesque, the line; heighten, in fact splash and plaster, the colour. But he has not left Nature behind here: he has only put her in a higher light.

One means of doing so has been condemned in him, as in others, as in its great earlier master, Swift, and its greatest later one, Thackeray, by some purists. They call it cheap and inartistic: but this is mere pedantry and prudery. Mis-spelling is not a thing to be employed every day or for every purpose: if you do that, you get into the ineffably dreary monotony which distinguishes the common comic journalist. But thrown in occasionally, and in the proper place, it gives an excellent zest: and it has seldom been employed—never, except in the two instances quoted—better than in the cases of Tabitha Bramble and her maid. For it is employed in the only legitimate way, that of zest, not substance. Tabitha and Winifred would still be triumphs of characterisation of a certain kind if they wrote as correctly as Uncle Matthew or Nephew Jery. Further, Lismahago is a bolder and a much less caricatured utilising of the " national " resource than Morgan. If Smollett had not been a perfectly undaunted, as well as a not very amiable, person he would hardly have dared to " *lacess* the thistle " in this fashion. But there are few sensible Scotsmen nowadays who would not agree with that most sensible, as well as greatest, of their compatriots, Sir Walter Scott, in acknowledging the justice (comic emphasis granted) of the twitch, and the truth of the grip, at that formidable plant. The way in which Smollett mixes up actual living persons, by their own names, with his fictitious characters may strike us as odd: but there is, for the most part, nothing offensive in it, and in fact, except a little of his apparently inevitable indulgence in nasty detail, there is nothing at all offensive in the book. The contrast of its general tone with that especially of his first two; the softening and mellowing of the general presentation—is very remarkable in a man of undoubtedly not very gentle disposition who had long suffered from extremely bad health, and whose chief original works recently—the *Journey* and the *Adventures*— had been, the first a tissue of grumbles, the second an outburst of savagery. But though the grumbles recur in Matthew Bramble's mouth, they become merely humorous there: and there is practically no savagery at all. Leghorn, it has been observed more than once, was in a fashion a Land of Beulah: a " season of calm weather " had set in for a rather stormy life just before the end.

Whatever may be his defects (and from the mere point of view of Momus probably a larger number may be found in him than either in Richardson or in Fielding), Smollett well deserves an almost equal place with them in the history of the novel. Richardson, though he had found the universal as far as certain aspects of it in humanity are concerned, had confined it within a very narrow space, or particular envelope, in tone and temper: the fact that he has been called " stifling," though the epithet may not be entirely just, is almost sufficient evidence of this. Fielding had taken the novel into a far larger air and, as has been said already, there was hardly anything to which his method might not lead, and in which it would not be effective. But he had been exclusively English in externals: and the result is that, to this day, he has had less influence abroad than perhaps any English writer of equal genius and than some of far less.[1] Smollett, by his remark-

---

[1] This is said not to have been quite the case at the *very* first: but it has been so since.

able utilisation of the characteristics of the other members of Magna-Britannia; by his excursions into foreign European and even transatlantic scenery, had widened the external if not the internal prospect; and had done perhaps even more by that chance-medley, as it perhaps was, of attention to the still more internal detail which was to be of such importance in the novel to come. Taking the three together (not without due allowance for the contemporary, if mainly imitative, developments which will be described in the next chapter), they had put prose fiction in a position which it had not attained, even in Spain earlier, even in France at more or less the same time: and had entirely antiquated, on the one hand, the mere *fabliau* or *novella*—the story of a single limited situation—on the other, the discursive romance with little plot and next to no character. One great further development, impossible at this time, of the larger novel, the historical, waited for Scott: but even this was soon, though very awkwardly, tried. It could not yet be born because the historic sense which was its necessary begetter hardly existed, and because the provision of historic matter for this sense to work on was rather scanty. But it is scarcely extravagant to say that it is more difficult to conceive even Scott doing what he did without Richardson, Fielding, and Smollett before him, than it is to believe that, with these predecessors, somebody like Scott was bound to come.

Great, however, as the three are, there is no need of any "injustice to Ireland"—little as Ireland really has to claim in Sterne's merit or demerit. He is not a fifth wheel to the coach by any means: he is the fourth and almost the necessary one. In Richardson, Fielding, and Smollett the general character and possibilities of the novel had been shown, with the exception just noted: and indeed hardly with that exception, because they showed the way clearly to it.   But its almost illimitable particular capabilities remained unshown, or shown only in Fielding's half extraneous divagations, and in earlier things like the work of Swift.   Sterne took it up in the spirit of one who wished to exhibit these capabilities; and did exhibit them signally in more than one or two ways.   He showed how the novel could present, in refreshed form, the *fatrasie*, the pillar-to-post miscellany, of which Rabelais had perhaps given the greatest example possible, but of which there were numerous minor examples in French.   He showed how it could be made, not merely to present humorous situations, but to exhibit a special kind of humour itself—to make the writer as it were the hero without his ever appearing as character in *Tristram*, or to humorise autobiography as in the *Sentimental Journey*.   And last of all (whether it was his greatest achievement or not is matter of opinion), he showed the novel of purpose in a form specially appealing to his contemporaries — the purpose being to exhibit, glorify, luxuriate in the exhibition of, sentiment or " sensibility."   In none of these things was he wholly original; though the perpetual upbraiding of " plagiarism " is a little unintelligent.   Rabelais, not to mention others, had preceded him, and far excelled him, in the *fatrasie ;*   Swift in the humour-novel; two generations of Frenchmen and Frenchwomen in the " sensibility " kind.   But he brought all together and adjusted the English novel, actually to them, potentially to much else.

To find fault with his two famous books is almost contemptibly easy.   The plagiarism which, if not found out at once, was found out very soon, is the least of these: in fact hardly a fault at all.   The indecency, which *was* found out at once, and which drew a creditable and not in the least Tartuffian protest from Warburton, is a far more serious matter—not so much because of the licence in subject as because of the unwholesome and sniggering tone. The sentimentality is very often simply maudlin, almost always tiresome *to us*, and in very, very few cases justified by brilliant success even in its own very doubtful kind. Most questionable of all, perhaps, is the merely mechanical mountebankery — the blanks, and the dashes, and the rows of stops, the black pages and the marbled pages which he employs to force a guffaw from his readers. The abstinence from any central story in *Tristram* is one of those dubious pieces of artifice which may possibly show the artist's independence of the usual attractions of story-telling, but may also suggest to the churlish the question whether his invention would have supplied him with any story to tell; and the continual asides and halts and parenthetic divagations in the *Journey* are not quite free from the same suggestion. In fact if you " can see a church by daylight " you certainly want no piercing vision, and no artificial assistance of light or lens, to discover the faults of this very unedifying churchman.

But he remains, for all that, a genius; and one of the great figures in our history. There is to his credit in general, as has been already pointed out, the great asset of having indicated, and in two notable instances patterned, the out-of-the-way novel—the novel eccentric, particular, individual. There is to that credit still more the brilliancy of the two specimens themselves in spite of their faults; their effectiveness in the literature of delight; the great powers of a kind more or less peculiar to the artist which they show, and the power, perhaps still greater, which they display in the actually general and ordinary lines of the novel, though adapted to this extraordinary use.

For though it pleased Sterne to anticipate the knife-grinder's innocent confession, " Story? God bless you! I have none to tell, sir! " in a sardonic paraphrase of half a score of volumes, he actually possessed the narrative faculty in an extraordinary degree. He does not merely show this in his famous inset short stories, accomplished as these are: he achieves a much greater marvel in the way in which he makes his *fatrasies* as it were novels. After one or two, brief but certainly not tedious, volumes of the *Life and Opinions of Tristram Shandy*, you know that you are being cheated, and are going to be: at the end you know still more certainly that you have been. You have had nothing of the " Life " but a great deal round rather than about the birth, and a few equivocal, merely glanced at, and utterly unco-ordinated incidents later. If you have had any " opinions " they have been chiefly those of Mr. Tristram Shandy's father and other members of his family, or those of its friends and circle, or of those shadowy personages outside the pretended story, such as Eugenius and Yorick, besides a few discourses which drop the slightest pretension of being Shandean or Tristramic and are plainly and simply the author's. In the *Journey* there is more unity; but it is, quite frankly, the unity of the temperament of that author himself. The incidents—sentimental, whimsical, fie-fie—have no other connection or tendency than the fact that they occur to the " gentleman in the black silk smalls " and furnish him with figures as it were for his performance. Yet you are *held* in a way in which nothing but the romance or the novel ever does hold you. The thing is a $\mu\tilde{\upsilon}\theta o\varsigma$ $\mathring{\alpha}\mu\upsilon\theta o\varsigma$— a story without story-end, without story-beginning, without story-connection or middle: but a story for all that. A dangerous precedent, perhaps; but a great accomplish-

ment: and, even as a precedent, the leader of a very
remarkable company. In not a few noteworthy later
books—in a very much greater number of parts of later
books—as we take our hats off to the success we are
saluting not a new but an old friend, and that friend
Sterne.

On the second great count—character—Sterne's record
is still more distinguished: and here there is no legerdemain
about the matter. There is a consensus of all sound
opinion to the effect that my Uncle Toby is an absolute
triumph—even among those who think that, as in the case
of Colonel Newcome later, it would have been possible to
achieve that triumph without letting his simplicity run
so near to something less attractive. It is not the sentiment that is here to blame, because Sterne has luckily not
forgotten (as he has in the case of his dead donkeys and his
live Marias) that humour is the only thing that will keep
such sentiment from turning mawkish, if not even rancid;
and that the antiseptic effect will not be achieved by
keeping your humour and your sentiment in separate
boxes. Trim is even better: he is indeed next to Sancho—
and perhaps Sam Weller—the greatest of all " followers "
in the novel: he supplies the only class-figure in which
Sterne perhaps beats Fielding himself. About Walter
Shandy there is more room for difference: and it is possible
to contend that, great as he is, he is not complete—that
he is something of a " humour " in the old one-sided and
over-emphasised Jonsonian sense. Nothing that he does
or says misbecomes him: but a good deal that he does not
do and say might be added with advantage, in order to
give us the portrait of a whole as well as a live man. As
for the other male characters, Sterne's plan excused him—
as it did not quite in Mr. Shandy's case—from making them

more than sketches and shadows.   But what uncommonly lively sketches and shadows they are!

Sterne's unlucky failing prevented him in most cases from touching the women off with a clean brush: but the quality of *liveness* pertains to them in almost a higher measure: and perhaps testifies even more strongly to his almost uncanny faculty of communicating it by touches which are not always unclean and are sometimes slight to an astonishing degree.   Even that shadow of a shade " My dear, dear Jenny " has a suggestion of verity about her which has shocked and fluttered some: the maids of the Shandean household, the grisettes and peasant girls and ladies of the *Journey*, have flesh which is not made of paper, and blood that is certainly not ink.   And the peculiarity extends to his two chief named heroines, Mrs. Shandy and the Widow.   Never were any two female personages more unceremoniously treated in the way of scanty and incidental appearance.   Never were any personages of scanty and incidental appearance made more alive and more female.

His details and accessories of all kinds, descriptive, literary, and other, would give subject for a separate chapter; but we must turn (for this chapter is already too long) to his phrase—in dialogue, narrative, whatever you please to call it.   For the fact is that these two things, and all others in which phrase and expression can be used, melt into each other with Sterne in a manner as " flibberti-gibbety " as most other things about him.   This phrase or expression is of course artificial to the highest degree: and it is to it that the reproach of depending on mechanical aids chiefly applies.   And yet laboriously figured, tricked, machined as it is—easy as once more it may be to prove that it is artifice and not art—the fact remains that, not merely (perhaps not by any means chiefly) in the stock extract-pieces which everybody knows, but almost everywhere, it is triumphant: and that English literature would be seriously impoverished without it. Certainly never was there a style which more fully justified the definition given by Buffon, in Sterne's own time, of style as " the *very* man." Falsetto, " faking," vamping, shoddy—all manner of evil terms may be heaped upon it without the possibility of completely clearing it from them. To some eyes it underlies them most when it is most ambitious, as in the Le Fevre story and the diatribe against critics. It leaves the court with all manner of stains on its character. Only, once more, if it did not exist we should be ignorant of more than one of the most remarkable possibilities of the English language.

Thus, in almost exactly the course of a technical generation—from the appearance of *Pamela* in 1740 to that of *Humphry Clinker* in 1771—the wain of the novel was solidly built, furnished with four main wheels to move it, and set a-going to travel through the centuries. In a sense, inasmuch as *Humphry Clinker* itself, though Smollett's best work, can hardly be said to show any absolutely new faculties, character, or method, the process was even accomplished in two-thirds of the time, between *Pamela* and *Tristram Shandy*. We shall see in the next chapter how eagerly the examples were taken up: and how, long before Smollett died, the novel of this and that kind had become one of the most prolific branches of literature. But, for the moment, the important thing is to repeat that it had been thoroughly and finally started on its high road, in general by Richardson, Fielding, and Smollett; in particular and wayward but promising side-paths by Sterne.

CHAPTER IV

THE MINOR AND LATER EIGHTEENTH-CENTURY
NOVEL [1]

IT is at last beginning to be recognised in principle, though
it is still much too often forgotten in practice, that the
minor work of a time is at least as important as the major
in determining general literary characteristics and tendencies. Nor is this anywhere much more noticeable than
in regard to the present period of our present subject.
The direct influence of Richardson and Fielding was no
doubt very great: but the development of the novel during
the middle and later century was too large and too various
to be all mere imitation. As a result, however, of their
influence, there certainly came over the whole kind a very
remarkable change. Even before them the *nisus* towards
it, which has been noticed in the chapter before the last,
is observable enough. Mrs. Manley's rather famous *New
Atlantis* (1709) has at least the form of a key-novel of the
political sort: but the whole interest is in the key and not
in the novel, though the choice of the form is something.
And the second, third, and fourth decades of the century
saw other work testifying to the vague and almost unconscious hankering after prose fiction which was becoming
endemic. A couple of examples of this may be treated, in

[1] A little of the work to be noticed in this chapter is not strictly
eighteenth century, but belongs to the first decade or so of the nineteenth.
But the majority of the contents actually conform to the title, and there
is hardly any more convenient or generally applicable heading for the
novel before Miss Austen and Scott, excluding the great names dealt with
in the last chapter.

passing, before we come to the work—not exactly of the first class in itself—of a writer who shows both the pre-Richardsonian and the post-Richardsonian phases of it most interestingly, and after a fashion to which there are few exact parallels.

A book, which counts here from the time of its appearance, and from a certain oddity and air of " key " about it, rather than from much merit as literature, or any as a story, is the *Adventures of Gaudentio di Lucca* by Simon Berington.[1] It appeared in 1737, between Defoe and Swift on the earlier, and Richardson on the later side, while the English world was to the novel as an infant crying for the light—and the bottle—at once. It begins and ends with adventures and discoveries of an ordinary romantic type. But the body consists of a revelation to certain Italian Inquisitors (who are not at all of the lurid type familiar to the Protestant imagination, but most equitable and well-disposed as well as potent, grave, and reverend signors) of an unknown country of " the Grand Pophar " in the centre of Africa. This country is civilised, but not yet Christianised: and the description of it of course gives room for the exercise of the familiar game of contrast—in this case not so much satiric as didactic—with countries nearer home which are at least supposed to be both civilised and Christian. It is a " respectable " book both in the French and the English sense: but it is certainly not very amusing, and cannot even be called very interesting in any way, save historically.

The other example which we shall take is of even less intrinsic attraction: in fact it is a very poor thing. There are, however, more ways than one in which

---

[1] The not infrequent attribution of this book to Berkeley is a good instance of the general inability to discriminate *style*.

corpora vilia are good for experiment and evidence: and we may find useful indications in the mere bookmaking of the time. Lowndes, the fortunate publisher of *Evelina*, some dozen years before that windfall came, had issued, or reissued, a collection called *The Novelist* and professedly containing *The select novels of Dr. Croxall* [the ingenious author of *The Fair Circassian* and the part destroyer of Hereford Cathedral] *and other Polite Tales*. The book is an unblushing if not an actually piratical compilation; sweeping together, with translations and adaptations published by Croxall himself at various times in the second quarter of the century and probably earlier, most of the short stories from the *Spectator* class of periodical which had appeared during the past two-thirds of a century. Most of the rest are obvious (and very badly done) translations from the French and even from Cervantes' *Exemplary Novels ;* seasoned with personal and other anecdotes, so that the whole number of separate articles may exceed four-score. Of these a few are interesting attempts at the historical novel or novelette—short sketches of Mary Queen of Scots (very sympathetic and evidently French in origin from the phrase " a *temple* which was formerly a church "), Jane Shore (an exquisitely absurd piece of eighteenth-century middle-class modernising and moralising), Essex, Buckingham, and other likely figures. There are cuts by the " Van-somethings and Back-somethings " of the time: and the whole, though not worthy of anything better than the " fourpenny box," is an evident symptom of popular taste. The sweetmeats or *hors d'œuvre* of the older caterings for that taste are here collected together to form a *pièce de résistance*. It is true that *The Novelist* is only a true title in the older sense—that the pieces are *novelle* not " novels " proper. But they are fiction, or fact treated like fiction: and though the popular taste itself was evidently ceasing to be satisfied with these morsels and demanding a substantial [joint, yet the substance was, after all, the same.

We rise higher, if not very high, with the novels of Mrs. Eliza Haywood (1693-1756), one of the damned of the *Dunciad*, but, like some of her fellows in that *Inferno*, by no means deserving hopeless reprobation. Every one who has devoted any attention to the history of the novel, as well as some who have merely considered it as a part of that of English literature generally, has noticed the curious contrast between the earlier and the later novels of this writer. *Betsy Thoughtless* (1751) and *Jemmy and Jenny Jessamy* (1753) could, without much difficulty, be transposed into novels of to-day. *Idalia* (1723) is of an entirely different mood and scheme. It is a pure Behnesque *nouvelle*, merely describing the plots and outrage which ruin the heroine (*The Unfortunate Mistress* is the second title), but attempting no character-drawing (the only hint at such a thing is that Idalia, instead of being a meek and suffering victim, is said to have a violent temper), and making not the slightest effort even to complete what story there is. For the thing breaks off with a sort of " *perhaps* to be concluded in *some* next," about which we have not made up our minds. Very rarely do we find such a curious combination or succession of styles so early: but the novel, for pretty obvious reasons, seems to offer temptations to it and facilities for it. For *Idalia's* above-named juniors, while not bad books to read for mere amusement, have a very particular interest for the student of the history of the novel. Taken in connection with their author's earlier work, they illustrate, for the first time, a curious phenomenon which has repeated itself often, notably in the case of Bulwer, and of a living novelist who need not be named. This is that the novel, more almost than any other kind of literature, seems to lend itself to what may be called the *timeserving* or " opportunism " of craftsmanship—to call out the adaptiveness and versatility of the artist. *Betsy* and *Jenny* are so different from *Idalia* and her group that a critic of the idle Separatist persuasion would, were it not for troublesome certainties of fact, have no difficulty whatever in proving that they must be by different authors. We know that they were *not*: and we know also the reason of their dissimilarity—the fact that *Pamela* and her brother and their groups *ont passé par là*.[1] This fact is most interesting: and it shows, among other things, that Mrs. Eliza Haywood was a decidedly clever woman.

At the same time the two books also show that she was not quite clever enough: and that she had not realised, as in fact hardly one of the minor novelists of this time did realise, the necessity of individualising character. Betsy is both a nice and a good girl—" thoughtless " up to specification, but no fool, perfectly " straight " though the reverse of prudish, generous, merry, lovable. But with all these good qualities she is not quite a person. Jenny is, I think, a little more of one, but still not quite— while the men and the other women are still less. Nor had Eliza mastered that practised knack of " manners-painting " which was to stand Fanny Burney, and many another after her, in the stead of actual character-creation. Her situations are often very lively, if not exactly decorous; and they sometimes have a real dramatic verisimilitude, for instance, the quarrel and reconciliation of the Lord and the Lady in *Jemmy and Jenny Jessamy*; but the higher

---

[1] The elect ladies about Richardson joined *Betsy* with *Amelia*, and sneered at both.

verisimilitude of prose fiction they lack. Neither again (though Smollett had given her a lead here) had she attained that power of setting and furnishing a scene which is so powerful a weapon in the novelist's armoury. Yet she had learnt much: and her later work would have been almost a wonder in her own earlier time.

She had even been preceded in the new line by one, and closely followed by another writer of her own sex, both of unblemished reputation, and perhaps her superiors in intellectual quality and accomplishment, though they had less distinct novel-faculty. Sarah Fielding, the great novelist's sister, but herself one of Richardson's literary seraglio, had a good deal of her brother's humour, but very little of his constructive grasp of life. *David Simple* (1744), her best known work, the *Familiar Letters* connected with it (to which Henry contributed), and *The Governess* display both the merit and the defect—but the defect is more fatal to a novel than the merit is advantageous. Once more—if the criticism has been repeated *ad nauseam* the occasions of it may be warranted to be much more nauseous in themselves—one looks up for interest, and is not fed. " The Adventures " of David—whose progeny must have been rapidly enriched and ennobled if Peter Simple was his descendant—were "in search of a Friend," and he came upon nobody in the least like O'Brien. It was, in fact, too early or too late for a *lady* to write a thoroughly good novel. It had been possible in the days of Madeleine de Scudèry, and it became possible in the days of Frances Burney: but for some time before, in the days of Sarah Fielding, it was only possible in the ways of Afra and of Mrs. Haywood, who, without any unjust stigma on them, can hardly be said to fulfil the idea of ladyhood, as no doubt Miss Fielding did.

There is an amusing and (in its context) just passage
of Thackeray's, in which he calls Charlotte Lennox, author
of *The Female Quixote* (1752), a " figment." But it would
be unlucky if any one were thereby prevented from reading
this work of the lady whom Johnson admired, and for
whom he made an all-night orgie of apple-pie and bay-
leaves. Her book, which from its heroine is also called
Arabella, is clever and not unamusing, though it errs (in
accordance with the moral-critical principles of the time)
by not merely satirising the " heroic " romances of the
Gomberville - La Calprenède - Scudèry type, but solemnly
discussing them. Arabella, the romance-bitten daughter
of a marquis, is, for all her delusion, or because of it,
rather a charming creature. Her lover Glanville, his
Richardsonian sister, and the inevitable bad Baronet (he
can hardly be called wicked, especially for a Baronet) are
more commonplace: and the thing would have been better
as a rather long *nouvelle* than as a far from short novel. It
alternately comes quite close to its original (as in the
intended burning of Arabella's books) and goes entirely
away from it, and neither as an imitation nor independently
is it as good as Graves's *Spiritual Quixote :* but it is very
far from contemptible.

Yet though the aptitude of women for novel-writing was
thus early exemplified, it is not to be supposed that the
majority of persons who felt the new influences were of
that sex. By far the larger number of those who crowded
to follow the Four were, like them, men.

That not exactly credit to the Tory party, Dr. John
Shebbeare, has had his demerits in other ways excused to
some extent on the score of *Lydia*—whose surname, by
the way, was " Fairchild," not unknown in later days of
fiction. Even one who, if critical conscience would in

any way permit it, would fain let the Tory dogs have a little the best of it, must, I fear, pronounce *Lydia* a very poor thing. Shebbeare, who was a journalist, had the journalist faculty of " letting everything go in "—of taking as much as he could from Richardson, Fielding, Smollett, etc., up to date (1755), and of throwing back to Afra for an interesting Indian, Canassatego. The book (like not a few other eighteenth-century novels) has very elaborate chapter headings and very short chapters, so that an immoral person can get up its matter pretty easily. A virtuous one who reads it through will have to look to his virtue for reward. The irony is factitious and forced; the sentiment unappealing; the coarseness quite destitute of Rabelaisian geniality; and the nomenclature may be sampled from " the Countess of Liberal " and " Lord Beef." I believe Shebbeare was once pilloried for his politics. If it had been for *Lydia*, I should not have protested.

The next book to be mentioned is an agreeable change. Why Hazlitt compared *The Life of John Buncle* (1756-1766) to Rabelais is a somewhat idle though perhaps not quite unanswerable question; the importance of the book itself in the history of the English novel, which has sometimes been doubted or passed over, is by no means small. Its author, Thomas Amory (1691 ?-1788), was growing old when he wrote it and even when he prefaced it with a kind of Introduction, the *Memoirs of several Ladies* (1755). It is a sort of dream-exaggeration of an autobiography; at first sight, and not at first sight only, the wildest of farragos. The author represents himself as a disinherited son who is devoted, with equal enthusiasm, to matrimony, eating and drinking as much as he can of the best things he can find, discussion of theological problems in a " Christian-deist "

or Unitarian sense, " natural philosophy " in the vague
eighteenth-century meaning, and rambling—chiefly in the
fell district which includes the borders of Lancashire, Yorkshire, Westmoreland, " Bishopric " (Durham), and Cumberland. With this district—which even now, though seamed
with roads and railways, does actually contain some of the
wildest scenery of the island; which only forty years ago
was much wilder; and which in Amory's time was a howling
wilderness in parts—he deals in the characteristic spirit of
exaggeration which perhaps, as much as anything else,
suggested Rabelais to Hazlitt. From Malham Cove and
Hardraw Scar, through the Wild Boar Fell district to the
head of Teesdale, you can find at this moment rough and
rugged scenery enough, some of which is actually recog-
nisable when " reduced " from Amory's extravagance.
But that extravagance extends the distances from furlongs
to leagues; deepens the caverns from yards to furlongs;
and exalts fell and scar into Alps and Andes. In the same
way he has to marry eight wives (not seven as has been
usually, and even by the present writer, said), who are
distractingly beautiful and wonderfully wise, but who
seldom live more than two years: and has a large number
of children about whom he says nothing, " because he has
not observed in them anything worth speaking about."
The courtships are varied between abrupt embraces soon
after introduction, and discussions on Hebrew, Babel,
" Christian-deism," and the binomial theorem. In the
most inhospitable deserts, his man or boy [1] is invariably
able to produce from his wallet " ham, tongue, potted
blackcock, and a pint of cyder," while in more favourable

---

[1] It has been observed, and is worth observing, that the eighteenth-
century hero, even in his worst circumstances, can seldom exist without a
" follower."

circumstances Buncle takes his ease in his inn by consuming
" a pound of steak, a quart of green peas, two fine cuts of
bread, a tankard of strong ale, and a pint of port " and
singing cheerful love-ditties a few days after the death of
an adored wife. He comes down the side of precipices by
a mysterious kind of pole-jumping—half a dozen fathoms
at a drop with landing-places a yard wide—like a chamois
or a rollicking Rocky Mountain ram. Every now and then
he finds a skeleton, with a legend of instructive tenor, in a
hermitage which he annexes: and almost infallibly, at the
worst point of the wilderness, there is an elegant country
seat with an obliging old father and a lively heiress ready
to take the place of the last removed charmer.

Mad, however, as this sketch may sound, and certainly
not quite sane as Amory may have been, there is a very
great deal of method in his, and some in its, madness.
The flashes of shrewdness and the blocks of pretty solid
learning (Rabelaisian again) do not perhaps so much concern us: but the book, ultra-eccentric as it is, does count
for something in the history of the English novel. Its
descriptions, rendered through a magnifying glass as they
are, have considerable power; and are quite unlike anything in prose fiction, and most things in prose literature,
before it. In Buncle himself there is a sort of extra-
natural, " four-dimension " nature and proportion which
assert the novelist's power memorably:—if a John Buncle
could exist, he would very probably be like Amory's John
Buncle. Above all, the book (let it be remembered that
it came before *Tristram Shandy*) is almost the beginning of
the Eccentric Novel—not of the satiric-marvellous type
which Cyrano and Swift had revived from Lucian, but of
a new, a modern, and a very English variety. Buncle is
sometimes extraordinarily like Borrow (on whom he prob-

ably had influence), and it would not be hard to arrange a very considerable spiritual succession for him, by no means deserving the uncomplimentary terms in which he dismisses his progeny in the flesh.

If there is an almost preposterous cheerfulness about *Buncle*, the necessary alterative can be amply supplied by the next book to which we come. The curious way in which Johnson almost invariably managed to hit the critical nail on the head is well illustrated by his remark to Frances Sheridan, author of the *Memoirs of Miss Sydney Bid[d]ulph* (1761), that he " did not know whether she had a right, on moral principles, to make her readers suffer so much." Substitute " æsthetic " for " moral " and " heroine " for " readers," and the remark retains its truth on another scheme of criticism, which Johnson was not ostensibly employing, and which he might have violently denounced. The book, though with its subsequent prolongation too long, is a powerful one: and though actually dedicated to Richardson and no doubt consciously owing much to his influence, practically clears off the debt by its own earnings. But Miss Bidulph (she started with only one *d*, but acquired another), whose journal to her beloved Cecilia supplies the matter and method of the novel, is too persistently unlucky and illtreated, without the smallest fault of her own, for anything but really, not fictitiously, real life. Her misfortunes spring from obeying her mother (but there was neither moral nor satire in this then), and husbands, lovers, rivals, relations, connections—everybody—conspire to afflict her. Poetical justice has been much abused in both senses of that verb: *Sydney Biddulph* shows cause for it in the very act of neglect.

But the eighteenth century, on the whole, loathed melancholy. The *Spiritual Quixote* (1772) of the Reverend

Richard Graves (1715-1804) has probably been a little injured by the ingenuous proclamation of indebtedness in the title. It is, however, an extremely clever and amusing book: and one of the best of the many imitations of its original, which, indeed, it follows only on broad and practically independent lines. During his long life (for more than half a century of which he was rector of Claverton near Bath) Graves knew many interesting persons, from Shenstone and Whitefield (with both of whom he was at Pembroke College, Oxford, though he afterwards became a fellow of All Souls) to Malthus, who was a pupil of his; and he had some interesting private experiences. He wove a good deal that was personal into his novel, which, as may easily be guessed, is a satire upon Methodism, and in which Whitefield is personally and not altogether favourably introduced. But even on him Graves is by no means savage: while his treatment of his hero, Geoffrey Wildgoose, a young Oxford man who, living in retirement with his mother in the country, becomes an evangelist, very mainly from want of some more interesting occupation, is altogether good-humoured. Wildgoose promptly falls in love with a fascinating damsel-errant, Julia Townsend; and the various adventures, religious, picaresque, and amatory, are embroiled and disembroiled with very fair skill in character and fairer still in narrative. Nor is the Sancho-Partridge of the piece, Jerry Tugwell, a cobbler (who thinks, though he is very fond of his somewhat masterful wife, that a little absence from her would not be unrefreshing), by any means a failure. Both Scott and Dickens evidently knew Graves well,[1] and knowledge of him might with advantage be more general.

---

[1] Julia Mannering reminds me a little of Julia Townsend: and if this be doubtful, the connection of Jerry's " Old madam gave me some higry-

The novels that have been noticed since those contrasted ones of Mrs. Haywood's, which occupy a position by themselves, all possess a sort of traditional fame; and cover (with the proper time allowed for the start given by Richardson and Fielding) nearly the same period of thirty years—in this case 1744 (*David Simple*) to 1772 (*The Spiritual Quixote*)—which is covered by the novels of the great quartette themselves. It would be possible to add a great many, and easy and not disagreeable to the writer to dwell on a few. Of these few some are perhaps necessary. Frank Coventry's *Pompey the Little*—an amusing satirical novel with a pet dog for the title-giver and with the promising (but as a rule ill-handled) subject of university life treated early — appeared in 1751 — the same year which saw the much higher flight (the pun is in sense not words) of *Peter Wilkins*, by Robert Paltock of Clement's Inn, a person of whom practically nothing else is known. It would be lucky for many people if they were thus singly yoked to history. It was once fashionable to dismiss *Peter* as a boy's book, because it discovers a world of flying men and women, modelled partly on Defoe, partly on Swift; it has more recently been fashionable to hint a sneer at it as " sentimental " because of its presentment of a sort of fantastic and unconventional Amelia (who, it may be remembered, made her appearance in the same year) in the heroine Youwarkee. Persons who do not care for fashion will perhaps sometimes agree that, though not exactly a masterpiece, it is rather a charming book. If anybody is sickened by its charm he may restore himself by a still better known story which no one can accuse of

pigry " and Cuddie's " the leddy cured me with some hickery-pickery " is not. While, for Dickens, compare the way in which Sam Weller's landlord in the Fleet got into trouble with the Tinker's Tale in *Spiritual Quixote*, bk. iv. chap. ii.

K

charm or sentiment, though it is clever enough—Charles Johnstone's *Chrysal* or *The Adventures of a Guinea* (1760). This, which is strongly Smollettian in more ways than one, derives its chief notoriety from the way in which the scandalous (and perhaps partly fabulous) orgies of Medmenham Abbey are, like other scandalous and partly fabulous gossip of the time, brought in. But it *is* clever; though emphatically one of the books which " leave a bad taste in the mouth." Indeed about this time the novel, which even in clean hands allowed itself not a little freedom, took, in others, excursions in the direction of the province of " prohibited literature," and sometimes passed the border.

One rather celebrated book, however, has not yet been mentioned: and it will serve very well, with two others greater in every way, as usher to a few general remarks on the weakness of this generation of minor novelists. Between 1766 and 1770 Henry Brooke, an Irishman of position, fortune, and literary distinction in other ways, who was at the time of more than middle age, published *The Fool of Quality* or *The Adventures of Henry Earl of Morland*. The hero is a sort of Grandison-Buncle, as proper though scarcely as priggish as the one, and as eccentric and discursive as the other; the story is chaos: the book is stuffed with disquisitions on all sorts of moral, social, and political problems. It is excellently written; it is clear from it that Brooke (who was for a time actually mad) did not belie the connection of great wits with madness. But it is, perhaps, most valuable as an evidence of the unconquerable set of the time towards novel.

Of this, however, as of some other points, we have greater evidence still in the shape of two books, each of them, as nothing else yet mentioned in this chapter can claim to be, a permanent and capital contribution to English literature—Johnson's *Rasselas* (1759) and Goldsmith's *Vicar of Wakefield* (1766).

It is not from the present writer that any one need look for an attempt to belittle Johnson: and there is no doubt (for the *Lives of the Poets* is but a bundle of essays) that *Rasselas* is Johnson's greatest *book*. But there may be, in some minds, as little doubt that attempts to defend it from the charge of not being a novel are only instances of that not wholly unamiable frenzy of eagerness to " say *not* ditto to Mr. Burke " which is characteristic of clever undergraduates, and of periods which are not quite of the greatest in literature. *Rasselas* is simply an extended and glorified moral apologue—an enlarged " Vision of Mirza." It has no real story; it has no real characters; its dialogue is " talking book; " it indulges in some but not much description. It is in fact a prose *Vanity of Human Wishes*, admirably if somewhat stiffly arranged in form, and as true to life as life itself. You will have difficulty in finding a wiser book anywhere; but although it is quite true that a novel need not be foolish, wisdom is certainly not its determining *differentia*. Yet for our purposes *Rasselas* is almost as valuable as *Tom Jones* itself: because it shows how imperative and wide-ranging was the struggle towards production of this kind in prose. The book is really— to adapt the quaint title of one of the preceding century — *Johnson al Mondo:* and at this time, when Johnson wanted to communicate his thoughts to the world in a popular form, we see that he chose the novel.

The lesson is not so glaringly obvious in the *Vicar of Wakefield*, because this *is* a novel, and a very delightful one. The only point of direct contact with *Rasselas* is the knowledge of human nature, though in the one book this takes the form of melancholy aphorism and apophthegm, in the other that of felicitous trait and dialogue-utterance. There is plenty of story, though this has not been arranged so as to hit the taste of the martinet in " fable; " the book has endless character; the descriptions are Hogarth with less of *peuple* about them; the dialogue is unsurpassable. Yet Goldsmith, untiring hack of genius as he was, wrote no other novel; evidently felt no particular call or predilection for the style; would have been dramatist, poet, essayist with greater satisfaction to himself, though scarcely (satisfactory as he is in all these respects) to us. That he tried it at all can hardly be set down to anything else than the fact that the style was popular: and his choice is one of the highest possible testimonies to the popularity of the style. Incidentally, of course, the *Vicar* has more for us than this, because it indicates, as vividly as any of the work of the great Four themselves, how high and various the capacities of the novel are—how in fact it can almost completely compete with and, for a time, vanquish the drama on its own ground. Much of it, of course—the " Fudge! " scene between Mr. Burchell and the town ladies may be taken as the first example that occurs—*is* drama, with all the cumbrous accessories of stage and scene and circumstance spared. One may almost see that " notice to quit," which (some will have it) has been, after nearly a century and a half, served back again on the novel, served by the *Vicar of Wakefield* on the drama.

At the same time even the *Vicar*, though perhaps less than any other book yet noticed in this chapter, illustrates the proposition to which we have been leading up—that, outside the great quartette, and even to a certain extent inside of it, the novel had not yet fully found its proper path—had still less made up its mind to walk freely and firmly therein. Either it has some *arrière pensée*, some second purpose, besides the simple attempt to interest and absorb by the artistic re-creation of real and ordinary life: or, without exactly doing this, it shows signs of mistrust and misgiving as to the sufficiency of such an appeal, and supplements it by the old tricks of the drama in "revolution and discovery;" by incident more or less out of the ordinary course; by satire, political, social, or personal; by philosophical disquisition; by fantastic imagination—by this, that, and the other of the fatal auxiliaries who always undo their unwise employers. Men want to write novels; and the public wants them to write novels; and supply does not fail desire and demand. There is a well-known *locus classicus* from which we know that, not long after the century had passed its middle, Lady Mary Wortley Montagu in Italy regularly received boxes of novels from her daughter in England, and read them, eagerly though by no means uncritically, as became Fielding's cousin and her ladyship's self. But while the kind had not conquered, and for a long time did not conquer, any high place in literature from the point of view of serious criticism—while, now and long afterwards, novel-writing was the Cinderella of the literary family, and novel-reading the inexhaustible text for sermons on wasted, nay positively ill-spent, time—the novelists themselves half justified their critics by frequent extravagance; by more frequent unreality; by undue licence pretty often; by digression and divagation still oftener. Except Fielding, hardly any one had dared boldly to hold up the mirror to nature, and be content with giving the reflection, in his own way, but with respect for it. For even Goldsmith, with infinite touches of nature, had not given quite a natural whole, and even Johnson, though absolutely true, had failed to accommodate his truth to the requirements of the novel.

The turning point in this direction of the kind was to be made by a person far inferior in ability to any one of the great quartette, and in a book which, *as* a book, cannot pretend to an equality with the worst of theirs—by a person indeed of less intellectual power, and in a book of less literary merit, than not a few of the persons and books just noticed. There is something, no doubt, paradoxical in this: and the paradox is connected, both with a real quality of the subject and with a surprising diversity of opinions about it. Frances Burney and her *Evelina* (1778), not to mention her subsequent works and her delightful *Diary*, have been the subject of a great deal of writing: but though more than a hundred years—more indeed than a century and a quarter—have passed since the book insidiously took London by gradual storm, it may, without too much presumption, be questioned whether either book or author has yet been finally or satisfactorily " placed." The immense advantage of not having a history, positively illustrated once for all in Shakespeare, could hardly be negatively illustrated better than in Madame d'Arblay. She had the curious, and actually very unpleasant, experience of being selected for a position at court on the strength of her literary achievements, of finding it intolerable, of breaking down, and of never doing any really good work after her release, through much more than half of her long life. On this fact critical biography has fastened almost exclusively. Macaulay, in one of his most brilliant and best known essays, represents the world as having been deprived of unknown quantities of admirable work by the misplaced kindness, and the positive unkindness, of Queen Charlotte. Some have agreed with him, some have differed

with him.   Some, in one of the natural if uncritical revul-
sions, have questioned whether even *Evelina* is a very remarkable book.   Some, with human respect for the great
names of its early admirers, have passed it over gingerly
—not exactly as willing to wound, but as quite afraid or reluctant to strike.   Nay, actual critical evaluations of the
novel-values of Miss Burney's four attempts in novel-writing
are very rare.   I dare say there are other people who have
read *The Wanderer* through: but I never met any one who
had done so except (to quote Rossetti) myself: and I could
not bring myself, even on this occasion, to read it again.
I doubt whether very many now living have read *Camilla*.
Even *Cecilia* requires an effort, and does not repay that
effort very well.   Only *Evelina* itself is legible and re-
legible—for reasons which will be given presently.   Yet
Cecilia was written shortly after *Evelina*, under the same
stimulus of abundant and genial society, with no pressure
except that of friendly encouragement and perhaps assistance, and long before the supposed blight of royal favour
and royal exigences came upon its author.   When *Camilla*
was published she had been relieved from these exigences,
though not from that favour, for five years: and was a
thoroughly happy woman, rejoicing in husband and child.
Even when the impossible *Wanderer* was concocted, she
had had ample leisure, had as yet incurred none of her
later domestic sorrows, and was assured of lavish recom-
pense for her (it must be said) absolutely worthless labours.
Why this steady declension, with which, considering the
character of *Cecilia*, the court sojourn can have had
nothing to do?   And admitting it, why still uphold, as the
present writer does uphold, *Evelina* as one of the *points de
repère* of the English novel?   Both questions shall be
answered in their order.

Frances Burney must have been, as we see not merely from external testimony, but from the infallible witness of her own diary, a most engaging person to any one who could get over her shyness and her prudery:[1] but she was only in a very limited sense a gifted one. Macaulay grants her a "fine understanding;" but even his own article contradicts the statement, which is merely one of his exaggerations for the sake of point. She had *not* a fine understanding: though she was neither silly nor stupid, her sense was altogether inferior to her sensibility. Although living in a most bookish circle she was, as Macaulay himself admits, almost illiterate: and (which he does not say) her comparative critical estimates of books, when she does give them, are merely contemptible. This harsh statement could be freely substantiated: but it is enough to say that, when a girl, she preferred some forgotten rubbish called *Henry and Frances* to the *Vicar of Wakefield:* and that, when a woman, she deliberately offended Chateaubriand by praising the *Itinéraire* rather than the *Génie du Christianisme*, or *Atala*, or *René*, or *Les Martyrs*. She had very little inventive power; her best novel, *Evelina*, has no plot worth speaking of. She never wrote really well. Even the *Diary* derives its whole charm from the matter and the *reportage*. *Evelina* is tolerable style of the kind that has no style; *Cecilia* is pompous and Johnsonian; *Camilla* was stigmatised by the competent and affectionate judgment of Mrs. Delany as "Gallicised;" and *The Wanderer* is in a lingo which suggests the translation of an ill-written French original by a person who does not know English.

[1] Also, perhaps, to one who had not yet discovered that intense concentration on herself and her family with which, after their quarrel, Mrs. Thrale, not quite an impartial judge, but a very shrewd one, charged her, and which does appear in the *Diary*.

What then was it in *Evelina*, and in part in *Cecilia* (with a faint survival even into *Camilla*), which turned the heads of such a " town " as Johnson and Burke, Walpole and Windham, and many others—which, to persons who can see it, makes the books attractive to-day, and which should always give their author a secure and distinguished place in the great torch-race of English fiction-writers? It is this—that Miss Burney had a quite marvellous faculty of taking impressions of actual speech, manners, and to a certain extent character: that she had, at any rate for a time, a corresponding faculty of expressing, or at least reporting, her impressions. Next (and perhaps most of all) that she had the luck to come at a moment when speech and manners were turning to the modern; and lastly, that she was content, in parts of her work at any rate, to let her faculty of expression work, automatically and uninterfered with, on the impressions: and thereby give us record of them for all time. Her acute critic " Daddy " Crisp lamented that we had not had a series of recorders of successive *tons* [fashions] like Fanny. But she was much more than a mere fashion-monger: and what has lasted best in her was not mere fashion. She could see and record life and nature : and she did so. Still, fashion had a good deal to do with it: and when her access to fashion and society ceased, the goodness of her work ceased likewise.

Even this gift, and this even in *Evelina* and the better parts of *Cecilia*, she had not always with her. The senti-mental parts of *Evelina* — the correspondence with Mr. Villars, the courtship with Lord Orville, and others—are very weak: and it cannot be said that Evelina herself, though she is a pleasant girl enough, gives the lie to Mr. Pope's libel about women. Cecilia has a little more in-dividuality. But the great strength of the former book lies in the admirable lower middle-class pictures of the Branghtons and Mr. Smith, whom Fanny had evidently studied from the life in the queer neighbourhood of Poland Street: as also in the justness and verisimilitude of the picture of the situation, which in different ways both books present—that of the introduction of a young girl to the world.[1] In these points, as in others which there is neither space nor need to particularise, Miss Burney showed that she had hit upon—stumbled upon one may almost say—the real principle and essence of the novel as distinguished from the romance—its connection with actual ordinary life—life studied freshly and directly "*from* the life," and disguised and adulterated as little as possible by exceptional interests and incidents. It is scarcely too much to say that one great reason why the novel was so long coming into existence was precisely this—that life and society so long remained subject to these exceptional interests and incidents. It is only within the last century or so that the " life of 'mergency " (to adapt Mr. Chucks slightly) ceased to be the ordinary life. Addison's " Dissenter's Diary" with its record of nothing but constitutionals and marrow-bones, and Mr. Nisby's opinions, has simply amused half a dozen generations. Yet, in a sense, it has nearly as much to do with the advent of the novel as Sir Roger de Coverley himself. For these things are, not merely in an allegory, the subjects of the novel. Not so very much earlier Mr. Nisby would have had a chance of delivering his opinions on the scaffold: and his disciple would have had prison bread and water for marrow-bones and " Brooks and Hellier." These would have been subjects for romance: the others were subjects for novel.

[1] Dunlop and others have directly or indirectly suggested a good deal of plagiarism in *Evelina* from *Miss Betsy Thoughtless :* but it is exactly in this *life*-quality that the earlier novelist fails.

All glory, therefore, be to Frances Burney; both that which her generous successor and superior gives her in *Northanger Abbey*, and more also—for Miss Austen, naturally enough, was not taking the view-point of literary history.   But it has been said that Fanny herself possessed her gift in two senses uncertainly—first, in that she did not very clearly perceive what it was, and, secondly, in that she soon lost grip of it.   It is, therefore, not wonderful that few others caught the trick from her for a long time— for indeed fully twenty years, till Miss Edgeworth made her appearance.   But these twenty years were years of extreme fertility in novels of different sorts, while—a phenomenon that occurs not seldom—the older kind of fiction made a kind of rally at the very time that the newer was at last solidly establishing itself.   There was, indeed, ample room for both.   You cannot kill Romance: it would be a profound misfortune, perhaps the profoundest that could befall the human race, if you could.   But the new romance was of rather a bastard kind, and it showed more of the bad blood than of the good till, by a curious coincidence, Scott once more found the true strain, just about the same time as that at which Miss Austen was making known the true strain of the novel proper.

This hybrid new romance had been stumbled upon more than a decade before Fanny Burney in her turn stumbled upon the pure novel: and most people know in what and by whom.   To this day it is by no means easy to be certain what Horace Walpole really meant to write, or thought he was writing, in *The Castle of Otranto* (1764). His own references to his own writings are too much saturated with affectation and pose to make it safe to draw any conclusions from them; there is little or no external evidence; and the book itself is rather a puzzle.

Taking the Preface to the second edition with a very large allowance of salt—the success of the first *before* this preface makes double salting advisable—and accommodating it to the actual facts, one finds it hardly necessary to go beyond the obvious and almost commonplace solution that *The Castle of Otranto* was simply the castle of Strawberry Hill itself with paper for lath and ink for plaster— in other words, an effort to imitate something which the imitator more than half misunderstood. Of mediæval literature proper, apart from chronicles and genealogies, Walpole knew nothing: and for its more precious features he had the dislike which sometimes accompanies ignorance. But he undoubtedly had positive literary genius—flawed, alloyed, incomplete, uncritical of itself, but existing: and this genius showed itself here. His paper-and-ink " Strawberry " is quite another guess structure from his lath-and-plaster one.   For itself in itself—for what it *is*— the present writer, though he has striven earnestly and often for the sake of the great things that it *did*, has never been able to get up any affection or admiration.   It is preposterous, desultory, tedious, clumsy, dull. But it made people (we know it on such excellent authority as Gray's) shudder: and the shudder was exactly what they wanted—in every sense of the verb " to want."   Moreover, quite independently of this shudder, it pointed the way to a wide, fertile, and delightful province of historical, social, literary, and other matter which had long been neglected, and which people had been assured was not worth exploring. Blair was just using, or about to use, " any romance of chivalry " as a hyperbolical exemplification of the contemptible in literature. Hume had been arguing against, and Voltaire was still sneering at, all sorts of superstition and supernaturalism. The common cant of criticism for generations had been that " sense " and " reason " were to be the only criteria. Walpole's egregious helmet dropped from no one knew (or knows) where on all these Philistinisms: and squelched them. How it did this, why it did it, and so forth, one knows not much more than one knows why and how all the things happened in the novel itself. *Après coup*, the author talked about " Shakespeare " (of whom, by the way, he was anything but a fervent or thorough admirer) and the like. Shakespeare had, as Sir Walter Raleigh has well pointed out, uncommonly little to do with it. But Shakespeare at least supplies us with an appropriate phrase for the occasion. *The Castle of Otranto* " lay in " Horace's " way, and he found it." And with it, though hardly in it, he found the New Romance.

In Horace's case also, as in that of Frances, though the success was even more momentous, the successors were slow and doubtful, though not quite so slow. In some dozen years Walpole read Miss Clara Reeve's *Old English Baron* (1777), and as in another celebrated case " thought it a bore." It *is* rather a bore. It has more consecutiveness than *Otranto*, and escapes the absurdities of the copiously but clumsily used supernatural by administering it in a very minute dose. But there is not a spark of genius in it, whereas that spark, though sometimes curiously wrapped up in ashes, was always present (Heaven knows where he got it!) in Sir Robert's youngest son. And the contagion spread. For general and epidemic purposes it had to wait till the Germans had carried it over the North Sea and sent it back again. For particular ones, it found a new development in one of the most remarkable of all novels, twenty years younger than *Otranto*, and a few years older than the new outburst of the " Gothic " supernatural in the works of Anne Radcliffe and Mat Lewis.

Vathek (1786) stands alone—almost independent even of its sponsors—it would be awkward to say godfathers—Hamilton and Voltaire; apart likewise from such work as it, no doubt, in turn partly suggested to Peacock and to Disraeli. There is, perhaps, no one towards whom it is so tempting to play the idle game of retrospective Providence as towards the describer of Batalha and Alcobaça, the creator of Nouronnihar and the Hall of Eblis. Fonthill has had too many vicissitudes since Beckford, and Cintra is a far cry; but though his associations with Bath are later, it is still possible, in that oddly enchanted city, to get something of the mixed atmosphere—eighteenth century, nineteenth, and of centuries older and younger than either —which, *tamisée* in a mysterious fashion, surrounds this extraordinary little masterpiece. Take Beckford's millions away; make him coin his wits to supply the want of them; and what would have been the result? Perhaps more *Vatheks;* perhaps things even better than *Vathek;* [1] perhaps nothing at all. On the whole, it is always wiser not to play Providence, in fact or fancy. All that need be said is that Anthony Hamilton and Voltaire are certainly not by themselves—good as they are, and admirable as the first is—enough to account for *Vathek*. Romance has passed there as well as persiflage and something like *coïonnerie;* it is Romance that has given us the baleful beauty of that Queen of Evil, Nouronnihar, and the vision of the burning hearts that make their own wandering but eternal Hell. The tendency of the novel had been on the

---

[1] Since the text was written—indeed very recently—the long-missing "Episodes" of *Vathek* itself have been at length supplied by the welcome diligence of Mr. Lewis Melville. They are not "better than Vathek," but they are good.

whole, even in its best examples, to prose in feeling as well as in form. It was Beckford who availed himself of the poetry which is almost inseparable from Romance. But it was Horace Walpole who had opened the door to Romance herself.

Still, *Vatheks* are not to be had to order: and as Romance was wanted, to order and in bulk, during the late years of the eighteenth century, some other kind had to be supplied. The chief accredited purveyors of it have been already named and must now be dealt with, to be followed by the list of secondary, never quite accomplished, exponents now of novel, now of romance, now of the two mixed, who filled the closing years of the eighteenth century.

It is, however, unjust to put the author of *The Mysteries of Udolpho* and the author of *The Monk* on the same level. Mat Lewis was a clever boy with a lively fancy, a knack of catching and even of anticipating popular tendencies in literature, a rather vulgar taste by nature, and no faculty of self-criticism to correct it. The famous *Monk* (1795), which he published when he was twenty, is as preposterous as *Otranto* and adds to its preposterousness a *haut goût* of atrocity and indecency which Walpole was far too much of a gentleman, and even of a true man of letters, to attempt or to tolerate. Lewis's other work in various forms is less offensive: but—except in respect of verse-rhythm which does not here concern us—hardly any of it is literature. What does concern us is that the time took it for literature, because it adopted the terror-style in fiction.

Anne Ward (she married a barrister named Radcliffe, of whom we do not hear much except that his engagements in journalism threw time on his wife's hands for writing) appears to have started on her career of terror-novelist, in which she preceded Lewis, with two fixed resolves of principle very contrary to his practice. The first was to observe strict " propriety " in her books—a point in which the novel had always been a little peccant. The second and more questionable, but also more original, was a curious determination to lavish the appearance of the supernatural, in accordance with the Walpolian tradition and the German adoption of it, but never to allow anything *really* supernatural in ultimate explanation or want of explanation. She applied these two principles to the working out, over and over again, of practically the same story—the persecutions of a beautiful and virtuous heroine, and her final deliverance from them. Her first attempt, *The Castles of Athlin and Dunbayne*, appeared as early as 1789: and she left a posthumous romance, *Gaston de Blondeville*, which did not come out till 1826, four years after her death. She also wrote some poems and a volume of *Travels* (1794) which is important for a reason to be noticed presently. But her fame rests upon four books, which she published in seven years, between her own twenty-sixth and thirty-third, *A Sicilian Romance* (1790), *The Romance of the Forest* (1791), the world-renowned *Mysteries of Udolpho* in 1794-1795, and *The Italian* two years later.

These stories owed their original attraction to the skill with which, by the use of a Defoe-like minuteness of detail, added to a pictorial faculty which Defoe had not, an atmosphere of terror is constantly diffused and kept up. Very little that is terrible actually happens: but the artist succeeds (so long as the trick has not become too familiar) in persuading you that something very terrible is *going* to happen, or has just happened. And so the delight of something " horrid," as the Catherines and Isabellas of the day put it, is given much more plentifully, and even

much more excitingly, than it could be by a real horror
now and then, with intervals of miscellaneous business.
In one sense, indeed, the process will not stand even the
slightest critical examination: for it is soon seen to consist
of a succession of serious mystifications and non-comic
much-ados-about-nothing. But these " ados " are most
cunningly made (her last book, *The Italian*, is, perhaps, the
best place to look for them, if the reader is not taking up
the whole subject with a virtuous thoroughness), and
Mrs. Radcliffe's great praise is that she induced her original
readers to suspend their critical faculties sufficiently to
enable them to take it all seriously. Scott, who undoubtedly owed her something, assigned her positive genius:
and modern critics, while, perhaps, seldom experiencing
much real delectation from her work, have discovered in
it not a few positive and many more indirect and comparative merits. The influence on Scott is not the least
of these: but there is even a more unquestionable asset
of the same kind in the fact that the Byronic villain-hero,
if not Byron himself, is Mrs. Radcliffe's work. Schedoni
did much more than beget or pattern Lara: he *is* Lara,
to all intents and purposes, in " first state " and before the
final touch has been put by the greater master who took
the plate in hand.

But there is more to be said for Mrs. Radcliffe than this.
Her " explained supernatural," tiresome as it may be to
some of us nowadays, is really a marvel of patience and
ingenuity: and this same quality extends to her plots
generally. The historical side of her novels (which she
does to some extent attempt) is a failure, as everything
of the kind was before Scott: that we may leave till we
come to Scott himself. But one important engine of the
novelist she set to work in a fashion which had never been

L

managed before, and that is elaborate description. She
shows an early adaptation of that " picturesque," of which
we see the beginnings in Gray, when she was in the nursery,
which was being directly developed by Gilpin, but which,
as we may see from her *Travels*, she had got not merely
from books, but from her own observation. She applies
it both within and without: at one moment giving pages
on the scenery of the Apennines, at another paragraphs on
the furniture of her abbeys and castles. The pine forests
and the cataracts; the skyline of Udolpho bathed in sun-
set glow, while a " melancholy purple tint " steals up the
slopes to its foundations—are all in the day's work now;
but they were not so then, and it is fair to say that Mrs.
Radcliffe does them well. The " high canopied tester of
dark green damask " and the " counterpane of black
velvet " which illustrate the introduction of the famous
chapter of the Black Pall in Chateau le Blanc may be mere
inventory goods now: but, once more, they were not so
then. And this faculty of description (which, as noted
above, could hardly have been, and pretty certainly was
not, got from books, though it may have been, to some
extent and quite legitimately, got from pictures) was applied in many minor ways—touches of really or supposedly
horrible objects in the dark, faint suggestions of sound,
or of appeals to the other senses—hints of all sorts, which
were to become common tricks of the trade, but were then
quite new.

At any rate, by these and other means she attained
that great result of the novel which has been noted in Defoe,
in Richardson, and in others — the result of what the
French vividly call *enfisting* the reader—getting hold of his
attention, absorbing him in a pleasant fashion. The
mechanism was often too mechanical: taken with the

author's steady and honest, but somewhat inartistic determination to explain everything it sometimes produces effects positively ridiculous to us. With the proviso of *valeat quantum*, it is not quite unfair to dwell, as has often been dwelt, on the fact that the grand triumph of Mrs. Radcliffe's terrormongering — the famous incident of the Black Veil—is produced by a piece of wax-work. But the result resulted—the effect *was* produced: and it was left to those who were clever enough to improve upon the means. For the time these means were "improved upon" in another sense; we shall glance at some of the caricatures, intended and unintended, later. For the present we may turn to other varieties of the curiously swarming novel-production of these two last decades of the century, and especially of the very last.

If Scott had not established Richard Cumberland's *Henry* (1795) in the fortress of the Ballantyne Novels, it would hardly be necessary to notice "Sir Fretful Plagiary's" contributions to the subject of our history. He preluded it with another, *Arundel* (1789), and followed it much later with a third, *John de Lancaster :* but there is no need to say anything of these. *Henry* displays the odd hit-*and*-miss quality which seems to have attached itself to Cumberland everywhere, whether as novelist, dramatist, essayist, diplomatist, poet, or anything else. It is, though by no means a mere "plagiarism," an obvious and avowed imitation of Fielding, and the writer is so intent on his *pastiche* that he seems quite oblivious himself, and appears to expect equal oblivion on the part of his readers, of the fact that nearly two generations had passed. Henry is Joseph; Susan May is a much more elaborate and attractive Betty; the doctor's wife a vulgarised and repulsive Lady Booby ; Ezekiel Daw, whom Scott admired, a *dissenting* Adams—the full force of the outrage of which variation Sir Walter perhaps did not feel. There are some good things in the story, but, as a whole, it is chiefly valuable as an early example of that great danger of modern literature—the influence of the " printed book " itself: and in a less degree of that forging ahead of the novel generally in public favour which we are chronicling. If the kind had not been popular, and if Fielding had not been its great prophet, one may be pretty sure that *Henry* would never have existed. The causes are important: the effect not quite so.

There was, however, at this time a novel-school, and not such a very small one, which had more legitimate reasons for existence, inasmuch as it really served as mouthpiece to the thoughts and opinions of the time, whether these thoughts and opinions were good or bad. This may be called the " revolutionary school," and its three most distinguished scholars were Bage, Holcroft, and Godwin, with Mrs. Inchbald perhaps to be added. The first began considerably before the outbreak of the actual French Revolution and shows the influence of its causes: the others were directly influenced by itself.

One of the most remarkable of English novel-writers who are not absolute successes, and one who, though less completely obscured by Fortune than some, has never had quite his due, is Robert Bage. It was unfortunate for him that he fell in with the crude generation contemporary in their manhood with the French Revolution, and so manifested the crudity in full. Bage, in fact, except for a certain strength of humour, is almost more French than English. He has been put in the school of Richardson, but it is certain that Richardson would have been shocked at the supposed scholar: and it is not certain that Bage would or need have felt complimented by the assignment of the master. He has the special laxity of the time in point of " morality," or at least of decency; its affectations of rather childish perfectibilism and anti-theism; and the tendency of at least a part of it to an odd Calibanic jesting. Bage is good-tempered enough as it is: but he rather suggests possible Carrier-and-Fouché developments in a favourable and fostering atmosphere. One does not quite know why Scott, who included in the Ballantyne Novels three of Bage's, *Mount Henneth* (1781), *Barham Downs* (1784), and *James Wallace* (1788), did not also include, if not *The Fair Syrian* (1787), two others, *Man as He is* (1792) and the still later *Hermsprong, or Man as He is Not* (1796). This last has sometimes been regarded as Bage's masterpiece: but it does not seem so to the present writer. It begins by the sketch of an illegitimate child, written in Bage's worst vein of hard rasping irony, entirely devoid of the delicate spring and " give " which irony requires, and which constitutes the triumph even of such things as *A Tale of a Tub* and *Jonathan Wild*. The rather impossibly named Hermsprong himself is not really so named at all, but is related (and in fact head-of-the-house) to the wicked or at least not good lord of the story. He is of the kind of Sir Charles Grandison, Rights-of-Mannified, which infests all these novels and is a great bore—as, indeed, to me is the whole book. The earlier *Man as He is* is far better. The hero, Sir George Paradyne, though of the same general class, is very much more tolerable and (being sometimes naughty) preferable to Grandison himself: while the heroine—a certain Miss Colerain, who is a merchant's daughter under a double cloud of her father's misfortune and of calumny as regards herself—though not an absolute success, is worth a dozen Harriets,

with thirteen Charlottes thrown in to make " 25 as 24 "
in bookseller's phrase. Bage's extravagant or perhaps
only too literal manners-painting (for it was an odd time)
appears not infrequently, as in the anecdote of a justly
enraged, though as a matter of fact mistaken, husband,
who finds a young gentleman sitting on his wife's lap, with
her arms round him, while he is literally and *en tout bien
tout honneur* painting her face — being a great artist in
that way. *Mount Henneth* is perhaps the liveliest of all:
though its liveliness is partly achieved by less merely
extravagant unconventionalities than this. But as a
matter of fact Bage never entirely " comes off ": though
there is cleverness enough in him to have made a dozen
popular and deservedly popular novelists at a better time
for the novel. For he was essentially a novelist of manners
and character at a transition time, when manners and
character had come out of one stage and had not settled
into another. Even Miss Edgeworth in *Belinda* shows
the disadvantage of this: and she was a lady of genius,
while Bage had only talent and was not quite a gentleman.

Thomas Holcroft was not a gentleman at all, never
pretended to the title, and would probably have been
rather affronted if any one had applied it to him: for he
was a violent Atheist and Jacobin, glorying in his extrac-
tion from a shoemaker and an oysterseller, and in his
education as a stable boy. He was, however, a man of
considerable intellectual power and of some literary gift,
which chiefly showed itself in his dramas (the best known,
The Road to Ruin), but is not quite absent from his novels
Alwyn (1780), *Anna St. Ives* (1792), and *Hugh Trevor*
(1794-1797). The series runs in curious parallel to that
of Bage's work: for *Alwyn*, the liveliest and the earliest
by far of the three, is little more than a study partly after

Fielding, but more after Smollett, with his own experiences brought in. The other two are purpose-novels of anarchist perfectibilism, and Holcroft enjoys the traditional credit of having directly inspired Godwin. Godwin himself acknowledged the obligation; indeed it is well known that — in pecuniary matters more particularly — Godwin had no hesitation either in incurring or in acknowledging obligations, always provided that he was not expected to discharge them. It is possible that Holcroft's rough and ready acceptance and exaggeration of the doctrines which Rousseau had (as seems most probable) developed from a paradox of Diderot's, gave an impetus to the rather sluggish but more systematic mind of Godwin. But it is certain that *Political Justice*, though it is not a novel at all, is a much more amusing book than *Anna St. Ives*, which is one. And though Holcroft (especially if the presence of this quality in his *Autobiography* is not wholly due to Hazlitt—there is some chance that it is) possessed a liveliness in narrative to which Godwin could never attain, there is no doubt that this enigmatical and many-sided spunger, philanderer, and corruptor of youth had a much higher general qualification for novel-writing than any one mentioned hitherto in this chapter, or perhaps than any to be mentioned, except the curiously contrasted pair, of Irish birth, who are to come last in it.

I have sometimes thought that the greatest testimony to Godwin's power in this respect is the idea (which even Hazlitt, though he did not share it, does not seem to have thought preposterous, and which seems to have been held by others who were not fools) that Godwin might be the author of *Waverley*. To us, looking back, the notion seems as absurd as that Bacon could be the author of Shakespeare or Steele of the *Tale of a Tub :* but if, instead of looking back, we throw ourselves back, the absurdity does not quite persist as it does in the other two instances. There are some who, of course, would say, "Why take this fanciful test of Godwin's ability when you have a real one in *Caleb Williams?*" The reasons are double: for, historically, such an estimate by contemporaries is of the very first value, and to the present writer *Caleb Williams* (1794) has never seemed a very interesting book. It is impossible to sympathise with a hero who is actuated by the very lowest of human motives, sheer inquisitiveness: and *my* sense of natural justice (which is different from Godwin's) demands not that he shall escape, but that he shall be broken on the wheel, or burnt at a slow fire, or made to read *Political Justice* after the novelty of its colossal want of humour has palled on him. One could sympathise with Falkland, but is not allowed to do so: because he is not human, except in his crime. But, as has been said, to those whose sporting interests are excited by the pleasures and hazards of the chase, these things no doubt do not occur. After all *Caleb* is, in a sense, the first "detective novel": and detective novels have always been popular, though they bore some people to extinction.

Far, however, be it from me to deny that this popularity, especially when, as in the present case, it has been continued for four whole generations, is a real and a very considerable asset. Even if it were now to cease, it is actually funded and vested to Godwin's credit in the *grand livre* of literary history: and it can never be written off. Perhaps *Caleb* is the one book of the later English eighteenth century in novel for which there must always be a public as soon as it is presented to that public. And when this is said and endorsed by those who do not personally much care for the book, it is at once a sufficient testimony to the position of the author, and a vindication of the not absolutely imbecile position of those who thought that he might have written *Waverley* and its successors. The way in which Godwin in his later novels came down from the mountain-tops of theory and paradox just as he came down from those of *Political Justice* itself is interesting and amusing, but not for us. As novels they are certainly inferior. The best parts of *St. Leon* (1799) and *Fleetwood* (1805) are perhaps better than anything in *Caleb : Mandeville* (1817) and *Deloraine* (1833) are *senilia*.[1] The graceful figure of the heroine Marguerite in *St. Leon* is said to be modelled on Mary Wollstonecraft, and there are some fresh pictures of youth and childhood in *Fleetwood*. But *St. Leon*, besides its historical shortcomings (which, once more, we may postpone), is full of faults, from the badly managed supernatural to an only too natural dullness and languor of general story: nor has *Fleetwood* anything like the absorbing power which *Caleb Williams* exercises, in its own way and on its own people. Yet again we may perhaps say that the chief interest of Godwin, from our point of view, is his repeated and further weighted testimony to the importance of the novel as an appeal to public attention. In this respect it was in fact displacing, not only the drama on one side, but the sermon on the other. Not so very long before these two had almost engrossed the domain of *popular* literature, the graver and more precise folk habitually reading sermons as well as hearing them, and the looser and lighter folk reading drama much oftener than (in then-existing circumstances) they had the opportunity of seeing it. With the novel the " address to the reader " became direct and stood by itself. The novelist could emulate Burke with his right

---

[1] Godwin had written novel-*juvenilia* of which few say anything.

barrel and Lydia Languish with his left. He certainly
did not always endeavour to profit as well as to delight:
but the double power was, from this time forward, shared
by him with his brother in the higher and older *Dichtung*.

Next to Godwin may be placed a lady who was much
adored by that curious professor of philandering, political
*in*justice, psychology, and the use of the spunge, but who
wisely put him off. Mrs. Inchbald's (1753-1821) command
of a certain kind of dramatic or at least theatrical situation,
and her propensity to Richardsonian " human-heart "-
mongering, have from time to time secured a certain
number of admirers for *A Simple Story* (1791) and *Nature
and Art* (1796). Some, availing themselves of the con-
fusion between " style " and " handling " which has
recently become fashionable, have even credited her with
style itself. Of this she has nothing — unless the most
conventional of eighteenth - century phraseology, dashed
with a kind of *marivaudage* which may perhaps seem
original to those who do not know Marivaux's French
followers, shall deserve the name. She is indeed very
much of an English Madame Riccoboni. But her situations—such as the meeting in *A Simple Story* of a father
with the daughter whom, though not exactly casting her
off, he has persistently refused to see, in revenge for her
mother's unfaithfulness, and the still more famous scene
in *Nature and Art* where a judge passes the death-sentence
on a woman whom he has betrayed—have, as has been
allowed, the dramatic or melodramatic quality which
attracts people in " decadent " periods. There seems,
indeed, to have been a certain decadent charm about Mrs.
Inchbald herself—with her beauty, her stage skill, her
strict virtue combined with any amount of " sensibility,"
her affectation of nature, and her benevolence not in the

least sham but distinctly posing. And something of this rococo relish may no doubt, with a little good will and sympathy, be detected in her books. But of the genuine life and the natural language which occasionally inspirit the much more unequal and more generally commonplace work of Miss Burney, she has practically nothing. And she thus falls out of the main line of development, merely exemplifying the revolutionary and sentimental episode.

We must now, for some pages, illustrate the course of the novel by minor examples: and we may begin with a brief notice of two writers, one of whom might have been taken before Miss Burney and the other just after her chronologically: but who, in the order of thought and method, will come better here. Both were natives of Scotland and both illustrate different ways of the novel. Henry Mackenzie, an Edinburgh advocate, in three books—the names of which at least are famous, while his friend Sir Walter has preserved the books themselves in the collection so often mentioned — produced, in his own youth and in rapid succession, *The Man of Feeling* (1771), *The Man of the World* (1773), and *Julia de Roubigné* (1777). John Moore, a Glasgow physician, wrote, when he was nearly sixty, the novel of *Zeluco* (1786) and followed it up with *Edward* ten years afterwards and *Mordaunt* (1800). Mackenzie did good work later in the periodical essay: but his fiction is chiefly the " sensibility "-novel of the French and of Sterne, reduced to the absolutely absurd. From his essay-work, and from Scott's and other accounts of him, he must have possessed humour of a kind: but the extremely limited character of its nature and operation may be exemplified by his representation of a whole press-gang as bursting into tears at the pathetic action and words of an old man who offers himself as substitute for his son.

This is one of the not rare, but certainly one of the most consummate, instances of fashion caricaturing itself in total unconsciousness. But it *was* the fashion: and Mackenzie, though perhaps he helped to bring it to an end, no doubt caused the shedding, by "the fair" of the time, of an ocean of tears as great as the ocean of port wine which was contemporaneously absorbed by "the brave."

Moore saw a good deal of continental society—he is indeed one of the first-hand witnesses for the events of the French Revolution—and he had a more considerable influence on the novel than has always been allowed him. *Zeluco* chiefly survives because of the exquisitely ludicrous and human trait of the English sailor who, discussing the French army, pronounces white uniforms "absurd" and blue "only fit for the artillery and the blue horse." But it is not quite certain that its villain-hero had not something, and perhaps a good deal, to do with those of Mrs. Radcliffe who were soon to follow, and, through these, with Byron who was not to be very long after. The later books are of much less importance, if only because they follow the outburst of fiction which the French Revolution itself ushered. But Moore, who was intimately connected with Smollett, carried on the practice of making national or sub-national characteristics important elements of novel interest: and is thus noteworthy in more ways than one.

He is a late instance—he was born in 1729 and so was only a few years younger than Smollett himself—of the writers who had, for all but half a century after Richardson's appearance, accumulated patterns and examples of the novel in all sorts of forms, hardly one of which lacked numerous and almost innumerable imitators and followers. By these later years of the century the famous "Minerva Press" and many others issued deluges of novel-work which were eagerly absorbed by readers. "Absorbed" in more senses than one: for the institution of circulating libraries, while it facilitated reading, naturally tended towards the destruction of the actual volumes read. Novels were rarely produced in a very careful or sumptuous fashion, and good copies of those that were in any way popular are now rather hard to obtain: while even in the British Museum it will frequently be found that only the later editions are represented. We shall finish this chapter with some instances, taken not quite at random, of the work of the last decades of the eighteenth and the beginning of the nineteenth century, winding up with more general notice of two remarkable writers who represent—though at least one of them lived far later—the period before Scott, and who also, as it happens, represent the contrast of novel and romance in a fashion unusually striking. The description, as some readers will have anticipated, refers to Miss Edgeworth and to Maturin. But the smaller fry must be taken first.

It is not uninteresting to compare two such books as Mrs. Bennett's *Anna* and Mrs. Opie's *Adeline Mowbray*. Published at twenty years' distance (1785 and 1804) they show the rapid growth of the novel, even during a time when nothing of the first class appeared. *Anna, or the Memoirs of a Welsh Heiress, interspersed with Anecdotes of a Nabob*, is a kind of bad imitation of Miss Burney, with a catchpenny " interspersion " to suit the day. *Adeline Mowbray*, written with more talent, chimes in by infusing one of the tones of *its* day—Godwinian theories of life. The space between was the palmy time of that now almost legendary " Minerva Press " which, as has been said, flooded the ever-absorbent market with stuff of which *The Libertine*, masterpiece of Mrs. Byrne, *alias* Charlotte Dacre, *alias* " Rosa Matilda," is perhaps best worth singling out from its companions, *Hours of Solitude, The Nun of St. Omers, Zofloya*, etc., because it specially shocked the censor of the style who will be mentioned presently. It is pure (or not-pure) rubbish. Angelo (the libertine) seduces the angelic Gabrielle de Montmorency, who follows him to Italy in male attire, saves him from the wicked courtesan Oriana and her bravo Fioren*za* (*sic*), is married by him, but made miserable, and dies. He continues his misbehaviour to their children, and finally blows his brains out. " Bah! it is bosh! " as the Master observes of something else.

It may seem iniquitous to say that some tolerably good novel-writers must be more summarily treated than some bad ones here: but there is reason for it. Such, for instance, as Charlotte Smith and the Miss Lees are miles above such others as the just-mentioned polyonymous " Rosa," as Sarah Wilkinson, or as Henrietta Mosse-Rouvière. The first three would make a very good group for a twenty-page causerie. Charlotte Smith, who was tolerably expert in verse as well as prose; who anticipated, and perhaps taught, Scott in the double use of the name " Waverley "; and whose *Old Manor House* (1793) is a solid but not heavy work of its kind—is something of a person in herself, but less of a figure in history, because she neither innovates nor does old things consummately. Harriet and Sophia Lee claimed innovation for the latter's *Recess* (1783-1786), as Miss Porter did for *Thaddeus of Warsaw*, but the claim can be even less allowed. There is nothing of real historical spirit, and very little goodness of any kind, in *The Recess*. *The Canterbury Tales* (1797-1805) (so named merely because they are supposed to be told by different persons) were praised by Byron, as he praised the

Percy Anecdotes and other things—either irresponsibly or impishly. They are not exactly bad: but also as far as possible from consummateness.

On the other hand, *The Convent of Grey Penitents*, one of the crops which rewarded Miss Wilkinson for tilling the lands of her imagination with the spade of her style, *is* very nearly consummate—in badness. It is a fair example of the worst imitations of Mrs. Radcliffe and Mat Lewis conjointly, though without the latter's looseness. The Marquis di Zoretti was an Italian nobleman—" one of those characters in whose bosom resides an unquenchable thirst of avarice " [" *thirst* of *avarice* " is good!], etc. He marries, however, a lovely signora of the odd name of Rosalthe, without a fortune, " which circumstance was overlooked by his lordship " for a very short time only. He plots to be free of her: she goes to England and dies there to the genteelest of slow music. Their son Horatio falls in love with a certain Julietta, who is immured by wicked arts in the " Convent of Grey Penitents," tormented by the head, Gradisca, but rescued, and so forth. The book, if harmless, is about as worthless as a book can be: but it represents, very fairly, the ruck, if not indeed even the main body, of the enormous horde of romances which issued from the press towards the end of the eighteenth century and the beginning of the nineteenth, and which, in their different action on persons of genius, gave us *Zastrozzi* on the one side and *Northanger Abbey* on the other.

As for Miss Henrietta Mosse, otherwise Rouvière, she represents the other school of abortive historical novel. *A Peep at Our Ancestors* (1807) is fairly worthy of its ridiculous name. It is preceded by expressions of thanks to the authorities of " the British Museum and the Heralds'

Office " for the " access to records " vouchsafed to its author. As the date of the story is 1146 (it was long before Mr. Freeman wrote) access to records would certainly not have been superfluous. The actual results of it are blocks of spiritless and commonplace historic narrative— it is nearly all narrative, not action—diversified by utterances like this of Malcolm III. of Scotland, " O my Edward! the deed which struck my son's life has centred [*sic*] thy noble youthful bosom also," or this of the heroine (such as there is), " the gentle *elegant* Adelaise," " And do I not already receive my education of thee, mamma ? " It is really a pity that the creator of this remarkable peep-show did not give references to her " records," so that one might look up this " elegant " young creature of the twelfth century who talked about " education " and said " mamma! " But this absolute failure in verisimilitude is practically universal before Scott.

The works of the very beautifully named Regina Maria Roche should probably be read, as they were for generations, in late childhood or early youth. Even then an intelligent boy or girl would perceive some of the absurdity, but might catch a charm that escapes the less receptive oldster. They were, beyond all question, immensely popular, and continued to be so for a long time: in fact it is almost sufficient evidence that there is, if I mistake not, in the British Museum no edition earlier than the tenth of the most famous of them, *The Children of the Abbey* (1798). This far-renowned work opens with the exclamation of the heroine Amanda, " Hail, sweet sojourn of my infancy! " and we are shortly afterwards informed that in the garden " the part appropriated to vegetables was divided from the part sacred to Flora." Otherwise, the substance of the thing is a curious sort of watered-down

Richardson, passed through successive filtering beds of Mackenzie, and even of Mrs. Radcliffe. It is difficult for even the most critical taste to find much savour or stimulus in the resulting liquid. But, like almost everybody mentioned here, Regina is a document of the demands of readers and the faculty of writers: and so she " standeth," if not exactly " crowned," yet ticketed.

Work—somewhat later—of some interest, but not of first-class quality, is to be found in the *Discipline* (1811) and *Self-Control* (1814) of Mary Brunton. A Balfour of Orkney on the father's side and a Ligonier on the mother's, the authoress had access to the best English as well as Scottish society, and seems to have had more than a chance of taking a place in the former: but preferred to marry a minister-professor and settled down to country manse life. She died in middle age and her husband wrote a memoir of her. *Discipline* seems to represent a sort of fancy combination of the life she might have led and the life she did lead. Ellen Percy, the heroine, starts in the highest circles; forgets herself so far as to " waltz*e* " with a noble ne'er-do-weel, thereby earning the " stern disapprobation " of a respectable lover; comes down in the world; has Highland experiences which, at the book's early date, are noteworthy; marries (like her creatress) a minister; but " retains a little of her coquettish sauciness." " Bless her, poor little dear! " one can imagine Thackeray exclaiming in his later and mellowed days. Mrs. Brunton's letters breathe a lady-like and not unamiable propriety, and she is altogether a sort of milder, though actually earlier, Miss Ferrier.

Ireland vindicated its claim to comparative liveliness in the work of a better known contemporary and survivor. Lady Morgan's (Miss Sydney Owenson's) *Wild Irish Girl*

M

(1806) is one of the books whose titles have prolonged for them a kind of shadowy existence. It is written in letters: and the most interesting thing about it for some readers now is that the heroine supplied Thackeray with the name Glorvina, which, it seems, means in Irish " sweet voice," if Lady Morgan is to be trusted *in rebus Celticis*. It is to be hoped she is: for the novel is a sort of *macédoine* of Irish history, folk-lore, scenery, and what not, done up in a syrup of love-making *quant. suff*. Its author wrote many more novels and became a butt for both good- and ill-natured satire with the comic writers of the twenties, thirties, and forties. The title was actually borrowed by Maturin in *The Wild Irish* " Boy," and it is fair to say that the book preceded Scott's, though not Miss Edgeworth's, experiments in the line of the " national " novel. The earlier Reviewers were discreditably savage on womenwriters, and Lady Morgan had her share of their truculence. She did not wholly deserve it: but it must be said that nothing she wrote can really be ranked as literature, save on the most indiscriminate and uncritical estimate. It is, however, difficult to see much harm in her.

Ida of Athens, for instance, which shocked contemporaries, and which, by the way, has the very large first title of *Woman*, could only bring a blush to cheeks very tickle of that sere: a yawn might come much more easily. The most shocking thing that the heroine, who is " an attempt to delineate woman in her natural state," does (and that not of malice) is to receive her lover in a natural bathroom. But her adventures are told in a style which is the oddest compound of Romantesque and Johnsonese. ("The hour was ardent. The bath was cool. *He calculated upon the probable necessity of its enjoyment*.") The spirit is the silliest and most ignorant Philhellenism—all the beauty, virtue, wisdom, of the ancient Greeks being supposed to be inherited by their mongrel successors of the early nineteenth century. An English and a Turkish lover dispute Ida's affection or possession. There are the elaborate pseudo-erudite notes which one has learnt to associate chiefly with Moore. The authoress boasts in her preface that she " has already written almost as many volumes as she has years," and that she has hardly ever corrected her proofs. Perhaps this silliness will make some think her not more an example of the savagery of contemporary criticism than a justification thereof.

It was in fact not only brutal man who objected to the preposterous excesses of pseudo-romance: and serious or jocular parables were taken up against it, if not before *Northanger Abbey* was written, long before it was published. In 1810 a certain " G." or " S. G.," whose full name was Sarah Green, wrote, besides some actual history and an attempt at the historical novel, a very curious and rather hybrid book entitled *Romance Readers and Romance Writers*. Its preface is an instance of " Women, beware Women," for though it stigmatises male creatures, such as a certain Curteis and a certain Pickersgill, it treats Lady Morgan (then only Sydney Owenson) and " Rosa Matilda " even more roughly and asks (as has been asked about a hundred years later and was asked about a hundred years before), " Is it not amazing that the [two] most licentious writers of romance are women ? " And it starts with a burlesque account of a certain Margaret Marsham who exclaims, " What then ? to add to my earthly miseries am I to be called Peggy? My name is Margaritta! " " I am sure that if I am called Peggy again I shall go into a fit." But this promise of something to complete the trio with *Northanger Abbey* and *The Heroine* (to be presently mentioned) is not maintained. Not only does the writer force the note of parody too much by making "Margaritta" say to herself, "Poor persecuted *dove* that I am," and adore a labourer's shirt on a hedge, but she commits the far more fatal fault of exchanging her jest for earnest. Margaritta— following her romance-models—falls a victim to an un-principled great lady and the usual wicked baronet—at whose head, one is bound to say, she flings herself with such violence as no baronet could possibly resist. Her sister Mary, innocent of romance-reading and all other faults, is, though not as guilty, as unlucky almost as Margaret: and by far the greater part of the book is an unreal present-ment, in nearly the worst manner of the eighteenth century itself, of virtuous curates, *un*virtuous "tonish" rectors, who calmly propose to seduce their curates' daughters (an offence which, for obvious reasons, must, in the worst times, have been unusual), libertine ladies, and reckless "fashionables" of all kinds. The preface and the opening create expectations, not merely of amusement but of power, which are by no means fulfilled. It is "S. G." who asserts that *Ida of Athens* "has brought a blush to the cheek of many," and one can only repeat the suggested substitution.

The only faults that can be found with *The Heroine* or *The Adventures of Cherubina*, by Eaton Stannard Barrett, which appeared in the same year, with no very different object and subject, though written in lighter vein, are one that it could not help and another that it could. Unjustly, but unavoidably, the first is the worst. That it is a burlesque rather overdone—a burlesque *burlesqué*—not in the manner of Thackeray, but in that of some older and some more recent writers—is unfortunate, but not fatal. One can forgive—one can even enjoy—the ghost who not only sneezes but says, " D—n, all is blown!" When the heroine is actually locked up with a man in a chest one is more doubtful: recovering when the Marquis de Furioso, " bowing gracefully to the bride," stabs himself to the heart, which is almost " the real Mackay " as they say in the North. The slight awkwardness of snow falling the day after the characters have been eating strawberries does not amuse us much, because this is a comparatively ordinary event of the early twentieth century, whatever it might be of the early nineteenth. But what is fatal, though the author could not help it, is that the infinitely lighter, more artistic, and more lethal dart of *Northanger Abbey* had been launched by the pen, if not the press, more than a dozen years before.

There are few more curious and interesting personages in the history of the English Novel than Maria Edgeworth. The variety of her accomplishment in the kind was extraordinary: and in more than one of its species she went very near perfection. One is never quite certain whether the perpetual meddling of her rather celebrated father Richard—one of the capital examples of the unpractical pragmatists and clever-silly crotcheteers who produced and were produced by the Revolutionary period—did her more harm than good. It certainly loaded her work with superfluous and (to us) disgusting didacticism: but it might be contended that, without its stimulus, she would have done much less, perhaps nothing. As it was, she lived for more than eighty years (till all but the middle of the nineteenth century) and wrote for more than sixty. Her work is thus very bulky: but it may be considered, for our present purpose, in three groups—her short stories written mainly but not wholly for children; her regular novels; and her Irish studies. Of these the middle division has been, and no doubt has deserved to be, the least popular: but its principal example, *Belinda* (1801) (*Patronage*, a longer and later book, and others are inferior), is considerably better than is usually admitted and, by its early date, deserves special notice here. It preceded Miss Austen's work in publication, and is specially cited by her as a capital example of novel in connection with the work of Miss Burney: and it is evidently founded on study of the latter, of which, indeed, it is the first really worthy continuation. Maria has nothing so good as Fanny's Smiths and Branghtons: but the whole book is far superior to *Evelina*. The extravagance of the *fin-de-siècle* society which it represents has probably disguised from not a few readers who do not know the facts, the other fact that it is a real attempt at realist observation of manners: and it has the narrative merit which was Miss Edgeworth's gift of nature. But the hero is patchy and improbable: the heroine, a good and quite possible girl, is not sufficiently " reliefed out "; and the most important figures of the book, Lord and Lady Delacour, almost great successes, are not helped by the peculiar academic-didactic moralising which she had caught from Marmontel.

The following of that ingenious and now too much undervalued writer stood her in better stead in the *Moral Tales* (1801) (which she deliberately called after his [1]), the

---

[1] The peculiar pedantic ignorance which critics sometimes show has objected to this rendering of Marmontel's *Contes Moraux*, urging that it should read " tales *of manners*." It might be enough to remark that the Edgeworths, father and daughter, were probably a good deal better acquainted both with French and English than these cavillers. But there is a rebutting argument which is less *ad hominem*. " Tales of Manners " leaves out at least as much on one side as " Moral Tales " does on the other: and the actual meaning is quite clear to those who know that of the Latin *mores* and the French *mœurs*. It is scarcely worth while to attempt to help those who do not know by means of paraphrases.

Popular Tales of the same kind, and (though Marmontel did not intentionally write for children) the delightful *Parent's Assistant* (1801) and *Frank*. In the two first-named divisions, the narrative faculty just mentioned appears admirably, together with another and still greater gift, that of character-painting, and even a grasp of literary and social satire, which might not be anticipated from some of her other books. The French governess (*Mlle. Panache*) and the satire on romantic young-ladyism (*Angelina*) are excellent examples of this. As for the pure child's stories, generation after generation of competent criticism, childish and adult, has voted them by acclamation into almost the highest place possible: and the gain-sayers have for the most part been idle paradoxers, ill-conditioned snarlers at things clean and sweet, or fools pure and simple.

The " Irish brigade " of the work—*Castle Rackrent* (1800), *Ormond*, and *The Absentee*, with the non-narrative but closely-connected *Essay on Irish Bulls*—have perhaps commanded the most unchequered applause. They are not quite free from the sentimentality and the didacticism which were both rampant in the novel of Miss Edgeworth's earlier time: but these are atoned for by a quite new use of the " national " element. Even Smollett and, following Smollett, Moore had chiefly availed themselves of this for its farcical or semi-farcical opportunities. Miss Edgeworth did not neglect these, but she did not confine herself to them: and such characters as Corny the " King of the Black Isles " in *Ormond* actually add a new province and a new pleasure to fiction.

Her importance is thus very great: and it only wanted the proverbial or anecdotic " That! " to make it much greater. " That! " as it generally is, was in her case the

last fusing touch of genius to accomplish the *grand œuvre*—
the perfect projection. She had humour, pathos, knowledge of the world, power of drawing it, acquaintance with
literature, shrewd common sense, an excellent style when
she was allowed to write in her own way, the feelings of
a lady who was also a good woman. King Charles is made
to say in *Woodstock* that "half the things in the world
remind him of the Tales of Mother Goose." It is astonishing, in the real complimentary sense, how many things
remind one of situations, passages, phrases, in Miss Edgeworth's works of all the kinds from *Castle Rackrent* to
Frank. She also had a great and an acknowledged
influence on Scott, a considerable and a certainly not
disavowed influence on Miss Austen. She is good reading
always, however much we may sometimes pish and pshaw
at the untimely poppings-in of the platitudes and crotchets
(for he was that most abominable of things, a platitudinous
crotcheteer) of Richard her father. She was a girl of
fourteen when the beginnings of the domestic novel were
laid in *Evelina*, and she lived to see it triumph in *Vanity
Fair*. But her own work, save in some of her short stories,
which are pretty perfect, represents the imperfect stage
of the development—the stage when the novel is trying
for the right methods and struggling to get into the right
ways, but has not wholly mastered the one or reached
the others.

There are those who would assign what they might call
"higher genius," or "rarer gift," or something similar, to
her countryman Charles Robert Maturin. The present
writer is not very fond of these measurings together of
things incommensurable — these attempts to rank the
"light white sea-mew" as superior or inferior to the
"sleek black pantheress." It is enough to say that while

Miss Edgeworth very deliberately adopted the novel, and even, as we have seen, slightly satirised at least pseudo-romance, Maturin was romantic or nothing. His life was hardly half hers in length, and his temperament appears to have been as discontented as hers was sunny: but he had his successes in drama as well as in novel, and one of his attempts in the latter kind had a wide-ranging influence abroad as well as at home, has been recently printed both in whole and in part, and undoubtedly ranks among the novels which any tolerably well instructed person would enumerate if he were asked to give a pretty full list of celebrated (and deservedly celebrated) books of the kind in English. The others fall quite out of comparison. *The Fatal Revenge* or the *Family of Montorio* (1807) is a try for the " furthest " in the Radcliffe-Lewis direction, discarding indeed the crudity of *The Monk*, but altogether neglecting the restraint of *Udolpho* and its companions in the use of the supernatural. *The Wild Irish Boy* (1808), *The Milesian Chief* (1812), *Women* (1818), and *The Albigenses* (1824) are negligible, the last, perhaps, rather less so than the others. But *Melmoth the Wanderer* (1820) is in quite a different case. It has faults in plenty—especially a narrative method of such involution that, as it has been said, " a considerable part of the book consists of a story told to a certain person, who is a character in a longer story, found in a manuscript which is delivered to a third person, who narrates the greater part of the novel to a fourth person, who is the namesake and descendant of the title-hero." Stripped of these tiresome lendings (which, as has been frequently pointed out, were a mania with the eighteenth century and naturally grew to such intricacy as this), the central story, though not exactly new, is impressive: and it is told and worked out in manner more impressive, because practically novel, save for, perhaps, a little suggestion from *Vathek*. Melmoth has bartered his soul with the devil for something like immortality and other privileges, including the unusual one of escaping doom if he can get some one to take the bargain off his hands. This leads up to numerous episodes or chapters in which Melmoth endeavours to obtain substitutes: and in one of these the love interest of the book—the, of course, fatal love of Melmoth himself for a Spanish-Indian girl Immalee or Isidora—is related with some real pathos and passion, though with a good deal of mere sentiment and twaddle. Maturin is stronger in his terror-scenes, and affected his own generation very powerfully: his influence being so great in France that Balzac attempted a variation and continuation, and that there are constant references to the book in the early French Romantics. In fact for this kind of " sensation " Maturin is, putting *Vathek* aside, quite the chief of the whole school. But it is doubtful whether he had many other gifts as a novelist, and this particular one is one that cannot be exercised very frequently, and is very difficult to exercise at all without errors and extravagances.

The child-literature of this school and period was very large, and, had we space, would be worth dealing with at length—as in the instances of the famous *Sandford and Merton* (1783-1789) by Thomas Day, Richard Edgeworth's friend, of Mrs. Trimmer's *Story of the Robins*, and others. It led up to the definitely religious school of children's books, first evangelical, then tractarian, with which we shall deal later: but was itself as a rule utilitarian—or sentimental—moral rather than directly religious. It is, however, like other things—indeed almost all things—in this chapter—a document of the fashion in which the novel was " filling all numbers " and being used for all purposes. It was, of course, in this case, nearest to the world-old " fable "—especially to the moral apologues of which the mediæval sermon-writers and others had been so fond. But its popularity, especially when taken in connection with the still surviving distrust of fiction, is valuable. It involves not merely the principle that " the devil shall not have all the best tunes," but the admission that this tune is good.

This point, and that other also frequently mentioned and closely connected with it, that the novel at this time overflows into almost every conceivable department of subject and object, are the main facts of a general historical kind, which should be in the reader's mind as the upshot of this chapter. But there is a third, almost as important as either, and that is the almost universal coming short of complete success—the lack of consummateness, the sense that if the Novel Israel is not exactly still in the wilderness, it has not yet crossed the Jordan. Even if we take in the last chapter, and its comparative giants, with the present and its heroes, ordinary folk, and pygmies, we shall scarcely find more than one great master, Fielding, and one little masterpiece, *Vathek*, deserving the adjective " consummate." No doubt the obvious explanation — that the hour was not because the man had not come except in this single case—is a good one: but it need not be left in the bare isolation of its fatalism. There are at least several subsidiary considerations which it is well to advance. The transition state of manners and language cannot be too often insisted upon: for this affected the process at both ends, giving the artist in fictitious life an uncertain model to copy and unstable materials to work in. The deficiency of classical patterns—at a time which still firmly believed, for the most part, that all good work in literature had been

so done by the ancients that it could at best be emulated—
should count for something: the scanty respect in which
the kind was held for something more. As to one of the
most important species, frequent allusions have been made,
and in the next chapter full treatment will be given, to the
causes which made the *historical* novel impossible until
very late in the century, and decidedly unlikely to be good
even then. Perhaps, without attempting further detail,
we may conclude by saying that the productions of this
time present, and present inevitably, the nonage and
novitiate of a branch of art which hardly possessed any
genuine representatives when the century was born and
which numbered them, bad and good, by thousands and
almost tens of thousands at its death. In the interval
there had been continuous and progressive exercise; there
had been some great triumphs; there had been not a little
good and pleasant work; and of even the work that was
less good and less pleasant one may say that it at least
represented experiment, and might save others from
failure.

CHAPTER V

In 1816 Sir Thomas Bernard, baronet, barrister, and philanthropist, published, having it is said written it three years previously, an agreeable dialogue on *Old Age*, which was very popular, and reached its fifth edition in 1820. The interlocutors are Bishops Hough and Gibson and Mr. Lyttleton, the supposed time 1740—the year, by accident or design, of *Pamela*. In this the aged and revered "martyr of Magdalen" is mildly reproached by his brother prelate for liking novels. Hough puts off the reproach as mildly, and in a most academic manner, by saying that he only admits them *speciali gratiâ*. This was in fact the general attitude to the whole kind, not merely in 1740, but after all the work of nearly another life-time as long as Hough's—almost in 1816 itself. Yet when Sir Thomas published his little book, notice to quit, of a double kind, had been served on this fallacy. Miss Austen's life was nearly done, and some of her best work had not been published: but the greater part had. Scott was in his actual hey-day. Between them, they had dealt and were dealing—from curiously different sides and in as curiously different manners—the death-blow to the notion that the novel was an inferior if not actually discreditable kind, suitable for weak intellects only, and likely to weaken strong ones, frivolous when not positively immoral, giving a distaste for serious reading, implying in the writer an inability to do anything more serious, and generally presenting a glaring contrast to real " literature."

Interesting as each of these two great novelists is individually, the interest of the pair, from our present historical point of view, is almost greater; and the way in which they complete each other is hardly short of uncanny. Before their time, despite the great examples of prose fiction produced by Bunyan, Defoe, Richardson, Fielding, Smollett, and Sterne, and the remarkable determination towards the life of ordinary society given, or instanced, by Miss Burney; despite the immense novel-production of the last half of the eighteenth century and the first decade of the nineteenth—it is hardly too much to say that " the novel," as such, had not found its proper way or ways at all. Bunyan's was an example of genius in a peculiar kind of the novel: as, in a very different one, was Sterne's. Defoe, possessing some of the rarest gifts of the novelist, was quite lacking in others. Richardson was not only *exemplar vitiis imitabile* and *imitatum*, but it might be doubted whether, even when not faulty, he was not more admirable than delightful. Smollett, like Defoe, was not much more than part of a novelist: and Miss Burney lacked strength, equality, and range. There remained Fielding: and it certainly is not here that any restrictions or allowances will be insinuated as to Fielding's praise. But Fielding's novels are a circle in which no one else save Thackeray has ever been able to walk. And what we are looking for now is something rather different from this—a masterpiece, or masterpieces, which may not only yield delight and excite admiration in itself or themselves, but may bring forth fruit in others—fruit less masterly perhaps, but of the same or a similar kind. In other words, nobody's work yet—save in the special kinds—

had been capable of yielding a novel-*formula :* nobody
had hit upon the most capital and fruitful novel-ideas.
And nearly everybody had, in the kind, done work curiously
and almost incomprehensibly faulty. Of these faults, the
worst, perhaps, were classable under the general head of
inverisimilitude. Want of truth to nature in character
and dialogue, extravagant and clumsy plotting, neglect of
(indeed entire blindness to) historic colour, unreal and
unobserved description—all these things might be raised
to a height or sunk to a bathos in the work of the Minerva
Press—but there was far too much of them in *all* the novel
work of these sixty or seventy years.

Although the facts and dates are well enough known,
it is perhaps not always remembered that Miss Austen,
while representing what may, using a rather objectionable
and ambiguous word, be called a more " modern " style
of novel than Scott's, began long before him and had
almost finished her work before his really began. If that
wonderful Bath bookseller had not kept *Northanger Abbey*
in a drawer, instead of publishing it, it would have had
nearly twenty years start of *Waverley*. And it must be
remembered that *Northanger Abbey*, though it is, perhaps,
chiefly thought of as a parody-satire on the school of Mrs.
Radcliffe, is, as these parody-satires have a habit of being,
a great deal more. If Catherine had not made a fool of
herself about the *Orphan of the Black Forest* and *Horrid
Mysteries* (or rather if everything relating to this were
" blacked out " as by a Russian censor) there would still
remain the admirable framework of her presentation at
Bath and her intercourse with the Tilneys; the more
admirable character-sketches of herself—the triumph of
the ordinary made not ordinary—and the Thorpes; the
most admirable flashes of satire and knowledge of human

nature, not "promiscuous" or thrown out *apropos* of things in general, but acting as assistants and invigorators to the story.

In the few words just used lies, as far as it can be comprehended in any few words, the secret both of Miss Austen and of Scott. It has been said—more than once or twice, I fear—that hardly until Bunyan and Defoe do we get an interesting story—something that grasps us and carries us away with it—at all. Except in the great eighteenth-century Four the experience is not repeated, save in parts of Miss Burney and Miss Edgeworth later—it is simulated rather than actually brought about by the Terror-novel—except in the eternal exception of *Vathek*—for Maturin did not do his best work till much later. The absence of it is mainly due to a concatenation of inabilities on the part of the writers. They don't know what they ought to do: and in a certain sense it may even be said that they don't know what they are doing. In the worst examples surveyed in the last chapter, such as *A Peep at Our Ancestors*, this ignorance plumbs the abyss—blocks of dull serious narrative, almost or quite without action, and occasional insertions of flat, insipid, and (to any one with a little knowledge) impossible conversation, forming their staple. Of the better class of books, from the *Female Quixote* to *Discipline*, this cannot fairly be said: but there is always something wanting. Frequently, as in both the books just mentioned, the writer is too serious and too desirous to instruct. Hardly ever is there a real *projection* of character, in the round and living—only pale, sketchy "academies" that neither live, nor move, nor have any but a fitful and partial being. The conversation is, perhaps, the worst feature of all—for it follows the contemporary stage in adopting a conventional lingo which, as we know from private letters as early as Gray's and Walpole's, if not even as Chesterfield's and those of men and women older still, was *not* the language of well-bred, well-educated, and intelligent persons at any time during the century. As for the Fourth Estate of the novel—description—it had rarely been attempted even by the great masters. In fact it has been pointed out as perhaps the one unquestionable merit of Mrs. Radcliffe that—following the taste for the picturesque which, starting from Gray and popularised by Gilpin, was spreading over the country—she did attempt to introduce this important feature, and did partly, in a rococo way, succeed in introducing it. As for plot, that has never been our strong point—we seem to have been contented with *Tom Jones* as payment in full of that demand.[1]

Now, this was all changed. It is doubtful whether if *Northanger Abbey* had actually appeared in 1796 it would have been appreciated—Miss Austen, like other writers of genius, had, not exactly as the common but incorrect phrase goes, to create the taste for her own work, but to arouse the long dormant appetite which she was born to satisfy. Yet, looking back a hundred years, it seems impossible that anybody of wits should have failed at once to discover the range, the perfection, and the variety of the new gift, or set of gifts. Here all the elements come in: and something with them that enlivens and intensifies them all. The plot is not intricate, but there is a plot— a good deal more, perhaps, than is generally noticed, and more than Miss Austen herself sometimes gave, as, for instance, in *Mansfield Park*. It is even rather artfully

---

[1] The frankness of the ingenious creator of Mr. Jorrocks should be imitated by 99 per cent. of English novelists. " The following story," says he of *Ask Mamma*, " does not involve the complication of a plot. It is a mere continuous narrative."

N

worked out—the selfish gabble of John Thorpe, who may look to superficial observers like a mere outsider, playing an important part *twice* in the evolution. There is not lavish but amply sufficient description and scenery—the Bath vignettes, especially the Beechencliff prospect; the sketch of the Abbey itself and of Henry's parsonage, etc. But it is in the other two constituents that the blowing of the new wind of the spirit is most perceptible. The character-drawing is simply wonderful, especially in the women—though the men lack nothing. John Thorpe has been glanced at—there had been nothing like him before, save in Fielding and in the very best of the essayists and dramatists. General Tilney has been found fault with as unnatural and excessive: but only by people who do not know what " harbitrary gents " fathers of families, who were not only squires and members of parliament, but military men, could be in the eighteenth century—and perhaps a little later. His son Henry, in common with most of his author's *jeunes premiers*, has been similarly objected to as colourless. He really has a great deal of subdued individuality, and it *had* to be subdued, because it would not have done to let him be too superior to Catherine. James Morland and Frederick Tilney are not to be counted as more than " walking gentlemen," Mr. Allen only as a little more: and they fulfil their law. But Isabella Thorpe is almost better than her brother, as being nearer to pure comedy and further from farce; Eleanor Tilney is adequate; and Mrs. Allen is sublime on her scale. A novelist who, at the end of the eighteenth century, could do Mrs. Allen, could do anything that she chose to do; and might be trusted never to attempt anything that she could not achieve. And yet the heroine is perhaps—as she ought to be—the greatest triumph of the whole, and the most indicative of

the new method. The older heroines had generally tried
to be extraordinary: and had failed. Catherine tries to
be ordinary: and is an extraordinary success. She is
pretty, but not beautiful: sensible and well-natured, but
capable, like most of us, of making a complete fool of
herself and of doing complete injustice to other people;
fairly well educated, but not in the least learned or accomplished. In real life she would be simply a unit in the
thousands of quite nice but ordinary girls whom Providence
providentially provides in order that mankind shall not
be alone. In literature she is more precious than rubies
—exactly because art has so masterfully followed and
duplicated nature.

Precisely to what extent the attractive quality of this
art is enhanced by the pervading irony of the treatment
would be a very difficult problem to work out. It is
scarcely hazardous to say that irony is the very salt of the
novel: and that just as you put salt even in a cake, so
it is not wise to neglect it wholly even in a romance. Life
itself, as soon as it gets beyond mere vegetation, is notori-
ously full of irony: and no imitation of it which dispenses
with the seasoning can be worth much. That Miss Austen's
irony is consummate can hardly be said to be matter of
serious contest.

It has sometimes been thought—perhaps mistakenly—
that the exhibition of it in *Northanger Abbey* is, though a
very creditable essay, *not* consummate. But *Pride and
Prejudice* is known to be, in part, little if at all later than
Northanger Abbey : and there can again be very little
dispute among judges in any way competent as to the
quality of the irony there. Nor does it much matter
what part of this wonderful book was written later and
what earlier: for its ironical character is all-pervading,

in almost every character, except Jane and her lover who are mere foils to Elizabeth and Darcy, and even in these to some extent; and in the whole story, even in the at least permitted suggestion that the sight of Pemberley, and Darcy's altered demeanour, had something to do with Elizabeth's resignation of the old romantic part of *Belle dame sans merci*. It may further be admitted, even by those who protest against the undervaluation of *Northanger Abbey*, that *Pride and Prejudice* flies higher, and maintains its flight triumphantly. It is not only longer; it is not only quite independent of parody or contrast with something previous; but it is far more intricate and elaborate as well as more original. Elizabeth herself is not merely an ordinary girl: and the putting forward of her, as an extraordinary yet in no single point unnatural one, is victoriously carried out. Her father, in spite of (nay, perhaps, including) his comparative collapse when he is called upon, not as before to talk but to act, in the business of Lydia's flight, is a masterpiece. Mr. Collins is, once more by common consent of the competent, unsurpassed, if not peerless: those who think him unnatural simply do not know nature. Shakespeare and Fielding were the only predecessors who could properly serve as sponsors to " this young lady " (as Scott delightfully calls her) on her introduction among the immortals on the strength of this character alone. Lady Catherine is not much the inferior (it would have been pleasing to tell her so) of her *protégé* and chaplain. Of almost all the characters, and of quite the whole book, it is scarcely extravagant to say that it could not have been better on its own scale and scheme— that it is difficult to conceive any scheme and scale on which it could have been better. And, yet once more, there is nothing out of the way in it—the only thing not of absolutely everyday occurrence, the elopement of Lydia, happens on so many days still, with slight variations, that it can hardly be called a licence.

The same qualities appear throughout the other books, whether in more or less quintessence and with less or more alloy is a question rather of individual taste than for general or final critical decision. *Sense and Sensibility*, the first actually to appear (1811), is believed to have been written about the same time as *Pride and Prejudice*, which appeared two years later, and *Northanger Abbey*, which did not see the light till its author was dead. It is the weakest of the three—perhaps it is the weakest of all: but the weakness is due rather to an error of judgment than to a lack of power. Like *Northanger Abbey* it has a certain dependence on something else: the extravagances of Marianne satirise the Sensibility-novel just as those of Catherine do the Terror-story of the immediate past. But it is on a much larger scale: and things of the kind are better in miniature. Moreover, the author's sense of creative faculty made her try to throw up and contrast her heroine with other characters, in a way which she had not attempted in *Northanger Abbey :* and good as these are in themselves, they make a less perfect whole. Indeed, in the order of thought, *Sense and Sensibility* is the " youngest " of the novels — the least self - criticised. Nothing in it shows lack of power (John Dashwood and his wife are of the first order); a good deal in it shows lack of knowledge exactly how to direct that power.

Mansfield Park (1814), though hardly as brilliant as *Pride and Prejudice,* shows much more maturity than *Sense and Sensibility*. Much of it is quite consummate, the character of Mrs. Norris especially: and for subtly

interwoven phrase without emphasis, conveying knowledge and criticism of life, it has few equals. But it has
an elopement. *Emma*, which has perhaps on the whole
been the most general favourite, may challenge that
position on one ground beyond all question, though possibly
not on all. It is the absolute triumph of that reliance
on the strictly ordinary which has been indicated as Miss
Austen's title to pre-eminence in the history of the novel.
Not an event, not a circumstance, not a detail, is carried
out of "the daily round, the common task" of average
English middle-class humanity, upper and lower. Yet
every event, every circumstance, every detail, is put *sub
specie eternitatis* by the sorcery of art. Few things could
be more terrible—nothing more tiresome—than to hear
the garrulous Miss Bates talk in actual life; few things are
more delightful than to read her speeches as they occur
here. An aspiring soul might feel disposed to "take and
drown itself in a pail" (as one of Dickens's characters says)
if it had to live the life which the inhabitants of Highbury
are represented as living; to read about that life—to read
about it over and over again—has been and is always likely
to be one of the chosen delights of some of the best wits of
our race. This is one of the paradoxes of art: and perhaps
it is the most wonderful of them, exceeding even the old
"pity and terror" problem. And the discovery of it, as
a possible source of artistic success, is one of the greatest
triumphs and one of the most inexhaustible discoveries of
that art itself. For by another paradox—this time not of
art but of nature—the extraordinary is exhaustible and
the ordinary is not. Tragedy and the more "incidented"
comedy, it is well known, run into types and reproduce
situations almost inevitably. "All the stories are told."
But the story of the life of Highbury never can be told,

because there is really nothing in it but the telling: and here the blessed infinity of Art comes in again.

Miss Austen's last book, like her first, was published posthumously and she left nothing else but a couple of fragments. One of these, *Lady Susan*, does not, so far as it extends, promise much, though it is such a fragment and such an evident first draft even of this, that judgment of it is equally unfair and futile. The other, *The Watsons*, has some very striking touches, but is also a mere beginning. *Persuasion*—which appeared with *Northanger Abbey* and which, curiously enough, has, like its nearly twenty years elder sister, Bath for its principal scene—has also some pretensions to primacy among the books, and is universally admitted to be of its author's most delicate, most finished, and most sustained work. And this, like *Emma*, resolutely abstains from even the slightest infusion of startling or unusual incident, of " exciting " story, of glaring colour of any kind: relying only on congruity of speech, sufficient if subdued description, and above all a profusion of the most delicately, but the most vividly drawn character, made to unfold a plot which has interest, if no excitement, and seasoned throughout with the unfailing condiment— the author's " own sauce "—of gentle but piquant irony and satire.

It is not to be supposed or inferred that Miss Austen's methods, or her results, have appealed to everybody. Madame de Staël thought her *vulgaire*—meaning, of course, not exactly our " vulgar " but " commonplace "; Charlotte Brontë was not much otherwise minded; her own Marianne Dashwood would doubtless have thought the same. Readers without some touch of letters may think her style old-fashioned: it has even been termed " stilted." Not merely may amateurs of blood and thunder, of passion and sensation, think her tame, but the more modern devotees of " analysis " may consider her superficial. On the other hand, it is notorious that, from her own day to this, she has never wanted partisans, often of superlative competence, and of the most strikingly different tempers, tastes, and opinions. The extraordinary quietness of her art is only matched by its confidence: its subtlety by its strength. She did not try many styles; she deliberately and no doubt wisely refused to try the other style which was already carrying all before it in her own later days. She seems to have confined herself (with what seems to some high-flying judges an almost ignoble caution) to the strata of society that she knew most thoroughly: and the curious have noted that she seldom goes above a baronet, and hardly even descends to a butler, in her range of person-ages who are not mere mutes. It is not at all unlikely— in fact it is almost certain—that she might have enlarged this range, and that of her incident, with perfect safety and to the great profit and delight of her readers. But these actual things she knew she could do consummately; and she would not risk the production of anything not consummate.

The value of her, artistically, is of course in the perfec-tion of what she did; but the value of her historically is in the way in which she showed that, given the treatment, any material could be perfected. It was in this way, as has been pointed out, that the possibilities of the novel were shown to be practically illimitable. Tragedy is not needed: and the most ordinary transactions, the most everyday characters, develop into an infinite series of comedies with which the novelist can amuse himself and his readers. The *ludicrum humani seculi* on the one hand, and the artist's power of extracting and arranging it on

the other—these two things supply all that is wanted.
This Hampshire parson's daughter had found the philo-
sopher's stone of the novel: and the very pots and pans,
the tongs and pokers of the house, could be turned into
novel-gold by it.

But even gold is not everything: and only a fanatic, and
a rather foolish fanatic, would say that this style of fiction
summed up and exhausted all the good that fiction could
give and do.   Miss Austen's art excludes (it has been said)
tragedy; it does not let in much pure romance; although
its variety is in a way infinite, yet it is not various in
infinite ways, but rather in very finite ones.   Everybody
who denies its excellence is to be blamed: but nobody is
to be blamed for saying that he should like some other
excellences as well.   The desire is innocent, nay commend-
able: and it was being satisfied, at practically the same
time, by the work of Sir Walter Scott in a kind of novel
almost as new (when we regard it in connection with its
earlier examples) as Miss Austen's own.   This was the Historical novel, which, in a way, not only subsumed many
though not quite all varieties of Romance, but also sum-
moned to its aid not a little—in fact a very great deal—
of the methods of the pure novel itself.

It is not very long since a critic, probably not very old,
sentenced the critical opinions of another critic, certainly
not very young, to " go into the melting pot " because they
were in favour of the historical novel: and because the
historical novel had for some time past done great harm
(I think the phrase was stronger) to the imaginative
literature of England.   Now there are several things
which might be said about this judgment—I do not say
" in arrest " of it, because it is of itself inoperative: as it
happens you cannot put critical opinions in the melting

pot. At least, they won't melt: and they come out again like the diabolic rat that Mr. Chips tried to pitch-boil. In the first place, there is the question whether the greater part by far of the imaginative and other literature of *any* time does not itself " go into the melting pot," and whether it much matters what sends it there. In the second, if this seems too cynical, there is the very large and grave question whether a still larger proportion of the novel of manners, in England, France, and all other countries during the same time, has not been as bad as, or worse than, the romantic division, historical or other. But the worst faults of the judgment remain. In the first place there is the fatal shortness of view. It is with the literature of two thousand, not with the literature of twenty, years that the true critic has to do: and no kind which—in two thousand, or two hundred, or twenty—has produced literature that is good or great can be even temporarily put aside because (as every kind of literature without exception has been again and again) it is for a time barren or fruitful only in weeds. And any one who does not count Scott and Dumas and Thackeray among the makers of good literature must really excuse others if they simply take no further count of him. The historical novel is a good kind, good friends, a marvellous good kind: and it has the advantage over the pure novel of manners that it is much less subject to obsolescence, if it be really well done; while it can practically annex most of the virtues of that novel of manners itself.

This excellent kind, however, had been wandering about in the wilderness—had indeed hardly got so far even as that stage, but had been a mere " bodiless childful of life in the gloom "—for more than two thousand years before *Waverley*. Of its earlier attempts to get into full existence

we cannot say much here: [1] something on the more recent
but rather abortive birth-throes has been promised, and
is now due. It is not improbable that considerable assistance was rendered to the kind by the heroic romance of
the seventeenth century in prose and verse, which often
attempted historic, and almost always pseudo-historic,
guise. As has been seen in regard to such collections as
Croxall's, historical stories were freely mingled with
fictitious: and it could not be for nothing that Horace
Walpole, the author of the *Castle of Otranto*, was a rather
ardent and even to some extent scholarly student of the
romance and the gossip of history.   Much earlier, Fielding
himself, in his salad days, had given something of an historic
turn to the story of *A Journey from this World to the Next.*
And when history itself became more common and more
readable, it could not but be that this inexhaustible source
of material for the new kind of literature, which was being
so eagerly demanded and so busily supplied, should suggest
itself.   Some instances of late eighteenth and early nineteenth century experiments have been given and discussed
in the last chapter: and when Scott (or " the Author of
Waverley ") had achieved his astonishing success, some
of the writers of these put in the usual claim of " That's
my thunder." This was done in the case of the Lees, it
was also done in the case of Jane Porter, the writer of
the once famous and favourite *Thaddeus of Warsaw* (1803)
and *Scottish Chiefs* (1810): while, as we have seen, there
had been historical colour enough in Godwin's novels to

---

[1] Those who are curious about the matter will find it treated in a
set of Essays by the present writer, which originally appeared in
Macmillan's Magazine during the autumn of 1894, and were reprinted among *Essays in English Literature*, Second Series, London,
1895.

make suggestion of *his* " authorship of *Waverley* " not absolutely preposterous. Even Mrs. Radcliffe had touched the style; and humbler persons like the egregious Henrietta Mosse had attempted it in the most serious spirit.

But with their varying degrees of talent—with, in one or two cases, even a little genius—all these writers had broken themselves upon one fatal difficulty — that of anachronism: not in the petty sense of the pedant, but in the wide one of the critic. The present writer is not prepared, without reading *A Peep at Our Ancestors* again (which he distinctly declines to do), to say that there are, in that remarkable performance, any positive errors of historic fact worse than, or as bad, as those which pedantry has pointed out in *Ivanhoe*. But whereas you may be nearly as well acquainted with the actual history of the time as the pedants themselves, and a great deal better acquainted with its literature, and yet never be shocked, disgusted, or contemptuously amused in *Ivanhoe* by such things as were quoted from the *Peep* a few pages back—so, to those who know something of " the old Elizabeth way," and even nowadays to those who know very little, and that little at second hand, Miss Lee's travesty of it in *The Recess* is impossible and intolerable. When Mrs. Radcliffe, at the date definitely given of 1584, talks about " the Parisian opera," represents a French girl of the sixteenth century as being "instructed in the English poets," and talks about driving in a " landau," the individual blunders are, perhaps, not more violent than those of the chronology by which Scott's Ulrica is apparently a girl at the time of the Conquest and a woman, not too old to be the object of rivalry between Front de Boeuf and his father, not long before the reign of Richard I. But this last oversight does not affect the credibility of the story, or the homogeneity of the manners, in the least. Mrs. Radcliffe jumbles up two (or more than two) utterly different states and stages of society, manners, and other things which constitute the very atmosphere of the story itself. Perhaps (we have very few easy conversations of the period to justify a positive statement) a real Bois-Guilbert and still more a real Wamba might not have talked exactly like Scott's personages: but there is no insistent and disturbing reason why they should not. When we hear an Adelaise of the mid-twelfth century asking whether she does not receive her education from her mamma, the necessary " suspension of disbelief " becomes impossible.

But these now most obvious truths were not obvious at all between 1780 and 1810: and it is perhaps the greatest evidence of Scott's genius that half, but by no means quite, unconsciously he saw them, and that he has made everybody see them since. It was undoubtedly fortunate that he began novel-writing so late: for earlier even he might have been caught in the errors of the time. But when he did begin, he had not only reached middle life and matured his considerable original critical faculty — criticism and wine are the only things that even the " kind calm years " may be absolutely trusted to improve if there is any original goodness in them—but he had other advantages. He had read, if not with minute accuracy, very widely indeed: and he possessed, as Lord Morley has well said, " the genius of history " in a degree which perhaps no merely meticulous scholar has ever reached, and which was not exceeded in *quality* even by the greatest historians such as Gibbon. He had an almost unmatched combination of common sense with poetic imagination, of knowledge of the world with knowledge of letters. He had shown himself to be possessed of the secret of semi-historical narrative itself in half a dozen remarkable verse romances, and therefore had less to do in engineering the prose romance. Last of all, he had seen what to avoid—not merely in his editing of Strutt's *Queenhoo Hall* (a valuable property-room for the novel, but nothing of a real novel), but in his reading of the failures of his predecessors and contemporaries. The very beginning of *Waverley* itself (which most people skip) is invaluable, because it shows us that at the time he wrote it (which, it need hardly be said, was a long time before its completion) he had not the knowledge or the courage to strike straight out into the stream of action and conversation, but troubled himself with accumulating bladders and arranging ropes for the possible salvation of his narrative if it got into difficulties. Very soon he knew that it would not get into difficulties: and away he went.

It ought not to be necessary, but from some symptoms it may be desirable, to point out that Scott is very far from being an historical novelist only. An acute French critic, well acquainted with both literatures, once went so far as to say that there were a good many professed " philosophical " novels which did not contain such keen psychology as Scott's: and I would undertake to show a good deal of cause on this side. But short of it, it is undeniable that he can do perfectly well without any historical scaffolding. There is practically nothing of it in his second and third novels, *Guy Mannering* and *The Antiquary*, each of which good judges have sometimes ranked as his very best: there is as little or less in *St. Ronan's Well*, a very fine thing as it is, and one which, but for James Ballantyne's meddling folly and prudery, would have been much finer. The incomparable little conversation - scenes and character-sketches scattered among the Introductions to the novels—

especially the history of Crystal Croftangry—show that
he could perfectly well have dispensed with all out-of-the-
way incident had he chosen. But, as a rule, he did not so
choose: and, in the majority of cases, he preferred to take
his out-of-the-way incident from historical sources. Not
here, unfortunately, can we allow ourselves even a space
proportionate to that given above in Miss Austen's case
to the criticism of individual novels: but luckily there is
not much need of this. The brilliant overture of *Waverley*
as such, with its entirely novel combination of the historical
and the " national " elements upon the still more novel
background of Highland scenery; the equally vivid and
vigorous narrative and the more interesting personages of
Old Mortality and *Rob Roy ;* the domestic tragedy, with the
historical element for little more than a framework, of the
Heart of Midlothian and the *Bride of Lammermoor ;* the
little masterpiece of *A Legend of Montrose ;* the fresh
departure, with purely English subject, of *Ivanhoe* and its
triumphant sequels in *Kenilworth, Quentin Durward,* and
others; the striking utilisation of literary assistance in the
Fortunes of Nigel ; and the wonderful blending of autobiographic, historical, and romantic interest in *Redgauntlet :*—
one cannot dwell on these and other things. The magic
continued even in *Woodstock*—written as this was almost
between the blows of the executioner's crow-bar on the
wheel, in the tightening of the windlasses at the rack—it
is not absent, whatever people may say, in *Anne of Geier-
stein,* nor even quite lacking in the better parts of *Count
Robert of Paris.* But we must not expatiate on its effects;
we must only give a little attention to the means by which
they are achieved.

Another of the common errors about Scott is to represent—perhaps really to regard—him as a hit-or-miss and

hand-to-mouth *improvisatore*, who bundled out his creations anyhow, and did not himself know how he created
them.   The fallacy is worse than a fallacy: for it is down-
right false witness.   We have numerous passages in and
out of the novels—the chief of them being the remarkable
conversation with Captain Clutterbuck in the Introduction
to the *Fortunes of Nigel* and the reflections in the *Diary*
on *Sir John Chiverton* and *Brambletye House*—showing
that Scott knew perfectly well the construction and the
stringing of his fiddle, as well as the trick of applying his
rosin.   But if we had not these direct testimonies, no one
of any critical faculty could mistake the presence of consciously perceived principles in the books themselves.   A
man does not suddenly, and by mere blind instinct, avoid
such a pitfall as that of incongruous speech and manners,
which has been noticed above.   It is not mere happy-go-
lucky blundering which makes him invariably decline
another into which people still fall — the selection of
historical personages of the first importance, and elaborately
known, for the *central* figures of his novels.   Not to believe
in luck is a mark of perhaps greater folly than to over-
believe in it: but luck will not always keep a man clear
of such perils as that unskilful wedging of great blocks of
mere history into his story, which the lesser historical
novelists always commit, or that preponderance of mere
narrative itself as compared with action and conversation
from which even Dumas, even Thackeray, is not free.

That he knew what he was doing and what he had to do
is thus certain; that he did it to an astounding extent
is still more certain; but it would not skill much to deny
that he did not always give himself time to do it perfectly
in every respect, though it is perhaps not mere paradox
or mere partisanship to suggest that if he had given him-

self more time, he would hardly have done better, and might have done worse. The accusation of superficiality has been already glanced at: and it is pretty certain that it argues more superficiality, of a much more hopeless kind, in those who make it. The accusation of careless and slovenly style is not much better: for Scott had, perfectly, the style suited to his own work, and you cannot easily have a better style than that. But there are two defects in him which were early detected by good and friendly judges: and which are in fact natural results of the extraordinary force and fertility of his creative power. One—the less serious, but certainly to some extent a fault in art and a point in which he is distinguished for the worse from Shakespeare—is that he is rather given to allow at first, to some of his personages, an elaborateness and apparent emphasis of drawing which seems to promise an importance for them in the story that they never actually attain. Mike Lambourne in *Kenilworth* is a good example of this: but there are many others. The fact evidently was that, in the rush of the artist's plastic imagination, other figures rose and overpowered these. It is an excuse: but it is hardly a justification. The other and more serious is a tendency—which grew on him and may no doubt have been encouraged by the astonishing pecuniary rewards of his work—to hurry his conclusions, to " huddle up the cards and throw them into the bag," as Lady Louisa Stuart told him. There is one of the numerous, but it would seem generic and classifiable, forms of unpleasant dream in which the dreamer's watch, to his consternation, suddenly begins to send its hands round at double and ten-fold speed. Scott is rather apt to do this, towards the close of his novels, in his eagerness to begin something else.

These defects, however, are defects much more from

o

the point of view of abstract criticism than from that of the
pleasure of the reader: while, even from the former, they
are outweighed many times by merits. And as regards
our present method of estimation, they hardly count at all.

For, in that calculus, the important thing is that Scott,
like Miss Austen, at once opened an immense new field to
the novelist, and showed how that field was to be cultivated. The complement-contrast of the pair can need
emphasising only to those on whom no emphasis would
be likely to impress it: but it may not be quite so evident
at once that between them they cover almost the entire
possible ground of prose fiction. The more striking and
popular as well as more strictly novel style of Scott
naturally attracted most attention at first: indeed it can
hardly be said that, for the next thirty years, much attempt
was made to follow in Miss Austen's steps, while such
attempts as were made were seldom very good.[1] But
there is no need to hurry Time: and he generally knows
what he is about. At any rate he had, in and through
these two provided—for generations, probably for centuries,
to come—patterns and principles for whoso would to follow
in prose fiction.

[1] Some work of distinction, actually later than hers in date, is
older in kind. This is the case not only with the later books of her
Irish elder sister, Miss Edgeworth (see last chapter), but with all
those of her Scotch younger one, Miss Ferrier, who wrote *Marriage*
just after *Sense and Sensibility* appeared, but did not publish it
(1818) till after Miss Austen's death, following it with *The Inheritance* (1824) and *Destiny* (1831). Miss Ferrier, who had a strong
though rather hard humour and great faculty of pronounced character-drawing, is better at a series of sketches than at a complete novel—
only *The Inheritance* having much central unity. And there is
still eighteenth - century quality rather than nineteenth in her
alternations of Smollettian farce-satire and Mackenziefied sentiment.
She is very good to read, but stands a little out of the regular historic
succession, as well as out of the ordinary novel classes.

CHAPTER VI

THE SUCCESSORS—TO THACKERAY

A PERSON inexperienced in the ways of life and literature might expect that such developments as those surveyed and discussed in the last chapter must have immediate and unbroken development further. Scott had thrown open, and made available, the whole vast range of history for the romancer: Miss Austen had shown the infinite possibilities of ordinary and present things for the novelist. And such a one might contend that, even if the common idea of definite precursorship and teachership be a mistake, the more subtle doctrine that such work as Scott's, and as Miss Austen's, is really the result of generally working forces, as well as of individual genius, would lead to the same conclusion. But the expectation would show his inexperience, and his ignorance of the fact that Art, unlike Science, declines to be bound by any calculable laws whatsoever.

It was indeed impossible that Scott's towering fame should not draw the nobler sort, and his immense gains the baser, to follow in his track: and they promptly did so. But, as he himself quoted in the remarkable comments (above alluded to) on his early imitators in the *Diary*, they had " gotten his fiddle, but not his rosin "—an observation the truth of which may be shown presently. Miss Austen's immediate influence in the other direction was almost *nil :* and this was hardly to be regretted, because a tolerably stationary state of manners, language, etc., such as her kind of novel requires, had not quite, though it had nearly, been reached. At any rate, the kind of ebb or half ebb, which so often, though not so certainly, follows flood-tides in literature, came upon the novel in the twenties and thirties. Even the striking appearance of Dickens and *Pickwick* in 1837 can hardly be said to have turned it distinctly: for the Dickensian novel is a species by itself—neither strictly novel nor strictly romance, but, as Polonius might say, a picaresque-burlesque - sentimental - farcical - realist - fantastic nonde-script. Not till *Vanity Fair* did the novel of pure real life advance its standard once more: while the historical novel-romance of a new kind may date its revival with—though it should scarcely trace that revival to — *Esmond*, or *Westward Ho!* or both.

Between Scott on the earlier side and Dickens and Thackeray on the other, there was an immense production of novels, illustrated by not a few names which should rank high in the second class, while some would promote more than one of them to the first. The lines of development, as well as the chief individual practitioners, may be best indicated by short discussions of Hook, Bulwer, Disraeli, Ainsworth, James, Marryat, and Peacock.

The most probable demur to this list is likely to be taken at the very first name. Theodore Hook has had no return of the immense popularity which his *Sayings and Doings* (1826-1829) obtained for him; nor, perhaps, is he ever likely to have any; nor yet, further, save in one respect, can he be said to deserve it. Flimsily constructed, hastily written, reflecting indeed the ways and speech of the time after a fashion, but in a distorted mirror and with a thin and superficial representation, nearer to bad drama than to good literature, full of horseplay and forced high jinks—

his stories have all the inseparable faults of improvisation together with those of art that is out of fashion and manners-painting (such as it is) of manners that are dead, and when alive were those of a not very picturesque, pleasing, or respectable transition. Yet, for all this, Hook has a claim on the critical historian of literature, and especially of the novel, which has been far too little acknowledged. And this claim does not even consist in the undoubted fact that his influence both on Dickens and on Thackeray was direct and very great. It lies in the larger and more important, though connected, fact that, at a given moment, his were the hands in which the torch of the novel-procession was deposited. He stands to fiction almost exactly as Leigh Hunt stands to the miscellaneous essay. He modernised and multiplied its subjects, attractions, appeals: he "vulgarised" it in the partly good French sense, as well as in the wholly bad English one; he was its journalist and *colporteur*. He broke up the somewhat stock-and-type moulds of eighteenth-century tale-telling; admitted a plurality, almost an infinity, of interest and incident; gave a sort of universal franchise to possible subjects of novel; and (perhaps most important of all) banished from that novel the tendency to conventional "lingo" which, though never so prevalent in it as in eighteenth-century drama, had existed. It may seem to some readers that there is an exaggerated and paradoxical opposition between this high praise and the severe censure pronounced a little above—that both cannot be true. But both are true: and it is a really natural and necessary cause and proof at once of their truth that Hook never wrote a really good novel, hardly even a really good tale ("Gervase Skinner" is probably the best), and yet that he deserves the place here given to him.

Ainsworth and James perhaps deserve to be taken next, not so much in point of merit as because both, though continuing (especially Ainsworth) very late, began pretty early. Indeed, a book in which Ainsworth had a hand, though it is said to be not wholly his, *Sir John Chiverton*, was, with Horace Smith's *Brambletye House* (1826), the actual subject of Scott's criticism above quoted. Both Ainsworth and James are unconcealed followers of Scott himself: and they show the dangers to which the historical romance is exposed when it gets out of the hands of genius. Of the two, James had the greater scholarship, the better command of English, and perhaps a nearer approach to command also of character: Ainsworth more "fire in his interior," more variety, somewhat more humour (though neither was strong in this respect), and a certain not useless or despicable faculty of splashy scene-painting and rough but not ineffective stage-management. But of Scott's combination of poetry, humour, knowledge of life, reading, grasp of character, and command of effective dialogue and description, both were utterly destitute: and both fell into the mistake (which even Dumas did not wholly avoid) of attempting to give the historical effect by thrusting in lardings of pure history, by overloading descriptions of dress, etc., and, in short, by plastering the historic colour on, instead of suffusing it, as Scott had managed to do. Popular as they were, not merely with youthful readers, they undoubtedly brought the historical novel into some discredit a little before the middle of the century.[1]

With Bulwer and Disraeli we get into a different sphere

[1] Here and in a good many cases to come it is impossible to particularise criticism. It matters the less that, from Ainsworth's *Rookwood* (1834) and James' *Richelieu* (1829) onwards, the work of both was very much *par sibi* in merit and defect alike.

of literature—whether into the same in both cases, and whether, if so, into one of the highest, are questions on which no general agreement has yet been reached—on which, perhaps, no general agreement is even possible.

With regard to the second, it must be remembered that to him, whether as Mr. Disraeli or as Lord Beaconsfield, novel-writing was always a " by-work "—partly a means to his real end of politics, partly a relaxation from the work necessary to that end. He called himself a " gentleman of the press "—with that mixture of sincerity, purpose, and ironical simulation which brought on him, from unintelligent or not very honest opponents, and even from others, the charge of affectation, if not of hypocrisy. And, undoubtedly, he did a good deal of work for the press, and very remarkable work too—almost wholly in the kind of novel-writing, from *Vivian Grey* (1826) to *Endymion* (1880). Yet it may be permitted—in the face of some more than respectable opinion on the other side—to doubt whether, except in some curious sports and by-products, he ever produced real novel-work of the highest class. In the satiric-fantastic tale—in a kind of following of Voltaire— such as *Ixion*, he has hardly a superior, unless it be Anthony Hamilton, who is the superior of Voltaire himself and the master of everybody. For a pure love-novel of a certain kind, *Henrietta Temple* (1837) is bad to beat—and in a curious cross between the historical, biographical, and the romantic, *Venetia* (same year) also stands pretty much alone. But all the rest, more or less political, more or less " of society," more or less fantastic—*Coningsby* (1844) as well as *Alroy* (1833), *Tancred* (1847) as well as *Vivian Grey*, *Sybil* (1845), as well as *The Young Duke* (1831), " leave to desire " in a strange way. Like the three which have been excepted for praise, each is in a manner *sui generis*, while the whole group stands, in a manner also, apart from others and by itself. There is astonishing cleverness everywhere, in regard to almost every point of novel-composition, though with special regard to epigrammatic phrase. But the whole is *inorganic* somehow, and more than somehow unreal; without (save in the cases mentioned) attaining that obviously unreal but persuasive phantasmagoria which some great writers of fiction have managed to put in existence and motion. How far this is due to the fact that most of the novels are political is a question rather to be hinted than to be discussed. But the present writer has never read a political novel, whether on his own side or on others, that seemed to him to be wholly satisfactory.

Bulwer—for it is perhaps here not impolite or improper still to call the first Lord Lytton by the name under which he wrote for forty years, and solidly niched himself in the novel-front of the minster of English Literature—had not a few points of resemblance to his rival and future chief. But their relations to politics and letters were reversed. Disraeli was a born politician who was also a very considerable man of letters: Bulwer was a born man of letters who was a by no means inconsiderable politician. His literary ability was extraordinarily diversified: but, once more, he was (here also) a born novelist, who was also a not inconsiderable dramatist; a critic who might not impossibly have been great, a miscellanist of ability, and a verse-writer than whom many a worse has somehow or other obtained the name of poet. He began novel-writing very early (*Falkland* is of 1827), he continued it all his life, and he was the very Proteus-chameleon of the novel in changing his styles to suit the tastes of the day. He never exactly copied anybody: and in all his various attempts

he went extremely near to the construction of master-
pieces. In the novel of society with *Pelham* (1828); the
novel of crime with *Eugene Aram* (1832) and *Zanoni* (1842);
the novel of passion and a sort of mystery with *Ernest Mal-
travers* and *Alice;* the historic romance with *The Last Days*
of Pompeii (1834), *The Last of the Barons* (1843), and *Harold*
(1848), he made marks deep and early. When the purely
domestic kind came in he made them, earlier and deeper
still, with *The Caxtons* (1850), *My Novel* (1853), etc. He
caught the " sensation " ball at nearly its first service with
his old " mystery " racket, and played the most brilliant
game of the whole tournament in *A Strange Story* (1862).
At the last he tried later kinds still in books like *The Coming*
Race (1871), *The Parisians* (1873), and *Kenelm Chillingly.*
And once, Pallas being kind, he did an almost perfect thing
(there is not a speck or a flaw in it except, perhaps, the
mechanical death of the bulldog) and produced one of the
best examples of one of the best and oldest classes of fiction
known to the world, in the ghost-story of *The Haunted and*
the Haunters (1859).

Such a mass, such a length, such a variety of production,
with so many merits in it, would be difficult to meet elsewhere in our department. And yet very few critics of
unquestionable competence, if any, have accorded the
absolute First Class to Lord Lytton as a novelist. That this
is partly (and rather unjustly) due to the singular and
sometimes positively ridiculous grandiloquence and to the
half-mawkish, half-rancid, sentimentality which too often
mar his earlier novels is probably true. But it is not all
the truth: if it were, it would be almost sufficient to point
out that he outgrew the first of these faults completely,
the second almost completely; and that from *The Caxtons*
(1850) onward there is hardly any stain on his literary

character in any such respect. But other faults—or at
least defects—remain. They may be almost summed up
in the charge of want of *consummateness*. Bulwer could be
romantic—but his romance had the touch of bad taste and
insincerity referred to above. He could, as in *The Caxtons*,
be fairly true to ordinary life—but even then he seemed
to feel a necessity of setting off and as it were apologising
for the simplicity and veracity by touches—in fact by
douches—of Sternian fantastry, and by other touches of
what was a little later to be called sensationalism. Even
his handling of the supernatural, which was undoubtedly
a strong point of his, was not wholly *de bon aloi*. To
pronounce him, as was once done by an acute and amiable
judge, " the *hum*miest of *bugs* " was excessive in life, and
would be preposterous in literature. But there undoubtedly was, with rare exceptions, a suspicion of what
is called in slang " faking " about his work. The wine is
not " neat " but doctored; the composition is *pastiche ;*
a dozen other metaphors—of stucco, veneer, glueing-up—
suggest themselves. And then there suggests itself, in
turn, a sort of shame at such imputations on the author
of such a mass of work, so various, so interesting, so
important as accomplishment, symptom, and pattern at
once. And perhaps one may end by pronouncing Bulwer
one of the very greatest of English novelists who are not
of the very greatest.

It is difficult to say whether the usual attitude of criticism
to Captain Marryat (1792-1848) is more uncritical than
ungrateful or more ungrateful than uncritical. Because
he has amused the boy, it seems to be taken for granted
that he ought not to amuse the man: because he does not
write with the artificial and often extremely arbitrary
graces of the composition books, that he is " not literature."

If it be so, why in the first case so much the worse for " the man," and in the second so much the worse for literature. As a matter of fact, he has many of the qualities of the novelist in a high degree: and if he were in the fortunate position of an ancient classic, whose best works only survive, these qualities could not fail of recognition. Much of his later work simply ought not to count; for it was mere hack-labour, rendered, if not necessary, very nearly so by the sailor's habit (which Marryat possessed in the highest degree) of getting rid of money. Even among this, *Masterman Ready* and *The Children of the New Forest*, " children's books," as they may be called, rank very high in their kind. But he counts here, of course, for his sea-novels mainly: and in them there are several things for us to notice. One is that Marryat had the true quality of the craftsman, as distinguished from the amateur or the chance-medley man who has a lucky inspiration. If it were the case that his books derived their whole attraction from the novelty and (within its limits) the variety of their sea-matter, then the first ought to be the best, as in nearly all such cases is the fact. But *Frank Mildmay* (1829), so far from being the best, is not far from being the worst of Marryat's novels. Much—dangerously much—as he put of his own experiences in the book, he did not know in the least how to manage them. And if Frank is something of a bravo, more of a blackguard, and nearly a complete ruffian, it is not merely because there was a good deal of brutality in the old navy; not merely because Marryat's own standard of chivalry was not quite that of Chaucer's Knight:—but partly, also, because he was aiming blunderingly at what he supposed to be part of the novelist's business—irregular as well as regular gallantry, and highly seasoned adventure.

But, like all good artists (and like hardly anybody who

has not the artistic quality in him), he taught himself by his failure, even though he sometimes relapsed. Of actual construction he was never a master. *The King's Own*, with its overdose of history at the beginning and of melo-drama at the end, is an example. But his two master-pieces, *Peter Simple* (1834) and *Mr. Midshipman Easy* (1836), are capital instances of what may be called " par-ticularist " fiction—the fiction that derives its special zest from the " colours " of some form of life unfamiliar to those who have not actually lived it. Even *Peter Simple* is unduly weighted at the end by the machinations of Peter's uncle against him and, at intervals during the book, by the proceedings connected therewith. But *Mr. Midshipman Easy* is flawless—except for the amiable but surely excessive sentimentalists who are shocked at the way in which Mr. Easy *père* quits the greater stage by mounting the lesser. Than this book there is not a better novel of special " humour " in literature; as much may be said of the greater part of *Peter Simple*, of not a little in *Jacob Faithful* (a great favourite with Thackeray, who always did justice to Marryat), and *Japhet in Search of a Father*, and of something in almost all. Nor were high jinks and special naval matters by any means Marryat's only province. Laymen may agree with experts in think-ing the clubhauling of the *Diomède* in *Peter Simple*, and the two great fights of the *Aurora* with the elements and with the Russian frigate in *Mr. Midshipman Easy*, to be extraordinarily fine things:—vivid, free from extravagance, striking, stirring, clear, as descriptive and narrative litera-ture of the kind can be only at its best, and too seldom is at all. An almost Defoe-like exactness of detail is one of Marryat's methods and merits: while it is very remarkable that he rarely attempts to produce the fun, in which Defoe is lacking and he himself so fertile, by mere exaggeration or caricature of detail. There are exceptions—the Dominie business in *Jacob Faithful* is one—but they are exceptions. Take Hook, his immediate predecessor, and no doubt in a way his model, as (it has been said) Hook was to almost everybody at the time; take even Dickens, his fellow-pupil with Hook and his own greater successor; and you will find that Marryat resorts less than either to the humour of simple *charge* or exaggeration.

The last name on our present list belongs to the class of " eccentric " novelists—the adjective being used, not in its transferred and partly improper sense so much as in its true one. Peacock never plays the Jack-pudding like Sterne: and his shrewd wit never permits him the sincere aberrations of Amory. But his work is out of the ordinary courses, and does not turn round the ordinary centres of novel writing. It belongs to the tradition—if to any tradition at all—of Lucian and the Lucianists— especially as that tradition was redirected by Anthony Hamilton. It thus comes, in one way, near part of the work of Disraeli; though, except in point of satiric temper, its spirit is totally different. Peacock was essentially a scholar (though a non-academic one) and essentially a humorist. In the progress of his books from *Headlong Hall* (1816) to *Gryll Grange* (1860)—the last separated from the group to which the first belongs by more than twice as many years as were covered by that group itself—he mellowed his tone, but altered his scheme very little. Except in *Maid Marian* and *The Misfortunes of Elphin,* where the Scott influence is evident, though Peacock was himself a rebel to Scott, the plan is always the same. *Headlong Hall* and *Nightmare Abbey, Melincourt* and *Crotchet Castle* (1831), as well as *Gryll Grange* itself, all have the uniform, though by no means monotonous, canvas of a party of guests assembled at a country-house and consisting of a number of " originals," with one or more common-sense but by no means commonplace characters to serve as contrast. It is in the selection and management of these foils that one of Peacock's principal distinctions lies. In his earlier books, and in accordance with the manners of the time, there is a good deal of " high jinks "—less later. In all, there is also a good deal of personal and literary satire, which tones and mellows as it proceeds. At first Peacock is extremely unjust to the Lake poets—so unjust indeed as to be sometimes hardly amusing—to the two universities (of which it so happened that he was not a member), to the Tory party generally, to clergymen, to other things and persons. In *Crotchet Castle* the progress of Reform was already beginning to produce a beneficent effect of reaction upon him, and in *Gryll Grange*, though the manners and cast are surprisingly modern, the whole tone is conservative—with a small if not even with a large C—for the most prominent and well treated character is a Churchman of the best academic Tory type.

It is not, however, in anything yet mentioned that Peacock's charm consists, so much as in the intensely literary, but not in the least pedantic, tone with which he suffuses his books, the piquant but not in the least affected turn of the phrases that meet us throughout, the peculiar quality of his irony (most quintessenced in *The Misfortunes of Elphin*, which is different in scheme from the rest, but omnipresent), and the crisp presentation of individual scene, incident, and character of a kind. Story, in the general sense, there is none, or next to none—the personages meet, go through a certain number of dinners (Peacock is great at eating and drinking), diversions, and difficulties, marry to a greater or less extent, but otherwise part. Yet such things as the character of Scythrop in *Nightmare Abbey* (a half fantastic, half faithful portrait of Shelley, who was Peacock's intimate friend), or of Dr. Folliott (a genial parson) in *Crotchet Castle*—as the brilliant picture of the breaking of the dyke in *Elphin*, or the comic one of the rotten-borough election in *Melincourt*—are among the triumphs of the English novel. And they are present by dozens and scores: while (though it is a little out of our way) there is no doubt that the attraction of the books is greatly enhanced by the abundance of inset verse—sometimes serious, more often light—of which Peacock, again in an eccentric fashion, was hardly less a master than he was of prose.

Here also it has seemed fit to dwell on a single writer, not perhaps generally held to be of the absolutely first class, because these " eccentrics " are of very great importance in the history of the English novel. The danger of the kind—even more than of other literary kinds—lies in the direction of mould and mechanism—of the production, by the thousand, of things of no individual quality and character. This danger has been and is being amply exemplified. But the Peacocks (would the plural were more justified!) save us from it by their own unconquerable individuality in the first place and, in the second, by the fact that even the best in this kind is " caviare to the general," while anything that is not the best has no attraction either for the general or the elect. They are, as it were, the salt of the novel-feast, in more senses than one: and it is cause for thankfulness that, in this respect as in the physical, England has been well off for salt-pits.

Besides these individual names—which in most literatures would be great, and even in English literature are not small—the second quarter of the century added to the history of the novel an infinity of others who can hardly appear here even on the representative or selective system. All the suns of the novel hitherto mentioned had moons and stars around them; all the *cadres* of the various kinds were filled with privates and non-commissioned officers to follow the leaders. Galt and Moir carried out the "Scotch novel" with something of Scott, but more of Smollett (Galt at least certainly, in part of his work, preceded Scott). Lady Morgan, who has been mentioned already, Banim, Crofton Croker, and others played a similar part to Miss Edgeworth. Glascock, Chamier, and Howard were, as it were, lieutenants (the last directly so) to Marryat. The didactic side of Miss Edgeworth was taken up by Harriet Martineau. Mrs. Shelley's *Frankenstein* (1818) is among the latest good examples of the "Terror" class, to which her husband had contributed two of its worst, and two of the feeblest books ever written by a man of the greatest genius, in *Zastrozzi* and *St. Irvyne*, some seven years earlier. Many women, not unnaturally, encouraged by the great examples of Miss Burney, Miss Edgeworth, Miss Austen, and Miss Ferrier, attempted novels of the most various kinds, sometimes almost achieving the purely domestic variety, sometimes branching to other sorts. The novels of Mrs. Gore, chiefly in the "fashionable" kind, are said to have attained the three-score and ten in number; Mrs. Crowe dealt with the supernatural outside of her novels if not also in them; the luckless poetess "L. E. L." was a novelist in *Ethel Churchill* (1837) and other books; Mrs. Trollope, prolific mother of a more prolific son, showed not a little power, if not quite so much taste, in *The Vicar of Wrexhill* (1837) and *The Widow Barnaby*. Single books, like Morier's *Hajji Baba* (1824), Hope's *Anastasius* (1819), Croly's *Salathiel* (1829), gained fame which they have not quite lost: and the little known Michael Scott (1789-1835) left in *Tom Cringle's Log* and *The Cruise of the Midge* a pair of stories of West Indian scenery and adventure which are nearly first rate. In 1839, not long after *Pickwick*, Samuel Warren's *Ten Thousand a Year* blended Bulwer and Dickens in a manner which to this day is a puzzle in its near approach to success. Yet he never repeated this approach, though he had earlier done striking things in the *Diary of a Late Physician* (1830). But in the latest thirties and early forties there arose two writers who were to eclipse every one of their contemporaries in this kind.

The remarkable originality and idiosyncrasy of Dickens have perhaps, to some extent and from not a few persons, concealed the fact that he was not, any more than other people, an earth-born wonder. Scanted of education as he was, he has in several places frankly and eagerly confessed his early acquaintance with the great older novelists, and his special fancy for Smollett—whose influence indeed is traceable on him from first to last, and not least in the famous " interiors " of which he made far more than his example had done. Even in *Pickwick* the expert will trace suggestions from others. But if the work is read in its proper order, and the *Sketches by Boz* are taken first, nobody who knows both Leigh Hunt and Theodore Hook will fail to see that Dickens owed a great deal to both. The fact is in no sense discreditable to him: on the contrary, it adds, in the estimation of all reasonable and critical judges, a very great deal of interest, and takes away none. The earth-born prodigy is seldom good for much and never for very much. The genius who fastens on the points in preceding literature most congenial to him, develops them,

P

builds on them with his own matter and form, and turns out something far greater than his originals is the really satisfactory person. Had Leigh Hunt lent to Hook his literature, his fund of trivial but agreeable observation and illustration, and his attractive style; had Hook communicated to Hunt his narrative faculty and his fecundity in character and manners:—neither could have written *Pickwick* or even the worst of its successors. Had there been no Hunt and no Hook, Dickens would no doubt have managed, in some fashion, to " do for himself." But it would have given him more trouble, he would have done it more slowly, and he would hardly have earned that generous and admirable phrase of his greatest contemporary in fiction which will be quoted shortly.

Neither from Smollett, however, nor from Hook, nor from Hunt, nor from anybody else did Dickens take what makes him Dickens. His idiosyncrasy, already mentioned, is so marked that everybody acknowledges its presence: but its exact character and nature are matter not so much of debate (though they are that also in the highest degree) as matter of more or less *questing*, often of a rather blind-man's-buff kind. There is probably no author of whom really critical estimates are so rare. He has given so much pleasure to so many people—perhaps there are none to whom he has given more pleasure than to some of those who have criticised him most closely—that to mention any faults in him is upbraided as a sort of personal and detestable ingratitude and treachery. If you say that he cannot draw a gentleman, you are told that you are a parrot and a snob, who repeats what other snobs have told you; that gentlemen are not worth drawing; that he *can* draw them; and so forth. If you suggest that he is fantastic, it is reproachfully asked if poetry is not fantastic,

and if you do not like poetry? If you intimate small
affection for Little Nell and Little Paul, you are a brute;
if you hint that his social crusades were often quite
irrational, and sometimes at least as mischievous as they
were beneficial, you are a parasite of aristocracy and a foe
of " the people." If you take exception to his repetitions,
his mannerisms, his tedious catch-processes of various
kinds, you are a " stop-watch critic " and worthy of all
the generous wrath of the exemplary and Reverend Mr.
Yorick. And yet all these assertions, objections, descriptions, are arch-true: and they can be made by persons
who know Dickens and enjoy Dickens a thousand times
better—who admire him in a manner a thousand times
more really complimentary—than the folk who simply
cry " Great is Dickens " and will listen to nothing but
their own sweet voices.

The real, the great, the unique merit of Dickens is that
he brought to the service of the novel an imagination
which, though it was never poetic, was plastic in almost
the highest degree: and that he communicated to the
results of it a kind of existence which, though distinctly
different from that of actual life, has a reality of its own,
and possesses the distinguishing mark of genius, so that if
it does not exactly force belief in itself, it forces suspension of disbelief. To have done this is not only to have
accomplished a wonderful artistic triumph, but to confer
an immense benefit on the human race. But in doing it
Dickens exhibits various foibles, prejudices, and dis-
abilities: though it is quite open to any one to maintain
that these rather assisted the flow of his imagination than
hindered it. He began very young; he had curiously little
literature; his knowledge of life, extraordinarily alert and
acute, was very one-sided, and the organs by which he

attained it seem absolutely to shut themselves and refuse communion with certain orders of society and classes of human creatures. The wealth of fantastic imagery which he used to such purpose not infrequently stimulated him to a disorderly profusion of grotesque; he was congenitally melodramatic; and before very long his habit of attributing special catch-words, gestures, and the like to his characters, exaggerated, degenerated, and stereotyped itself in a fashion which it is difficult to think satisfactory to anybody. He was, moreover, a "novelist of purpose" in the highest degree; he had very strong, but very crude—not to say absurd—political ideas; and he was apt to let the great powers of pathos, of humour, of vivid description, which he possessed to "get out of hand" and to land him in the maudlin, the extravagant, and the bombastic.

But—to put ourselves in connection with the main thread of our story once more—he not only himself provided a great amount of the novel pleasure for his readers, but he infused into the novel generally something of a new spirit. It has been more than once pointed out that there is almost more danger with the novel of "getting into ruts" than with any kind of literature. Nobody could charge the Dickens novel with doing this, except as regards mannerisms of style, and though it might inspire many, it was very unlikely to create a rut for any one else. He liked to call himself "the inimitable," and so, in a way, he was. Imitations of him were, of course, tried: but they were all bad and obvious failures. Against the possible tameness of the domestic novel; against the too commonly actual want of actuality of the historic romance; he set this new fantastic activity of his, which was at once real and unreal, but where the reality had a magical touch of the unfamiliar and the very unreality was stimulating. He might have a hundred faults—he was in fact never faultless, except in *Pickwick*, which is so absolutely unique that there is nothing to compare with it and show up faults (if it has any) by the comparison. But you can read him again and again with unceasing delight, and with delight of a kind given by no other novelist.[1]

The position of Thackeray in the history of the novel is as different from that of Dickens as the fortunes of the two were in their own progress and development. In fact, though a sort of pseudo-Plutarchian parallel between them is nearly as inevitable as it is common, it is a parallel almost entirely composed of differences, carried out in matter almost incommensurable. In the first place, Dickens, as we have seen, and as Thackeray said (with the generous and characteristic addition " at the head of the whole tribe "), " came and took his place calmly " and practically at once (or with the preliminary only of " Boz ") in *Pickwick*. Whether he ever went further may at least be questioned. But Thackeray did not take his place at once—in fact he conspicuously failed to take it for some sixteen years: although he produced, for at least the last ten of these, work containing indications of extraordinary power, in a variety of directions almost as extraordinary.

To attempt to assign reasons for this comparative failure would be idle—the fact is the only reasonable reason. But some phenomena and symptoms can be diagnosed. It is at least noteworthy that Thackeray—in this approaching Dickens perhaps nearer than in any other point—began with extravaganza — to adopt perhaps the most con-

---

[1] It has not been thought necessary to insert criticism of Dickens's individual novels. They are almost all well known to almost everybody: and special discussion of them would be superfluous, while their general characteristics and positions in novel-history are singularly uniform and can be described together.

venient general name for a thing which cannot be quite satisfactorily designated by any. In both cases the adoption was probably due to the example and popularity of Theodore Hook. But it was also due, in a higher and more metaphysical sense, to the fact that the romance, which had had so mighty a success in Scott's hands, was for the time overblown, and that the domestic novel, despite the almost equally wonderful, though much quieter and less popular achievement of Miss Austen, was not thoroughly and genuinely ready. From extravaganza in a certain sense Dickens, as has been said, never really departed: and he achieved most of his best work in his own peculiar varieties of it. Thackeray was, if not to leave it entirely aside, to use it in his later days merely as an occasional variation and seasoning. But at first he could not, apparently, get free from it: and he might have seemed unable to dispense with its almost mechanical externalities of mis-spelling and the like. It must also be remembered that circumstances were at first curiously unfavourable to him: and that loss of fortune, domestic affliction, and other things almost compelled him to write from hand to mouth —to take whatever commission offered itself: whereas the, if not immediate, speedy and tremendous success of *Pickwick* put the booksellers entirely at Dickens's feet. Still, a certain vacillation—an uncertainty of design not often accompanying genius like his—must be acknowledged in Thackeray. For a time he hesitated between pen and pencil, the latter of which implements he fortunately never abandoned, though the former was his pre-destined wand. Then he could not, or would not, for years, get out of the " miscellaneous " style, or patchwork of styles—reviews, short stories, burlesques, what not. His more important attempts seemed to have an attendant

guignon.[1] *Catherine* (1839-1840), a very powerful thing
in parts, was ill-planned and could not be popular.
A Shabby Genteel Story (1841), containing almost the
Thackerayan *quiddity*, was interrupted partly by his wife's
illness, partly, it would seem, by editorial disfavour, and
moreover still failed to shake off the appearance of a want
of seriousness. Even *The Great Hoggarty Diamond* (1841-
1842) was apparently cut short by request, and still lay
open to an unjust, but not quite inexcusable, question on
this same point of " seriousness." In all there was, or
might seem to be, a queer and to some readers an unsatisfactory blend of what they had not learnt to call " realism "
with what they were quite likely to think fooling. During
these years Thackeray was emphatically of the class of
writers of whom people " do not know what to make."
And it is a true saying of English people—though perhaps
not so pre-eminently true of them as some would have it—
that " not to know what to make " of a thing or a person
is sufficient reason for them to distrust, dislike, and " wash
their hands of " it or him.

Some would have it that *Barry Lyndon* (1843) marks
the close of this period of indecision and the beginning of
that of maturity. The commoner and perhaps the juster
opinion is that this position belongs to *Vanity Fair* (1846-
1848). At any rate, *after* that book there could be no
doubt about the fact of the greatness of its writer, though
it may be doubted whether even now the quality of this
greatness is correctly and generally recognised. It is this
—that at last the novel of real life on the great scale has
been discovered. Even yet a remnant of shyness hangs

---

[1] For this reason, and for the variety of kind of his later novels a little
more individual notice must be given to them than in the case of Dickens,
but still only a little, and nothing like detailed criticism.

on the artist. He puts his scene a little though not very far back; he borrows a little, though not much, historical and romantic interest in the Waterloo part; the catastrophe of the Becky-Steyne business, though by no means outside of the probable contents of any day's newspaper, is slightly exceptional. But on the whole the problem of " reality, the whole reality, and nothing but reality " is faced and grasped and solved—with, of course, the addition to the " nothing but " of " except art."

He had struck his path and he kept to it: even when, as in *Esmond* (1852) and *The Virginians* (1858-1859) actually, and in *Denis Duval* prospectively, he blended the historical with the domestic variety. *Pendennis* (1849-1850) imports nothing out of the most ordinary experience; *The Newcomes* (1854-1855) very little; *Philip* (1861-1862) only its pantomime conclusion; while the two completely historical tales are in nothing more remarkable than in the way in which their remoter and more unfamiliar main subject, and their occasional excursions from everyday life, are subdued to the scheme of the realist novel in the best sense of the term—the novel rebuilt and refashioned on the lines of Fielding, but with modern manners, relying on variety and life, and relying on these only.

There is thus something of similarity (though with attendant differences, of the most important kind) between the joint position of Dickens and Thackeray towards the world of the novel, and the joint position of Scott and Miss Austen. They *overlap* more than their great forerunners of the preceding generation. Both wrote historical novels: it is indeed Thackeray's unique distinction that he was equally master of the historical novel and of the novel of pure modern society, almost uneventful. In parts of some of his later books, especially *Little Dorrit*,

Great Expectations, and *Our Mutual Friend,* Dickens at least tried to exchange his picaresque-fantastic cloudland for actual ordinary modern life. But on the whole the method of Thackeray was the method of the novel, though shot with a strong romantic spirit, and the method of Dickens the method of the romance applied, for the most part, to material which could hardly be called romantic. Both, therefore, in a manner, recalled the forces of fiction from the rather straggling and particularist courses which it had been pursuing for the last quarter of a century.

In fact, even in the two mighty men of genius whom we have just been discussing, there may be seen—at their beginnings at least — something of that irresolution, uncertainty, and want of reliance on the powers of the novel, it-by-itself-it, which we have noticed before: and which the unerring craftsmanship of Scott had already pointed out in the " Conversation of the Author of *Waverley* with Captain Clutterbuck " more than once referred to. They want excuses and pretexts, bladders and spring-boards. Even Dickens, despite his irrepressible self-reliance, burdens himself, at the beginning of *Pickwick,* with the clumsy old machinery of a club which he practically drops: and, still later, with the still more clumsy framework of " Master Humphrey's Clock " which he has not quietly to drop, but openly to strip off and cast away, before he has gone very far. Thackeray takes sixteen years of experiment before he trusts his genius, boldly and on the great scale, to reveal itself in its own way, and in the straight way of the novel.

Yet in this time also a great advance was made, as is shown not only by the fact that Dickens and Thackeray themselves became possible, but by the various achievements of the principal writers mentioned in this chapter, of one or two who might have been, but are perhaps, on the whole, best postponed to the next, such as Lever, and of the great army of minorities who have been of necessity omitted. In every direction and from every point of view novel is *growing*. Although it was abused by precisians, the *gran conquesta* of Scott had forced it into general recognition and requisition. Even the still severe discipline of family life in the first half of the nineteenth century, instead of excluding it altogether, contented itself with prescribing that " novels should not be read in the morning." A test which may be thought vulgar by the superfine or the superficial, but a pretty good one, is the altered status and position of the writers of novels. In the eighteenth, especially the earlier eighteenth, century the novelist had not merely been looked down upon *as* a novelist, but had, as a rule, resorted to novel-writing under some stress of circumstance. Even when he was by birth a " gentleman of coat armour " as Fielding and Smollett were, he was usually a gentleman very much out at elbows: the stories, true or false, of *Rasselas* and Johnson's mother's funeral expenses, of the *Vicar of Wakefield* and Goldsmith's dunning landlady, have something more than mere anecdote in them. Mackenzie, though the paternity of his *famille déplorable* of novels was no secret, preserved a strict nominal incognito. Women, as having no regular professions and plenty of time at their disposal, were allowed more latitude: and this really perhaps had something to do with their early prominence in the novel; but it is certain that Scott's rigid, and for a long time successful, maintenance of the mask was by no means mere prudery, and still less merely prudent commercial speculation. Yet he, who altered so much in the novel, altered this also. Of the novelists noticed in the early part of this chapter, one became Prime Minister of England, another rose to cabinet rank, a baronetcy, and a peerage; a third was H.M. consul in important posts abroad; a fourth held a great position, if not in the service directly of the crown, in what was of hardly less importance, that of the East India Company; a fifth was a post-captain in the navy and Companion of the Bath.

And all this had been rendered possible partly by the genius of novel-writers, partly by the appetite of the novel-reader. This latter was to continue unabated: whether the former was to increase, to maintain itself, or slacken must be, to some extent of course, matter of opinion. But we have still two quarter-centuries to survey, in the first of which there may perhaps be some reason for thinking that the novel rose to its actual zenith. Nearly all the writers mentioned in this chapter continued to write—the greater part, in genius, of Thackeray's accomplished work, and the greater part, in bulk, of Dickens's, had still to appear. But these elders were reinforced by fresh recruits, some of them of a prowess only inferior to the very greatest: and a distinct development of the novel itself, in the direction of self-reliance and craftsmanlike working on its own lines, was to be seen. In particular, the deferred influence of Miss Austen was at last to be brought to bear with astonishing results: while, partly owing to the example of Thackeray, the historical variety (which had for the most part been a pale and rather vulgarised imitation of Scott), was to be revived and varied in a manner equally astonishing. More than ever we shall have to let styles and kinds " speak by their foremen "— in fact to some extent to let them speak for themselves with very little detailed notice even of these foremen. But we shall still endeavour to keep the general threads in hand and to exhibit their direction, their crossing, and their other phenomena, as clearly as possible to the reader. For only so can we complete the picture of the course of fiction throughout English literature—with the sole exclusion of living writers, whose work can never be satisfactorily treated in such a book as this—first, because they are living and, secondly, because it is not done.

CHAPTER VII

At about the very middle of the nineteenth century—say from 1845 to 1855 in each direction, but almost increasingly towards the actual dividing line of 1850—there came upon the English novel a very remarkable wind of refreshment and new endeavour. Thackeray and Dickens themselves are examples of it, with Lever and others, before this dividing line: many others yet come to join them. A list of books written out just as they occur to the memory, and without any attempt to marshal them in strict chronological order, would show this beyond all reasonable possibility of gainsaying. Thackeray's own best accomplished work from *Vanity Fair* (1846) itself through *Pendennis* (1849) and *Esmond* (1852) to *The Newcomes* (1854); the brilliant centre of Dickens's work in *David Copperfield* (1850)—stand at the head and have been already noticed by anticipation or implication, while Lever had almost completed the first division of his work, which began with *Harry Lorrequer* as early as the year of *Pickwick*. But such books as *Yeast* (1848), *Westward Ho!* (1855); as *The Warden* (1855); as *Jane Eyre* (1847) and its too few successors; as *Scenes of Clerical Life* (1857); as *Mary Barton* (1848) and the novels which followed it, with others which it is perhaps almost unfair to leave out even in this allusive summary by sample, betokened a stirring of the waters, a rattling among the bones, such as is not common in literature. Death removed Thackeray early and Dickens somewhat less prematurely, but after a period rather barren in direct novel work. The others continued and were constantly reinforced: nor was it till well on in the seventies that any distinct drop from first- to second-growth quality could be observed in the general vintage of English fiction.

One is not quite driven, on this occasion, to the pusillanimous explanation that this remarkable variety and number of good novels was simply due to the simultaneous existence of an equally remarkable number of good novelists. The fact is that, by this time, the great example of Scott and Miss Austen—the great wave of progress which exemplified itself first and most eminently in these two writers—had had time to work upon and permeate another generation of practitioners. The novelists who have just been cited were as a rule born in the second decade of the century, just before, about, or after the time at which Scott and Miss Austen began to publish. They had there-fore—as their elders, even though they may have had time to read the pair, had not—time to assimilate thoroughly and early the results which that pair had produced or which they had first expressed. And they had even greater advantages than this. They had had time to assimilate, likewise, the results of all the rest of that great literary generation of which Scott and Miss Austen were themselves but members. They profited by thirty years more of constant historical exploration and realising of former days. One need not say, for it is question-begging, that they also *profited* by, but they could at least avail themselves of, the immense change of manners and society which made 1850 differ more from 1800 than 1800 had differed, not merely from 1750 but from 1700. They had, even though all of them may not have been sufficiently grateful for it, the stimulus of that premier position in Europe

which the country had gained in the Napoleonic wars, and
which she had not yet wholly lost or even begun to lose.
They had wider travel, more extended occupations and
interests, many other new things to draw upon. And,
lastly, they had some important special incidents and
movements—the new arrangement of political parties, the
Oxford awakening, and others — to give suggestion and
impetus to novels of the specialist kind. Nay, they had
not only the great writers, in other kinds, of the immediate past, but those of the present, Carlyle, Tennyson,
latterly Ruskin, and others still to complete their education
and the machinery of its development.

The most remarkable feature of this *renouveau*, as has
been both directly and indirectly observed before, is the
resumption, the immense extension, and the extraordinary
improvement of the domestic novel. Not that this had
not been practised during the thirty years since Miss
Austen's death. But the external advantages just
enumerated had failed it: and it had enlisted none of the
chief talents which were at the service of fiction generally.
A little more gift and a good deal more taste might have
enabled Mrs. Trollope to do really great things in it: but
she left them for her son to accomplish. Attempts and
" tries " at it had been made constantly, and the goal had
been very nearly reached, especially, perhaps, in that now
much forgotten but remarkable *Emilia Wyndham* (1846)
by Anne Caldwell (Mrs. Marsh), which was wickedly
described by a sister novelist as the " book where the
woman breaks her desk open with her head," but which
has real power and exercised real influence for no short
time.

This new domestic novel followed Miss Austen in that it
did not necessarily avail itself of anything but perfectly

ordinary life, and relied chiefly on artistic presentment—on treatment rather than on subject. It departed from her in that it admitted a much wider range and variety of subject itself; and by no means excluded the passions and emotions which, though she had not been so prudish as to ignore their results, she had never chosen to represent in much actual exercise, or to make the mainsprings of her books.

The first supreme work of the kind was perhaps in *Vanity Fair* and *Pendennis*, the former admitting exceptional and irregular developments as an integral part of its plot and general appeal, the latter doing for the most part without them. But *Pendennis* exhibited in itself, and taught to other novelists, if not an absolutely new, a hitherto little worked, and clumsily worked, source of novel interest. We have seen how, as early as Head or Kirkman, the possibility of making such a source out of the ways of special trades, professions, employments, and vocations had been partly seen and utilised. Defoe did it more; Smollett more still; and since the great war there had been naval and military novels in abundance, as well as novels political, clerical, sporting, and what not. But these special interests had been as a rule drawn upon too onesidedly. The eighteenth century found its mistaken fondness for episodes, inset stories, and the like, particularly convenient here: the naval, military, sporting, and other novels of the nineteenth were apt to rely too exclusively on these differences. Such things as the Oxbridge scenes and the journalism scenes of *Pendennis*—both among the most effective and popular, perhaps *the* most effective and popular, parts of the book—were almost, if not entirely, new. There had been before, and have since been, plenty of university novels, and their record has been a record of almost uninterrupted failure; there have since, if not before, *Pendennis* been several " press " novels, and their record has certainly not been a record of unbroken success. But the employment here, by genius, of such subjects for substantial *parts* of a novel was a success pure and unmixed. So, in the earlier book, the same author had shown how the most humdrum incident and the minutest painting of ordinary character could be combined with historic tragedy like that furnished by Waterloo, with domestic *drame* of the most exciting kind like the discovery of Lord Steyne's relations with Becky, or the at least suggested later crime of that ingenious and rather hardly treated little person.

Most of the writers mentioned and glanced at above took—not of course always, often, or perhaps ever in conscious following of Thackeray, but in consequence of the same " skiey influences " which worked on him—to this mixed domestic-dramatic line. And what is still more interesting, men who had already made their mark for years, in styles quite different, turned to it and adopted it. We have seen this of Bulwer, and the evidences of the change in him which are given by the " Caxton " novels. We have not yet directly dealt with another instance of almost as great interest and distinction, Charles Lever, though we have named him and glanced at his work.

Lever, who was born as early as 1806, had, it has been said, begun to write novels as early as his junior, Dickens, and had at once developed, in *Harry Lorrequer*, a pretty distinct style of his own. This style was a kind of humour-novel with abundant incident, generally with a somewhat " promiscuous " plot and with lively but externally drawn characters—the humours being furnished partly

Q

by Lever's native country, Ireland, and partly by the
traditions of the great war of which he had collected a
store in his capacity of physician to the Embassy at
Brussels. He had kept up this style, the capital example
of which is *Charles O'Malley* (1840), with unabated *verve*
and with great popular success for a dozen years before
1850. But about that time, or rather earlier, the general
" suck " of the current towards a different kind (assisted
no doubt by the feeling that the public might be getting
tired of the other style) made him change it into studies
of a less specialised kind—of foreign travel, home life, and
the like—sketches which, in his later days still, he brought
even closer to actuality. It is true that in the long run
his popularity has depended, and will probably always
depend, on the early " rollicking " adventure books: not
only because of their natural appeal, but because there is
plenty of the other thing elsewhere, and hardly any of
this particular thing anywhere. To almost anybody, for
instance, except a very great milksop or a pedant of construction, *Charles O'Malley* with its love-making and its
fighting, its horsemanship and its horse-play, its " devilled
kidneys " [1] and its devil-may-care-ness, is a distinctly
delectable composition; and if a reasonable interval be
allowed between the readings, may be read over and over
again, at all times of life, with satisfaction. But the fact
of the author's change remains not the less historically
and symptomatically important, in connection with the
larger change of which we are now taking notice, and with
the similar phenomena observable in the work of Bulwer.

At the same time it has been pointed out that the
following of Miss Austen by no means excluded the follow-

[1] Edgar Poe has a perfectly serious and very characteristic explosion at
the prominence of these agreeable viands in the book.

ing of Scott: and that the new development included " crosses " of novel and romance, sometimes of the historical kind, sometimes not, which are of the highest, or all but the highest, interest. Early and good examples of these may be found in the work of the Brontës, Charlotte and Emily (the third sister Anne is but a pale reflection of her elders), and of Charles Kingsley. Charlotte (*b.* 1816) and Charles (*b.* 1819) were separated in their birth by but three years, Emily (*b.* 1818) and Kingsley by but one.

The curious story of the struggles of the Brontë girls to get published hardly concerns us, and Emily's work, *Wuthering Heights*,[1] is one of those isolated books which, whatever their merit, are rather ornaments than essential parts in novel history. But this is not the case with *Jane Eyre* (1847), *Shirley* (1849), *Villette* (1852), and *The Professor* (1857) (but written much earlier). These are all examples of the determination to base novels on actual life and experience. Few novelists have ever kept so close to their own part in these as Charlotte Brontë did, though she accompanied, permeated, and to a certain extent transformed her autobiography and observation by a strong romantic and fantastic imaginative element. Deprive Thackeray and Dickens of nearly all their humour and geniality, take a portion only of the remaining genius of each in the ratio of about 2 *Th.* to 1 *D.*, add a certain dash of the old terror-novel and the German fantastic tale, moisten with feminine spirit and water, and mix thoroughly: and you have something very like Charlotte Brontë. But it is necessary to add further, and it is her great glory, the perfume and atmosphere of the Yorkshire moors, which she had in not quite such perfection as her sister Emily,

---

[1] Some will have it that this was really Charlotte's: but not with much probability.

but in combination with more general novel-gift. Her actual course of writing was short, and it could probably in no case have been long; she wanted wider and, perhaps, happier experience, more literature, more man-and-woman-of-the-worldliness, perhaps a sweeter and more genial temper. But the English novel would have been incomplete without her and her sister; they are, as wholes, unlike anybody else, and if they are not exactly great they have the quality of greatness. Above all, they kept novel and romance together—a deed which is great without any qualification or drawback.

Charles Kingsley is one of the most precious documents for the cynics who say that while, if you please the public in only one way, you may possibly meet with only tolerable ingratitude; if you attempt to please it in more ways than one, you are certain to be suspected, and still more certain to have the defects of your weakest work transferred to to your best. He was a novelist, a poet, an essayist, a preacher, a historian, and a critic. His history, though less positively inaccurate than the " dead set " against him of certain notorious persons chose to represent it, was uncritical: and his criticism, sometimes acute and luminous, was decidedly unhistorical. But he was a preacher of remarkable merit, a charming and original essayist, a poet of no wide range but of true poetical quality, and a novelist of great variety and of almost the first class. He let his weakest qualities go in with his strongest in his novels, and had also the still more unfortunate tendency to " trail coats " of the most inconceivably different colours for others to tread upon. Liberals, Radicals, and Tories; Roman Catholics, High Churchmen, Low Churchmen, and No-Churchmen; sentimentalists and cynics; people who do not like literary and historical allusion, and people who

are meticulous about literary and historical accuracy—all
these and many others, if they cannot disregard flings at
their own particular tastes, fancies, and notions, are sure
to lose patience with him now and then.   Accordingly, he
has met with some exacerbated decriers, and with very
few thorough-going defenders.

Yet *almost* thoroughing-going defence is, as far as the
novels (our only direct business) are concerned, far from
difficult; and the present writer, though there are perhaps
not a dozen consecutive pages of Kingsley's novels to which,
at some point or other, he is not prepared to append the
note, " This is Bosh," is prepared also to exalt him miles
above writers whose margins he would be quite content to
leave without a single annotation of this—or any other—
kind.   In particular the variety of the books, and their
vividness, are both extraordinary.   And perhaps the
greatest notes of the novel generally, as well as those in
which the novel of this period can most successfully
challenge comparison with those of any other, are, or should
be, vividness and variety.   His books in the kind are seven;
and the absence of *replicas* among them is one of their
extraordinary features.   *Yeast*, the first (1848), and *Alton
Locke*, the second (next year), are novels of the unrest of
thought which caused and accompanied the revolutionary
movement of the period throughout Europe.   But they
are quite different in subject and treatment.   The first is
a sketch of country society, uppermost and lowermost: [1]
the second one of town-artisan and lower-trade life with
passages of university and other contrast.   Both are
young and crude enough, intentionally or unintentionally;

---

[1] It is curious to compare this (dealing as it does largely with sport) and
the " Jorrocks " series of Robert Surtees (1803-1864).   Kingsley was
nearly as practical a sportsman as Surtees: but Surtees's characters and
manners have the old artificial-picaresque quality only.

both, intentionally beyond all doubt, are fantastic and extravagant; but both are full of genius. Argemone Lavington, the heroine of *Yeast*, is, though not of the most elaborately drawn, one of the most fascinating and real heroines of English fiction; an important secondary character of the second book, the bookseller Sandy Mackaye, is one of its most successful " character-parts." Both, but especially *Yeast*, are full of admirable descriptive writing, not entirely without indebtedness to Mr. Ruskin, but very often independently carried out, and always worthy of a " place on the line " in any gallery. There is much accurate and real dialogue, not a little firm character-drawing. Above all, both are full of blood—of things lived and seen, not vamped up from reading or day-dreaming—and yet full of dreams, day and other, and full of literature. Perhaps " the malt was a little above the meal," the yeast present in more abundant quality than the substances for fermentation, but there was no lack even of these.

Hypatia—which succeeded after some interval (1853) and when the writer's Christian Socialist, Churchman-Chartist excitement had somewhat clarified itself — is a more substantial, a more ambitious, but certainly also an even more successful book. It has something of—and perhaps, though in far transposed matter, owes something to—*Esmond* in its daring blend of old and new, and it falls short of that wonderful creation. But it is almost a second to it: and, with plenty of faults, is perhaps the only classical or semi-classical novel of much value in English.

But it was in the next year, 1854, that Kingsley's work reached its greatest perfection in the brilliant historical novel of *Westward Ho !* where the glories of Elizabethan adventure and patriotism were treated with a wonderful kindred enthusiasm, with admirable narrative faculty, with a creation of character, suitable for the purpose, which is hardly inferior to that of the greatest masters, and with an even enhanced and certainly chastened exercise of the descriptive faculty above noticed. The book to some extent invited—and Kingsley availed himself of the opportunity in a far more than sufficient degree—that " coat-trailing " which, as has been said, inevitably in its turn provokes " coat-treading ": and it has been abused from various quarters. But that it is one of the very greatest of English novels next to the few supreme, impartial and competent criticism will never hesitate to allow. Of his remaining books of novel kind one was of the " eccentric " variety: the others, though full of good things, were perhaps on the whole failures. The first referred to (the second in order of appearance), *The Water Babies* (1863), is a half Rabelaisian though perfectly inoffensive *fatrasie* of all sorts of things, exceedingly delightful to fit tastes. But *Two Years Ago* (1857), though containing some fine and even really exquisite things, shows a relaxing hand on the crudity and promiscuousness which had been excusable in his two first books and had been well restrained in *Hypatia* and *Westward Ho!* by central and active interests of story and character. " Spasmodic " poetry, the Crimean War, Pre-Raphaelitism, Tractarianism, the good and bad sides of science, and divers other things make a mixture that is not sufficiently concocted and " rectified." While in the much later *Hereward the Wake* (1866), though the provocation offered to the Dryasdust kind of historian is no matter, there is a curious relapse on the old fault of incorporating too much history or pseudo-history, and the same failure as in *Two Years Ago*, or perhaps a greater one in degree, to concoct the story (which is little more than a chronicle) together with a certain neglect to conciliate the sympathies of the reader. But the whole batch is a memorable collection; and it shows, rather exceptionally, the singular originality and variety of the novel at this time.

This remarkable pair may be supplemented by an in some ways more remarkable trio, all of them pretty close contemporaries, but, for different reasons in each case, coming rather late into the novel field—Charles Reade (*b.* 1814), Anthony Trollope (*b.* 1815), and Mary Ann Evans (*b.* 1819). It would be difficult to find three persons more different in temperament; impossible to find more striking instances of the way in which the new blend of romance and novel lent itself to the most various uses and developments. Reade—who thought himself a dramatist and wasted upon drama a great deal of energy and an almost ideal position as a possessor of an unusually rich fellowship at Magdalen College, Oxford, with no duties — came rather closer to Dickens than to any novelist previously named, not merely in a sort of non-poetic but powerful imagination, but also in the mania for attacking what seemed to him abuses—in lunatic asylums (on which point he was very nearly a monomaniac himself), prisons, and many other things. But he is almost more noteworthy, from our point of view, because of his use—it also must, one fears, be called an abuse—of a process obviously invited by the new demand for truth to life, and profitable up to a certain point. This was the collection, in enormous scrapbooks, of newspaper cuttings on a vast variety of subjects, to be worked up into fiction when the opportunity served. Reade had so much genius—he had perhaps the most, in a curious rather incalculable fashion, of the whole group—that he very nearly succeeded in digesting these " marine stores " of detail and document into real books. But he did not always, and could not always, quite do it: and he remains, with Zola, the chief example of the danger of working at your subject too much as if you were getting up a brief, or preparing an article for an encyclopædia. Still, his greatest books, which are probably *It is Never too Late to Mend* (1856) and *The Cloister and the Hearth* (1861), have immense vigour and, in the second case, an almost poetic attraction which Dickens never reaches, while over all sparks and veins of genius are scattered. Moreover, he is interesting because, until his own time, he would have been quite impossible; and, even at that time, without the general movement which we are describing, very unlikely.

There is not so much object here in discussing the much discussed question of the merits and defects of " George Eliot " (Mary Ann Evans or Mrs. Cross) as a novelist, as there is in pointing out her relations to this general movement. She began late, and almost accidentally; and there is less unity in her general work than in some others here mentioned. Her earliest and perhaps, in adjusted and " reduced " judgments, her best work—*Scenes of Clerical Life* (1857-1858), *Adam Bede* (1859), *The Mill on the Floss* (1860), *Silas Marner* (1861)—consists of very carefully observed and skilfully rendered studies of country life and character, tinged, especially in *Adam Bede* and *The Mill on the Floss*, with very intense and ambitious colours of passion. The great popularity of this tempted her into still more elaborate efforts of different kinds. Her attempt in quasi-historical romance, *Romola* (1865), was an enormous *tour de force* in which the writer struggled to get historical and local colour, accurate and irreproachable, with all the desperation of the most conscientious relater of actual history. *Felix Holt the Radical* (1866), *Middle March* (1872), and *Daniel Deronda* (1876) were equally elaborate sketches of modern English society, planned and engineered with the same provision of carefully laboured plot, character, and phrase. Although received with enthusiasm by the partisans whom she had created for herself, these books have seemed to some *over*-laboured, and if not exactly unreal, yet to a certain extent unnatural. But the point for us is their example of the way in which the novel—once a light and almost frivolous thing—had come to be taken with the utmost seriousness—had in fact ceased to be light literature at all, and begun to require rigorous and elaborate training and preparation in the writer, perhaps even something of the athlete's processes in the reader. Its state may or may not have advanced in grace *pari passu* with the advance in effort and in dignity: but this later advance is at least there. Fielding himself took novel-writing by no means lightly, and Richardson still less so: but imagine either, imagine Scott or even Miss Austen, going through the preliminary processes which seemed necessary, in different ways, to Charles Reade and to Mary Ann Evans!

In a certain sense, however, the last of the three, though he may give less impression of genius than the other two (or even the other four whom we have specially noticed), is the most interesting of all: and qualms may sometimes arise as to whether genius is justly denied to him. Anthony Trollope, after a youth, not exactly *orageuse*, but apparently characterised by the rather squalid yet mild dissipation which he has described in *The Three Clerks* (1858) and *The Small House at Allington* (1864), attained a considerable position in the Post Office which he held during great part of his career as a novelist. For some time that career did not look as if it were going to be a successful one, though his early (chiefly Irish) efforts are better than is sometimes thought. But he made his mark first with

The Warden (1855), and then, much more directly and triumphantly, with its sequel *Barchester Towers* (1857). When the first of these was published Dickens had been a successful novelist for nearly twenty years and Thackeray had " come to his own " for nearly ten. *The Warden* might have been described at the time (I do not know whether it was, but English reviewing was only beginning to be clever again) as a partial attempt at the matter of Dickens in a partial following of the manner of Thackeray. An " abuse "—the distribution in supposed unjust proportion of the funds of an endowed hospital for aged men— is its main avowed subject.   But Trollope indulged in no tirades and no fantastic-grotesque caricature—in fact he actually drew a humorous sketch of a novel *à la Dickens* on the matter.   His real object was evidently to sketch faithfully, but again not without humour, the cathedral society of " Barchester " as it actually spoke, dressed, thought, and lived: and he did it.   The first book had a little too much talk about the nominal subject, and not enough actual action and conversation. *Barchester Towers* remedied this, and presented its readers with one of the liveliest books in English fiction.   There had been nothing like it (for Thackeray had been more discursive and less given to small talk) since Miss Austen herself, though the spirits of the two were extremely different.   Perhaps Trollope never did a better book than this, for variety and vigour of character drawing.   The masterful wife of Bishop Proudie, the ne'er-do-weel canon's family (the Stanhopes), and others stand out against an interest, not intense but sufficient, of story, a great variety of incident, and above all abundant and lifelike conversation.   For many years, and in an extraordinary number of examples, he fell little below, and perhaps once or twice went above, this standard.   It was rather a fancy

of his (one again, perhaps, suggested by Thackeray) to run
his books into series or cycles—the chief being that actually opened as above, and continuing through others to the
brilliant *Last Chronicle of Barset* (1867), which in some
respect surpasses *Barchester Towers* itself, with a second
series, not quite disconnected, dealing with Lady Glencora
Palliser as centre, and yet others. His total production
was enormous: it became in fact impossibly so, and the
work of his last *lustrum* and a little more (say 1877-1882),
though never exactly bad or painful to read, was obvious
hack-work. But between *The Warden* and *The American
Senator*, twenty-two years later, he had written nearer
thirty than twenty novels, of which at least half were much
above the average and some quite capital.[1] Moreover, it is
a noteworthy thing, and contrary to some critical explanations, that, as his works drop out of copyright and are
reprinted in cheap editions, they appear to be recovering
very considerable popularity. This fact would seem to
show that the manners, speech, etc., represented in them
have a certain standard quality which does not—like the
manner, speech, etc., of novels such as those of Hook and
Surtees—lose appeal to fresh generations; and that the
artist who dealt with them must have had not a little
faculty of fixing them in the presentation. In fact it is
probably not too much to say that of the *average* novel of
the third quarter of the century—in a more than average
but not of an extraordinary, transcendental, or quintessential
condition—Anthony Trollope is about as good a representative as can be found. His talent is individual enough,

---

[1] His most ambitious studies in strict *character* are the closely connected
heroines of *The Bertrams* (1859) and *Can you Forgive Her ?* (1864-1865). But
the first-named book has never been popular; and the other hardly owes
its popularity to the heroine.

but not too individual: system and writer may each have the credit due to them allotted without difficulty.

A novelist who might have been in front of the first flight of these in point of time, and who is actually put by some in the first flight in point of merit, is Mrs. Gaskell. Born in 1810, she accumulated the material for her future *Cranford* at Knutsford in Cheshire: but did not publish this till after Dickens had, in 1850, established *Household Words*, where it appeared in instalments. She had a little earlier, in 1848, published her first novel, *Mary Barton*—a vivid but distinctly one-sided picture of factory life in Lancashire. In the same year with the collected *Cranford* (1853) appeared *Ruth*, also a " strife-novel " (as the Germans would say) though in a different way: and two years later what is perhaps her most elaborate effort, *North and South*. A year or two before her death in 1865 *Sylvia's Lovers* was warmly welcomed by some: and the unfinished *Wives and Daughters*, which was actually interrupted by that death, has been considered her maturest work. Her famous and much controverted *Life of Charlotte Brontë* does not belong to us, except in so far as it knits the two novelists together.

From hints dropped already, it may be seen that the present writer does not find Mrs. Gaskell his easiest subject. There is much in her work which, in Hobbes's phrase, is both " an effect of power and a cause of pleasure ": but there appears to some to be in her a pervading want of actual success—of *réussite*—absolute and unquestionable. The sketches of *Cranford* are very agreeable and very admirable performances in the manner first definitely thrown out by Addison, and turned to consummate perfection in the way of the regular novel (which be it remembered *Cranford* is not) by Miss Austen. But the mere mention of the last name kills them. The author of *Emma* would have treated Miss Matty and the rest much less lovingly, but she would have made them persons. Mrs. Gaskell has left them mere types of amiable country-townishness in respectable if not very lively times. Excessive respectability cannot be charged against *Mary Barton* and *Ruth*, but here the " problem "—the " purpose"—interposes its evil influence: and we have got to take a side with men or with masters, with selfish tempters of one class and deluded maidens of another. *North and South* is perhaps on the whole the best place in which to study Mrs. Gaskell's art: for *Wives and Daughters* is unfinished and the books just named are tentatives. It begins by laying a not inconsiderable hold on the reader: and, as it is worked out at great length, the author has every opportunity of strengthening and improving that hold. It is certain that, in some cases, she does not do this: and the reason is the same— the failure to project and keep in action definite and independent characters, and the attempt to make weight and play with purposes and problems. The heroine's father—who resigns his living and exposes his delicate wife and only daughter, if not exactly to privation, to discomfort and, in the wife's case, fatally unsuitable surroundings, because of some never clearly defined dissatisfaction with the creed of the Church (*not* apparently with Christianity as such or with Anglicanism as such), and who dies " promiscuously," to be followed, in equally promiscuous fashion, by a friend who leaves his daughter Margaret a fortune—is one of those nearly contemptible imbeciles in whom it is impossible to take an interest. In respect to the wife Mrs. Gaskell commits the curious mistake of first suggesting that she is a complainer about nothing, and then showing her to us as a suffering victim of her husband's folly and of hopeless disease. The lover (who is to a great extent a replica of the masterful mill-owner in *Shirley*) is uncertain and impersonal: and the minor characters are null. One hopes, for a time, that Margaret herself will save the situation: but she goes off instead of coming on, and has rather less individuality and convincingness at the end of the story than at the beginning. In short, Mrs. Gaskell seems to me one of the chief illustrations of the extreme difficulty of the domestic novel—of the necessity of exactly proportioning the means at command to the end to be achieved. Her means were, perhaps, greater than those of most of her brother-and-sister-novelists, but she set them to loose ends, to ends too high for her, to ends not worth achieving: end thus produced (again as it seems to me) flawed and unsatisfactory work. She " means " well in Herbert's sense of the word: but what is meant is not quite done.

To mention special books and special writers is not the first object of this survey, though it would be very easy to double and redouble its size by doing this, even within the time-limits of this, the last, and the next chapters. It may, however, be added that in this remarkable central period, and in the most central part of it from 1840 to 1860, there appeared the first remarkable novel of Mr. George Meredith, *The Ordeal of Richard Feverel* (1859), first of a brilliant series that was to illustrate the whole remaining years of the century; and the isolated masterpiece of *Phantastes*, which another prolific writer, George Macdonald, was never to repeat; while Mrs. Oliphant and Mrs. Craik, both of whom will also reappear in the next chapter, began as early as 1849. In 1851 appeared the first of two remarkable books, *Lavengro* and *The Romany Rye*, in which George Borrow, if he did not exactly create, brought to perfection from some points of view what may be called the autobiographic novel.

Indeed the memory of the aged and the industry of the young could recall or rediscover dozens and scores of noteworthy books, some of which have not lost actual or traditional reputation, such as the *Paul Ferroll* (1855) of Mrs. Archer Clive, a well-restrained crime-novel, the story of which is indicated in the title of its sequel, *Why Paul Ferroll killed his Wife*. Henry Kingsley, George Alfred Lawrence, Wilkie Collins, and others began their careers at this time. The best book ever written about school, *Tom Brown's School Days* (1857), and the best book in lighter vein ever written about Oxford, *Mr. Verdant Green* (1853-1856), both appeared in the fifties.

Although, indeed, the intenser and more individual genius of the great novelists of this time went rather higher than the specialist novel, it was, in certain directions, well cultivated during this period. Men likely to write naval novels of merit were dying out, and though Lever took up the military tale, at second hand, with brilliant results, the same historical causes were in operation there. But a comparatively new kind—the "sporting" novel—developed itself largely and in some cases went beyond mere sport. Such early books as Egan's *Tom and Jerry* (1821) can hardly be called novels: but as the love of sport extended and the term itself ceased to designate merely on the one side the pleasures of country squires, and on the other the amusements (sometimes rather blackguard in character) of men about town, the general subject made a lodgment in fiction. One of its most characteristic practitioners was Robert Smith Surtees, who, before Dickens and perhaps acting as suggester of the original plan of *Pickwick* (*not* that which Dickens substituted), excogitated (between 1831 and 1838) the remarkable fictitious personage of " Mr. Jorrocks," grocer and sportsman, whose adventures, and those of other rather hybrid characters of the same kind, he pursued through a number of books for some thirty years. These (though in strict character, and in part of their manners, deficient as above noticed) were nearly always readable—and sometimes very amusing—even to those who are not exactly Nimrods: and they were greatly commended to others still by the admirable illustrations of Leech. There is not a little sound sport in Kingsley and afterwards in Anthony Trollope: while the novels of Frank Smedley, *Frank Fairlegh* (1850), *Lewis Arundel* (1852), and *Harry Coverdale's Courtship* (1855), mix a good deal more of it with some good fun and some rather rococo romance. The subject became, indeed, very popular in the fifties, and entered largely into, though it by no means exclusively occupied, the novels of George John Whyte-Melville, a Fifeshire gentleman, an Etonian, and a guardsman, who, after retiring from the army, served again in the Crimean War, and, after writing a large number of novels, was killed in the hunting field. Some of Whyte-Melville's books, such as *Market Harborough* (1861), are hunting novels pure and simple, so much so that it has been said (rashly) that none but hunting men and women can read them. Others, such as *Kate Coventry* (1856), a very lively and agreeable book, mix sport with general character and manners-painting. Others, such as *Holmby House* (1860), *The Queen's Maries* (1862), etc., attempt the historical style. But perhaps this mixed novel of sport, society, and a good deal of love-making reached its most curious development in the novels of George Alfred Lawrence, from the once famous *Guy Livingstone* (1857) onwards—a series almost typical, which was developed further, with touches of original but

R

uncritical talent, which often dropped into unintentional caricature, by the late " Ouida " (Louise de La Ramée). All the three last writers mentioned, however, especially the last two, made sport only an ingredient in their novel composition (" Ouida," in fact, knew nothing about it) and at least endeavoured, according to their own ideas and ideals, to grapple with larger parts of life. The danger of the kind showed less in them than in some imitators of a lower class, of whom Captain Hawley Smart was the chief, and a chief sometimes better than his own followers. Some even of his books are quite interesting: but in a few of them, and in more of other writers, the obligation to tell something like a story and to provide something like characters seems to be altogether forgotten. A run (or several runs) with the hounds, a steeplechase and its preparations and accidents, one at least of the great races and the training and betting preliminary to them—these form the real and almost the sole staple of story; so that a tolerably intelligent office-boy could make them up out of a number or two of the *Field*, a sufficient list of proper names, and a commonplace book of descriptions. This, in fact, is the danger of the specialist novel generally: though perhaps it does not show quite so glaringly in other cases. Yet, even here, that note of the fiction of the whole century—its tendency to " accaparate " and utilise all the forms of life, all the occupations and amusements of mankind—shows itself notably enough.

So, too, one notable book has, here even more than elsewhere, often set going hosts of imitations. *Tom Brown's School Days*, for instance (1857), flooded the market with school stories, mostly very bad. But there is one division which did more justice to a higher class of subject and produced some very remarkable work in what is called the religious novel, though, here as elsewhere, the better examples did not merely harp on one string.

A very interesting off-shoot of the domestic novel, ignored or despised by the average critic and rather perfunctorily treated even by those who have taken it as a special subject, is the " Tractarian " or High-Church novel, which, originating very shortly after the movement itself had began, had no small share in popularising it. The earlier Evangelicals had by no means neglected fiction as a means of propagating their views, especially among the young. Mrs. Sherwood in *Little Henry and his Bearer* and *The Fairchild Family* (1818) and " Charlotte Elizabeth " (Browne or Tonna) are examples. But the High-Church party, in accordance with its own predecessors and patterns in the seventeenth century, always maintained, during its earlier and better period, a higher standard of scholarship and of general literary culture. Its early efforts in fiction— according to the curious and most interesting law which seems to decree that every subdivision of a kind shall go through something like the vicissitudes of the kind at large —were not strictly novels but romance, and romance of the allegorical kind. In the late thirties and early forties the allegorists, the chief of whom were Samuel Wilberforce and William Adams, were busy and effective. The future bishop's *Agathos* (before 1840) is a very spirited and well-written adaptation of the " whole armour of God " theme so often re-allegorised: and Adams's *Shadow of the Cross* is only the best of several good stories—of a rather more feminine type, but graceful, sound enough in a general way, and combining the manners of Spenser and Bunyan with no despicable skill. If, however, the Tractarian fiction-writers had confined themselves to allegory there would be no necessity to do more than glance at them, for allegory, on the obvious Biblical suggestion, has been a constant instrument of combined religious instruction and pastime. But they went much further afield. Sometimes the excursions were half satirical, as in the really amusing *Owlet of Owlstone Edge* and *The Curate of Cumberworth and the Vicar of Roost* of Francis Paget, attacking the slovenly neglect and supineness which, quite as much as unsound doctrine, was the *bête noire* of the early Anglo-Catholics. William Gresley and others wrote stories mostly for the young. But the distinguishing feature of the school, and that which gives it an honourable and more than an honorary place here, was the shape which, before the middle of the century, it took in the hands of two ladies, Elizabeth Sewell and Charlotte Mary Yonge.

The first, who was the elder but survived Miss Yonge and died at a very great age quite recently, had much less talent than her junior: but undoubtedly deserves the credit of setting the style. In her novels (*Gertrude*, *Katharine Ashton*, etc.) she carried, even farther than Miss Austen, the principle of confining herself rigidly to the events of ordinary life. Not that she eschews the higher middle or even the higher classes: though, on the other hand, Katharine Ashton, evidently one of her favourite heroines, is the daughter of a shopkeeper. But the law of average and ordinary character, incident, atmosphere, is observed almost invariably. Unfortunately Miss Sewell (she was actually a schoolmistress) let the didactic part of her novels get rather too much the upper hand: and though she wrote good English, possessed no special grace of style, and little faculty of illustration or ornament from history, literature, her own fancy, current fashions, even of the most harmless kind, and so forth. The result is that her books have a certain dead-aliveness—that the characters, though actually alive, are neither interestingly alive nor, as Miss Austen had made hers, interesting in their very uninterestingness. Sometimes, for a scene or two, her truth to nature and fact is rewarded by that curious sense of recognition which the reader feels in the presence of actual *mimesis*—of creation of fictitious fact and person. But this is not common: and the epithet " dull," which too commonly only stigmatises the person using it, may really suggest itself not seldom in reference to Miss Sewell. A " success of esteem " is about the utmost that can be accorded her.

With Miss Yonge the case was very different. She was a lady of wide reading and, even according to the modern rather arbitrary restrictions of the term, something of an historical scholar; she had humour, of which there was scarcely a particle in Miss Sewell's composition; she had a very considerable understanding, and consequently some toleration of the infinite varieties, and at least the more venial foibles, of human temperament. She possessed an inexhaustible command of dialogue which was always natural and sometimes very far from trivial; and if she had no command of the greater novelists' imagination in the creation of character and story, she had an almost uncanny supply of invention, of what may be called the second or third class, in these respects. She wrote too much and too long; but it cannot be said that she ever merely repeated herself. And her best books—the famous *Heir of Redclyffe* (1853), which captivated William Morris and his friends at Oxford, and which, with a little unnecessary sentimentality and a little " unco-guidness," is full of cleverness, nature, good sense, good taste, and good form; *Heartsease* (1854), perhaps the best of all; *Dynevor Terrace* (1857), less of a general favourite but full of good things; and the especially popular *Daisy Chain* (1856), with not a few others—are things which no courageous and catholic critic of fiction will ever be tired of defending or (which is not always the same thing) of reading.   Some of her early tales, before these, were a little " raw ": and most of her later work showed (as did Anthony Trollope's and that of other though not all very prolific novelists) that the field had been overcropped.   But she was hardly ever dull: and she always had that quality—if not of the supreme artist, of the real craftsman—which prevents a thing from being a failure.   What is meant is done: though perhaps it might have been meant higher.

The comparison, backwards and forwards, of this great company of novels is of endless interest; perhaps one of many aspects of that interest may be touched on specially, because it connects itself with much else that has been said. If we read, together or in near sequence, three such books as, say, *Emilia Wyndham*, *Pendennis*, and *Yeast*, all of which appeared close together, between 1846 and 1849, the differences, in quality and volume of individual genius, will of course strike every one forcibly.   But some will also be struck by something else—the difference between the first and the other two in *style* or (as that word is almost hope- lessly ambiguous) let us perhaps say *diction*.   Both Thackeray and Kingsley are almost perfectly modern in this.   We may not speak so well to-day, and we may have added more slang and jargon to our speech, but there is no real differ- ence, except in these respects, between a speech of Pen's (when not talking book) or one of Colonel Bracebridge's, and the speech of any gentleman who is a barrister or a guardsman at this hour.   The excellent Mrs. Marsh had not arrived at that point; what some people call the " stilted " forms and phrases of fifty or almost a hundred years earlier clung to her still.   The resulting lingo is far better than that part of the lingo of to-day where literary and linguistic good manners have been forgotten altogether: but it is distinctly deficient in *ease*. There are endless flourishes and periphrases—the colloquialisms which Swift and others had denounced (and quite properly) in their ugliest and vulgarest forms are not even permitted entrance in improved and warranted varieties. You must never say "won't" but always "will not," whereas the ability to use the two forms adds infinite propriety as well as variety to the dialogue. You say, "At length a most unfortunate accident aggravated (if aggravation were possible) the unfortunate circumstances of the situation." You address your own characters in the oratorical manner of Mr. Burke and other great men, "Ah, Mr. Danby! if instead, etc." In short, instead of reserving the grand manner (and a rather different grand manner) for grand occasions, you maintain a sort of cheap machine-made kind of it throughout. The real secret of the novel was not found out till this was discarded. Perhaps that real secret does not lie so much anywhere else as here.

A few words may not improperly be said about some of the circumstances and details of novel-appearance and distribution, etc., at this palmy day of English fiction. At what time the famous "three-decker" was consecrated as the regular novel line-of-battle-ship I have not been able to determine exactly to my own satisfaction. Richardson had extended his interminable narrations to seven or eight volumes: Miss Burney latterly had not been content with less than five. From the specimens I have examined, I have an idea that with the "Minerva Press" and its contemporaries and successors at the end of the eighteenth and beginning of the nineteenth century, *four* was a very favourite if not the most usual number. But these volumes were usually small—not much larger than those of the Belgian reprints of Dumas which, as one remembers, used to run into the dozen or something like it in the case of his longer books. Three, however, has obvious advantages; the chief of them being the adjustment to "beginning, middle, and end," though there is a corresponding disadvantage which soon developed itself—and in fact, finally, I have no doubt helped to ruin the form—the temptation to make the *second* volume a place of mere padding. But the actual popularity of "the old three-decker" continued for quite two generations, if not more, and was unmistakable. Library subscriptions were generally adjusted to it; and any circulating-library keeper would tell you that, putting this quite aside, even subscribers to more or fewer volumes than three would take the three-volume by preference. More than this, still, there is a curious fact necessarily known to comparatively few people. Although it was improper of Mr. Bludyer to sell his novel, and dine and drink of the profits before "smashing" it, there were probably not many reviewers who did not get rid of most of their books of this kind, if for no other reasons than that no house, short of a palace, would have held them all. And, in the palmy days of circulating libraries, the price given by second-hand booksellers for novels made a very considerable addition to the reviewer's remuneration or guerdon. But these booksellers would not pay, in proportion, for two or one volume books—alleging, what no doubt was true, that the libraries had a lower tariff for them. Further, the short story, now so popular, was very *un*popular in those days: and library customers would refuse collections of them with something like indignation or disgust. Indeed, there are reviewers living who may perhaps pride themselves on having done something to drive the dislike out and the liking in.

The circulating library itself, though not the creation of the novel, was very largely extended by it, and helped no doubt very largely to extend the circulation of the novel in turn. Before it, to some extent, and long before so-called " public " or " free " libraries, books in general and novels in particular had been very largely diffused by clubs, " institutions," and other forms of co-operative individual enterprise, the bookplates of which will be found in many a copy of an old novel now. Sometimes these were purely private associations of neighbours: sometimes they belonged to more or less extensive establishments, like that defunct " Russell Institution in Great Coram Street," which a great author, who was its neighbour, once took for an example of desolation; or the still existing and flourishing " Philosophical " examples in Edinburgh and Bath. In these latter cases, of course, novels were not allowed to be the main constituents of the library; in fact in some, but few, they may have been sternly excluded. On the other hand, the private-adventure circulating libraries tended more and more, with few exceptions, to rely on novels only—" Mudie's " and a few more being exceptions. Very few people, I suppose, ever bought three-volume novels; and the fact that they went almost wholly to the libraries, and were there worn to pieces, accounts for the comparative rarity of good copies. The circulating library has survived both the decease of the three-volume novel and the competition of the so-called free library. But it is pretty certain that it was a chief cause— and almost the whole *sustaining* cause—of the three-volume system itself. Nor was the connection between nature of form and system of distribution limited to England: for the single-volume novel, though older in France than with us, is not so very old.

But a very considerable proportion of these famous books made appearances previous to that in three volumes, and not distantly connected with their popularity. For the most part these previous appearances were either in magazines or periodicals of one kind and another, or else in " parts."

Neither process was exactly new, though both were largely affected by changed conditions of general literature and life. The magazine-appearance traces itself, by almost insensible gradations, to the original periodical-essay of the Steele-Addison type—the small individual bulk of which necessitated division of whatsoever was not itself on a very small scale. If you run down the " Contents " of the *British Essayists* you will constantly find " Continuation of the story of Alonso and Imoinda " and the like. But when, in the early years of the nineteenth century, the system of newspapers and periodicals branched out into endless development, coincidently with the increase of demand and supply in regard to the novel, it was inevitable that this latter should be drawn upon to supply at once the standing dishes and the relishes of the entertainment. *Blackwood* and the *London*, the first fruits of the new kind, did not at once take to the novel by instalments: and the *London* had no time to do so. But *Blackwood* soon became celebrated—a reputation which it has never lost—for the excellence of its short stories, and by degrees took to long ones; while its followers—*Fraser*, *Bentley's Miscellany*, *The Dublin University Magazine*, the *New Monthly*, and others—almost from the first bated their hooks with this new *appât*. A very large proportion of the work of the novelists mentioned in the last chapter, as well as of Lever, appeared in one or other of these. *Fraser* in particular was Thackeray's chief refuge in the Days of Ignorance of the public as to his real powers and merits, while, just as he was going off, the very different work of Kingsley came on there. And the tradition, as is well known, has never been broken. The particular magazines may have died in some cases: but the magazine-appearance of novels is nearly as vivacious as ever.

Publication in parts is nearly as old, but has a less continuous history, and has seen itself suffer an interruption of life. There are scattered examples of it pretty far back both in France and England. Marivaux had a particular fancy for it: with the result that he left not a little of his work unfinished. Such volume-publication as that of *Tristram Shandy*, in batches really small in quantity and at fairly regular if long intervals, is not much different from part-issue. As the taste for reading spread to classes with not much ready money, and perhaps, in some cases, living at a distance from libraries, this taste spread too. But I do not think there can be much doubt that the immense success of Dickens—in combination with his own very distinct predilection for keeping the ring himself and being his own editor—had most to do with its prevalence during the period under present consideration. Thackeray took up the practice from him: as well as others both from him and from Thackeray. The great illustrators, too, of the forties, fifties, and sixties, from Cruikshank and Browne to Frederick Walker, were partly helped by the system, partly helped to make it popular. But the circulating libraries did not like it for obvious reasons, the parts being fragile and unsubstantial: and the great success of cheap magazines, on the pattern of *Macmillan's* and the *Cornhill*, cut the ground from under its feet. The last remarkable novel that I remember seeing in the form was *The Last Chronicle of Barset*. *Middlemarch* and *Daniel Deronda* came out in parts which were rather volumes than parts.

This piece-meal publication, whether in part or periodical, could not be without some effects on the character of the production. These were neither wholly good nor wholly bad. They served to some extent to correct the tendency, mentioned above, of the three-volume novel to "go to seed" in the middle—to become a sort of preposterous sandwich with meat on the outsides and a great slab of ill-baked and insipid bread between. For readers would not have stood this in instalments: you had to provide some bite or promise of bite in each—if possible—indeed to leave each off at an interesting point. But this itself rather tended to a jumpy and ill-composed whole — to that mechanical shift from one part of the plot to another which is so evident, for instance, in Trollope: and there was worse temptation behind. If a man had the opportunity, the means, the courage, and the artistic conscience necessary to finish his work before any part of it appeared, or at least to scaffold it thoroughly throughout in advance, no harm was done. But perhaps there is no class of people with whom the temptation—common enough in every class—of hand-to-mouth work is more fatal than with men of letters. It is said that even the clergy are human enough to put off their sermon-writing till Saturday, and what can be expected of the profane man, especially when he has a whole month apparently before him? It is pretty certain that Thackeray succumbed to this temptation: and so did a great many people who could much less afford to do so than Thackeray. It was almost certainly responsible for part of the astonishing medley of repetitions and lapses in Lever: and I am by no means sure that some of Dickens's worst faults, especially the ostentatious plot-

that-is-no-plot of such a book as *Little Dorrit*—the plot
which marks time with elaborate gesticulation and really
does not advance at all—were not largely due to the system.

Let it only be added that these expensive forms of
publication by no means excluded cheap reprints as soon
as a book was really popular. The very big people kept
up their prices: but everybody else was glad to get into
" popular libraries," yellow-backed railway issues, and the
like, as soon as possible.

It will have been seen that the present writer puts the
novel of 1845-1870 very high: he would indeed put it, in
its own compartment, almost on a level with the drama of
1585-1625 or the poems of 1798-1825. Just at the present
moment there may be a pretty general tendency to consider this allowance exaggerated if not preposterous: and to
set it down to the well-known foible of age for the period of
its own youth. There is no need to do more than suggest that
those who were young when Shakespeare, or when Byron,
died, would not have been exactly in their dotage if, forty
years later, they had extolled the literature of their nonage.
One does not care to dwell long on such a point: but it
may just be observed that the present writer's withers are
hardly even pinched, let alone wrung, by the strictest application, to his case, of this rather idle notion. For some of
what he is praising as the best novels were written before
he was born; many while he was in the nursery; most
before he had left school, and practically all before he had
ceased to be an undergraduate. Now acute observers
know that what may be called the disease of contemporary
partisanship rarely even begins till the undergraduate
period, and is at its severest from twenty-five to thirty-five.
I would undertake that most of our reviewers who discover
Shakespeares and Sainte-Beuves, improved Thackerays

and bettered Molières, week by week or day by day, count their years between these limits. *Beati illi* from some points of view, but from others, if they go on longer, Heaven help them indeed!

But all this is really idle. A critic is not right or wrong because he is young or old as the case may be; because he follows the taste of his age or runs counter to it; because he likes the past or because he likes the present. He is right or wrong according as he does or does not like the right things in the right way. And it is a simple historical fact, capable now of being seen in a proper perspective, and subjected to the proper historical tests, that, in the large sense, the two generations from the appearance of Scott and Miss Austen to the death of Dickens (and considering the ebb which followed Scott and Miss Austen themselves, specially the latter of these two), supplied the spring tide of the novel-flood, the flower-time of its flowering season, the acme of its climax.

The comparison, both in the longer and shorter time, to the great summer of the drama may be too complimentary—I do not think it is, except in so far as that drama necessarily involved poetry, a higher thing by far than either drama itself or novel—but it is certainly not an altogether comfortable one. For we know that the drama, thereafter, has never had a more than galvanised life, except in the imagination of the gentlemen who discover Shakespeares and Molières as aforesaid. And there are those who say that, not only at the moment, but for some time past, the state of the novel is, and has been, not much more promising. The student who is thoroughly broken to the study of literary history is never a pessimist, though he may be very rarely an optimist: for the one thing of which he should be thoroughly convinced is its

incalculableness. But he might admit—while reserving
unlimited trust in the Wind of the Spirit and its power to
blow exactly as it listeth, and to awaken the dryest of
dry bones—that circumstances are not incompatible with
something like a decay in the novel: just as they were
with a decay in the drama. The state of society and temper
in the late sixteenth and early seventeenth century—
enthusiastic; not too well regulated; stirred at once by
the sinking force of the mediæval and the rising force of
the modern spirit; full of religious revival which had
happily not gone wholly wrong, as it had in some other
countries; finding ready to its hand a language which had
cast most of its sloughs of accidence and prosody, and was
fresh, limber, ready for anything; enterprising but not
buried in business—was favourable to the rise and flourishing of this disorderly abundance of dramatic creation—
tragic, comic, and in all the varieties that *Hamlet* cata-
logues or satirises. The mid-nineteenth century had something of the same hot-bed characteristic, though sufficiently
contrasted and fitted to produce a different growth. It
had, if at a little distance, the inspiriting memory of a great
war, where the country had taken the most glorious part
possible. It also had a great religious revival, which had
taken no coarse or vulgar form. Although the middle class
had seized, and the lower classes were threatening to seize,
the government, even the former had not monopolised the
helm. There was in society, though it was not strait-
laced or puritanical, a general standard of " good form."
Scholarship and knowledge of literature had not yet been
exchanged for " education " and ignorance of letters.
The national fancy for sport was in about its healthiest
condition, emerging from one state of questionableness
and not yet plunged in another. The chair of the chief of

the kinds of literature—poetry—which always exercises a singular influence over the lower forms, was still worthily occupied and surrounded. And, above all, the appetite for the novel was still eager, fresh, and not in the least sated, jaded, or arrived at that point when it has to be whetted by asafœtida on the plates or cigarettes between the courses. Few better atmospheres could be even imagined for the combined novel - romance — the story which, while it did not exclude the adventurous or even the supernatural in one sense, insisted on the rational in another, and opened its doors as wide as possible to every subject, or combination of subjects, that would undertake to be interesting. That the extraordinary reply made by genius and talent to the demand thus created and encouraged should last indefinitely could not be expected: that the demand itself should lead to overproduction and glut was certain. But, as we shall see, there was no sudden decadence; the period even of best or nearly best production went on with no important intermission; and was but yesterday still represented by two great names, is still represented by one, among the older writers, by more than one or two names of credit among the middle-aged and younger. To these in some degree, and to those who have finished their career in the last thirty years to a greater, we must now turn.

CHAPTER VIII

IN regard to a large part of the subject of the present chapter the present writer possesses the knowledge of a reviewer, week by week and almost day by day, of contemporary fiction between 1873 and 1895. It so happened that the beginning of this period coincided very nearly with the beginning of that slightly downward movement of the nineteenth-century novel which has been referred to at the end of the last chapter: and he thus had opportunities of observing it all along its course, till we parted company. It must again, and most strongly, be insisted that this " downward movement," like such movements generally in literature, is only so to be characterised with considerable provisos and allowances. Literary " down-grades " are not like the slopes of an inclined plane: they are like portions of a mountain range, in which isolated peaks may shoot up almost level with the very highest of the central group, but in which the table lands are lower, the *average* height of the hills inferior, and the general sky-line a nearer and nearer approximation to the plain. At the actual death of Dickens there was no reason for any one less hopelessly pessimist than Peacock's Mr. Toobad, or Sydney Smith's Tuxford waiter, to take a gloomy view of the future of the novel. Of the greater novelists mentioned in the last chapter Charlotte Brontë and Mrs. Gaskell were indeed dead, and if Kingsley had not wholly ceased writing novels, he had, before ceasing, given signs that he had better do so. Yet, at least to the admirers of "George Eliot," she was at her most admirable; some of the very best stuff of Trollope was but just past, and some of all but his best was still to appear; Charles Reade was writing busily with that curious unsatisfactory genius of his; others were well at work.

There was also no lack of newer comers. Mr. Meredith had been writing for some dozen years: and though he had achieved no general popularity, though even critics might make reserves as to points in his procedure, there could be no competent doubt of his great powers. Mr. Blackmore had made his late beginning some time before: and had just caught the public ear unmistakably with *Lorna Doone* (1869). Mr. Hardy was on the eve of catching it with the new and powerful attractions of *Under the Greenwood Tree* (1872). In the heart of the sixties (1863-4-6), the *Chronicles of Carlingford* had seemed the promissory notes of a novelist of the absolutely first class in Mrs. Oliphant, though somehow the bills were rather renewed than met. Others to be noticed immediately had come or were coming on. Let us take a little more detailed notice of them.

In the cases of Mr. Meredith and of Mr. Hardy—not to speak of others on whom the bar still luckily rests—the "great ox" was, until the original composition of this book was actually finished, "on the tongue" of any one who does not disregard the good old literary brocard "*de* vivis *nil nisi* necessarium.*" You may and must criticise, with as much freedom as consists with courtesy, the successive stages of the work of the living master as he submits it to your judgment by publication. But justice no less than courtesy demands that, until the work is finished, and sealed as a whole—till the *ne varietur* and *ne plus ultra* of death have been set on it—you shall abstain from a more general judgment, which can

hardly be judicial, and which will have difficulty in steering
between the fulsome if it be favourable and the uncivil if
it be adverse.   Fortunately there was little difficulty in any
of our three excepted cases.   As has been already hinted
in one case, the chorus of praise, ever since it made itself
heard, has not been quite unchequered.   It has been
objected both to Mr. Meredith and to Mr. Hardy that
there is in them a note, perhaps to be detected also
generally in the later fiction which they have so powerfully influenced—the note of a certain *perversity*—of an
endeavour to be peculiar in thought, in style, in choice of
subject, in handling of it; in short in general attitude.
And with this has been connected—not in their cases with
any important or really damaging effect, though undoubtedly
so in regard to some of their followers—a suggestion that
this " perversity " is the note of a waning period—
that just as the excessive desire to be *like* all the best
models is the note of Classical decadence, so the excessive
desire to be *unlike* everything else is the note of Romantic
degeneration.

There is truth in this, but it damages neither Mr.
Meredith nor Mr. Hardy on the whole; though it may
supply a not altogether wholesome temptation to some
readers to admire them for the wrong things, and may inter-
pose a wholly unnecessary obstacle in the way of their full
and frank enjoyment by others.   The intellectual power and
the artistic skill which have been shown in the long series
that has followed *The Ordeal of Richard Feverel;* the fresh-
ness and charm of the earlier, the strenuous workmanship
and original handling of the later, novels of the author of
Far from the Madding Crowd and of *Tess of the D'Urber-
villes*, simply disable off-hand the judgment of the critic—
and in fact annul his jurisdiction—if he fails to admire

them; while in some cases universal, in many general, in
all considerable and not trivial delight has been given by
them to generations of novel readers.   Above all, it may
be said of both these veterans that they have held the
standard high, that—in Mr. Meredith's case more specially
and for a longer preliminary period, but virtually in both
—they have had to await the taste for their work: and that
in awaiting it they have never stooped for one moment to
that dastardly and degrading change of sail to catch the
popular breeze, which has always been the greatest curse
of politics and of literature—the two chief worldly occupations and ends of the mind of man—that they have been
and are artists who wait till the world comes to them, and
not artisans who haunt the market places to hire themselves out to the first comer who will pay their price, or
even bate their price to suit the hirer.   If it were possible to
judge the literary value of a period by its best representatives—which is exactly what is *not* possible—then the
period 1870-1908 might, as far as novel-writing is concerned,
point to these two names and say, " These are mine; what
does it matter what you choose to say against me ? "

The foregoing remarks were actually written before Mr.
Meredith's death: and I have thought it better to leave
them exactly as they then stood with hardly any correc-
tion; but it may justly be expected that they should
now be supplemented.   The history of Mr. Meredith's
career and reputation, during the half century which
passed between the appearance of *Richard Feverel* and his
death, has a certain obvious resemblance to that of
Browning's, but with some differences.   His work at once
arrested attention, but it did not at once in all, or in many,
cases fix it, even with critical readers: and for a long time
the general public turned an obstinately deaf ear.   He

followed *The Ordeal* itself—a study of very freely and deeply drawn character; of incident sometimes unusual and always unusually told; of elaborate and disconcerting epigram or rather of style saturated with epigrammatic quality; and of a strange ironic persiflage permeating thought, picture, and expression in the same way—unhastingly but unrestingly with others. *Evan Harrington* (1861) is generally lighter in tone; and should be taken in connection with the ten years later *Harry Richmond* as an example of what may be called a sort of new picaresque novel—the subjects being exalted from the gutter—at least the street gutter—to higher stories of the novel house. *Emilia in England* (1864), later called *Sandra Belloni,* and its sequel *Vittoria* (1866), embody, especially the latter, the Italomania of the mid-century. Between them *Rhoda Fleming* (1865), returning to English country life, showed, with the old characteristics of expression, tragic power superior perhaps to that of the end of *Feverel*. In fact some have been inclined to put *Rhoda* at the head. In 1875 *Beauchamp's Career* showed the novelist's curious fancy for studying off actual contemporaries; for it is now perfectly well known who " Beauchamp " was: and four years later came what the true Meredithian regards as the masterpiece, *The Egoist*. Two other books followed, to some extent in the track of *Beauchamp's Career, Diana of the Crossways* (1886), utilising the legend of Mrs. Norton's betrayal of secrets, and *The Tragic Comedians* (1881), the story of the German socialist Lassalle. The author's prediction, never hurried, now slackened, and by degrees ceased, but the nineties saw three books, *One of Our Conquerors* (1891), *Lord Ormont and his Aminta* (1894), and *The Amazing Marriage* (1895).

No bibliography of Mr. Meredith being here necessary

or possible, smaller and miscellaneous things need not
detain us; and we are not concerned with his sometimes
charming verse. It is the character, and especially the
" total-effect " character, of the major novels with which
we have to do. This has been faintly adumbrated above,
but the lines must be a little deepened and the contour
filled in to some extent here.

By invoking (practically at the outset of his work) " the
Comic Spirit " as the patron of his endeavours and the
inspirer of his art, Mr. Meredith of course did no more than
assert his claim to place himself in the right race and
lineage of Cervantes and Fielding. Nor, though the claim
be a bold one, can there be much dispute among competent
judges that he made it out. To the study, not in a
frivolous or even merely satirical, but in a gravely ironic
mode, of the nature of humanity he addicted himself
throughout: and the results of his studies undoubtedly
enlarge humanity's conscious knowledge of itself in the
way of fictitious exemplification. In a certain sense no
higher praise can be given. To acknowledge it is at once to
estate him, not only with Cervantes and Fielding themselves,
but with Thackeray, with Swift, with Molière, with Shakespeare. It places him well above Dickens, and, in the
opinion of the present writer, it places him above even
Balzac. But there are points wherein, according to that
same opinion, he approaches much nearer to Balzac and
Dickens than to the other and greater artistic creators:
while in one of these points he stands aloof even from these
two, and occupies a position—not altogether to his advantage—altogether by himself in his class of artistic creation. All the six from Thackeray to Shakespeare — one
might even go farther back and, taking a more paradoxical
example, add Rabelais—are, even in extravaganza, in parody,

in what you please, at once pre-eminently and *prima facie* natural and human.   To every competent human judgment, as soon as it is out of its nonage, and barring individual disqualifications of property or accident, this human nature attests itself.   You may dislike some of its manifestations; you may decline or fail to understand others; but there it is, and there it is *first*.   In Balzac and Dickens and Mr. Meredith it is not first.   Of course it is there to some extent and even to a large one: or they would not be the great writers that they are, or great writers at all. But it is not merely disguised by separable clothings, as in Rabelais wholly and in parts of others, or accompanied, as in Swift and others still, by companions not invariably acceptable.   It is to a certain extent adulterated, sophisticated, made not so much the helpmeet, or the willing handmaid, of Art as its thrall, almost its butt.   I do not know how early criticism, which now seems to have got hold of the fact, noticed the strong connection-contrast between Dickens and Meredith: but it must always have been patent to some.   The contrast is of course the first to strike: — the ordinariness, in spite of his fantastic grotesque, of Dickens, and the extraordinariness of Meredith; the almost utter absence of literature in Dickens, and the prominence of it in Meredith—divers other differences of the same general kind.   But to any one reflecting on the matter it should soon emerge that a spirit, kindred in some way, but informed with literature and anxious " to be different," starting too with Dickens's example before him, might, and probably would, half follow, half revolt into another vein of not anti- but extra-natural fantasy, such as that which the author of *The Ordeal of Richard Feverel* actually worked.

" Extra- not anti-" that is the key.   The worlds of

Dickens, of Balzac, and of Meredith are not impossible worlds: for the only worlds which are impossible are those which are inconsistent with themselves, and none of these is that. Something has been said of the " four dimensions " which are necessary to work Dickens's world, and our business here is not with Balzac's. But something must now be said of the fourth dimension—some would say the fifth, sixth, and almost tenth dimensions—which is or are required to put Mr. Meredith's in working order. I do not myself think that more than a fourth is needed, and I have sometimes fancied that if Mohammedan ideas of the other world be true, and an artist is obliged to endow all his fictitious creations with real life, it will be by the reduction and elimination of this dimension that Mr. Meredith will have to proceed. There will be great joy in that other world when he has done it: and, alarming as the task looks, I think it not impudent to say that no one who ever enjoyed his conversation will think it impossible.

The intrusive element can, however, only be designated singly by rather enlarging the strict and usual sense of the term Style so as to include not merely diction, but the whole manner of presentation—what, in short, is intended by the French word *faire*. For this, or part of this, he made, in relation to his poems, a sort of apology-explanation in the lines prefixed to the collected edition, and entitled " The Promise in Disturbance." I am not sure that there is any single place where a parallel excuse-defiance musters itself up in the novels: but there are scores (the prelude to *The Egoist* occurs foremost) where it is scattered about all of them; and it is certainly much more required there. Indeed as far as the narrow sense of " style " goes, the peculiarity, whether they admit it to be a fault or not, is practically admitted as a fact by all

but Meredith-monomaniacs. Here is a *sors Meredithiana*,
taken from *Rhoda Fleming*, one of the simplest of the
books:—

" Algernon waited dinnerless until the stealthy going
minutes distended and swelled monstrous and horrible as
viper-bitten bodies, and the venerable Signior Time became
of unhealthy hue."

To match that—it would be exceedingly easy to match
and beat it out of the author himself—you must go to
the maddest of the seventeenth-century metaphysicals—
say to Edward Benlowes himself. But this is nothing: it is
at worst an obvious playful exaggeration, very like some
things of Dickens's own transposed into another key.
But take this opening of the fifteenth chapter of *Diana of
the Crossways*:—

" The Gods of this world's contests, against whom our
poor stripped individual is commonly in revolt, are, as we
know, not miners, they are reapers; and if we appear no
longer on the surface, they cease to bruise us: they will
allow an arena character to be cleansed and made present-
able while enthusiastic friends preserve discretion.   It is
of course less than magnanimity; they are not proposed
to you for your worship; they are little Gods, temporary
as that great wave, their parent human mass of the hour.
But they have one worshipful element in them, which is,
the divine insistency upon there being two sides to a case
—to every case.   And the People so far directed by them
may boast of healthfulness.   Let the individual shriek,
the innocent, triumphant, have in honesty to admit the fact.
One side is vanquished according to decree of Law, but the
superior Council does not allow it to be extinguished."

Here undoubtedly there is something more than a simile,
an image, or a *pointe ;* there is a thought, and the author's

admirers would, I suppose, rely triumphantly on it as a marriage of original thought and phrase. But is it so? Is the thought really anything more than the perfectly correct and obvious one that, if you let scandal alone it will die, or at least go into abeyance? Does that thought really gain anything from being tricked out with not always very congruously arranged paraphernalia of Gods, and arenas, and reapers, and miners, and the People with a large P, and shrieks, and innocency, and the rest? A palate or an appetite so jaded that it cannot appreciate thought put before it plainly, or so sluggish that it requires to be stung or puzzled into thinking, may derive some advantage. But are these exactly the tastes and appetites that should be accepted as arbiters?

Again, partly through this perpetual mirage and steam-cloud of style, partly by other methods, Mr. Meredith manages, with consummate cleverness no doubt, to colour his whole representation of character and story in the same extra-natural way. Take the rick-burning at the beginning of *Feverel;* take the famous wine scene (a very fascinating one, though I never heard anywhere else, in some researches on the subject, of port that would keep ninety years) in *The Egoist.* The things may have happened this way in some Georgium Sidus, where the Comic Spirit has arranged the proper Fourth Dimension: but that is not the way they happen here. The Wise Youth, Diana, Edward Blancove, Roy Richmond—but why begin a list which would never end?—are inhabitants of the same region. They are not impossible: they could be translated into actual tellurian beings, which the men and women of the bad novelist never can be. But at present they are not translated: and you must know a special language, in a wide sense, in order to translate them. I do not

say that the language is impossible or even very hard
to learn: but it is required. And Meredithians say you
ought to learn it. An extremely respectable book of reference before me rebukes " those who lack the intelligence and
sensibility that can alone admit them to the charmed
circle of appreciative readers " and who " have not
patience to apply themselves to the study of the higher
fiction with the same ardour that they think necessary in
the case of any other art."

Now " Fudge! " is a rude word: but I fear we must
borrow it from Goldsmith's hero, and apply it here. As
for " charmed circles " there is uncommonly good company
outside them, where, as Beatrice says, we may "be as merry
as the day is long," so that the Comic Spirit cannot entirely
disdain us. And as for art—the present writer will fight
for its claims as long as he has breath. But the proof of
the art of the novelist is that—at first hand or very shortly
—he " enfists," absorbs, delights you. You may discover
secrets of his art afterwards with much pleasure and profit:
but the actual first-hand delight is the criterion. There
ought to be no need of sitting down before the thing with
tools and dynamite like burglars at a safe; of mustering
crucibles and reagents like assayers at some doubtful and
recalcitrant piece of ore. Now these not very adept
defenders of Mr. Meredith seem to assert that these processes are desirable in any case, and necessary in his. As
a matter of fact the necessity is not omnipresent: but it is
present far too frequently. It is the first duty of the
novelist to " let himself be read "—anything else that he
gives you is a *bonus*, a trimming, a dessert.

It is not unamusing to those who regarded Mr. Meredith
during almost his whole career with those mingled feelings of
the highest admiration and of critical reserve which this

notice has endeavoured to express, to note a new phase which seems to be coming over the youngest criticism. The original want of appreciation has passed, never, one may hope, to return; and the middle *engouement*, which was mainly engineered by those doughty partisans, Mr. Stevenson and Mr. Henley, is passing likewise. But the most competent and generous juniors seem to be a little uncomfortable, to have to take a good deal on trust, and not quite to " like the security." To those who know the history of critical opinion these signs speak pretty clearly, though not so as to authorise them to anticipate the final judgment absolutely. Genius, all but of the highest, can hardly be denied to Mr. Meredith: but it is genius marred, perhaps by unfortunate education, certainly by undue egotism, by a certain Celtic *tapage*, and by a too painful and elaborate endeavour to be unlike other people.

A very interesting subject for examination from the present point of view is Mr. Blackmore, because, on the one hand there is complete *parrhesia*, and on the other (here at least) enthusiastic admiration. Few of our modern novelists have combined so much scholarship with so much command of mother wit and racy English, so much close study of minor character and local speech with such wealth of romantic fancy; such a thorough observance of " good form " with so complete a freedom from priggishness and prudery. To this day there are lively controversies whether he worked up the Doone story from local tradition or made it " out of his own head." But whichever he did (and the present historian owns that he cares very little about the point) the way in which he has turned a striking, but not extraordinary, and certainly not very extensive West Country glen into an *Arabian Nights* valley, with the figures and action of a mediæval romance and the human interest of a modern novel, is really wonderful. And there is hardly a book of his last thirty years' production, from *Clara Vaughan* to *Perlycross*, which has not vigour, variety, character, " race " enough for half a dozen. In such books, for example, as *The Maid of Sker* and *Cripps the Carrier* the idiosyncrasy is extraordinary: the quaint and piquant oddity of phrase and apophthegm is as vivid as Dickens, rather more real, and tinged somehow with a flavour of literature, even of poetry, which was Dickens's constant lack.

And yet when one comes to consider the books critically, either one by one, or in pairs and batches, or as a whole, it is somehow or other difficult to pronounce any one exactly a masterpiece. There is a want of " inevitableness " which sometimes amounts to improbability, as in the case particularly of that most vivid and racy of books, *Cripps the Carrier*, where the central incident or situation, though by no means impossible, is almost insultingly unlikely, and forces its unlikeliness on one at almost every moment and turn. Never, perhaps, was there a better instance of that " possible-improbable " which contrasts so fatally with the " probable-impossible." In not a few cases, too, there is that reproduction of similar *dénouements* and crucial occurrences which is almost necessary in a time when men write many novels. In almost all there is a want of central interest in the characters that should be central; in some an exaggeration of dialect; or of quaint non-dialectic but also non-catholic locutions on the author's part. One rather hates oneself for finding such faults—no one of which is absolutely fatal—in a mass of work which has given, and continues to give, so much pleasure: but the facts remain. One would not have the books *not* written on any account; but one feels that they were written rather because the author chose to do so than because he could not help it.   Now it is possible to exaggerate the necessity of " mission " and the like: but, after all, *Ich kann nicht anders* must be to some extent the mood of mind of the man who is committing a masterpiece.

Something of the sort is still more noticeable in the work of other writers of the period.   We have seen that two ladies of great talent, Mrs. Oliphant and Mrs. Craik, began to write, long before Mr. Meredith published *Richard Feverel* and very little later than the time of *Vanity Fair*.   They produced, the one in *Salem Chapel* (1863), a book which contemporaries might be excused for thinking likely to herald a new George Eliot at least; the other, in *John Halifax, Gentleman* (1857), a book of more sentimentalism, but of great interest and merit.   Both were miracles of fecundity, Mrs. Craik producing, in the shorter life of the two, not much fewer than fifty novels; Mrs. Oliphant, besides a great deal of work in other departments, a tale which did not stop very far short of the hundred.   The latter, moreover, gave, at a comparatively late period of her career, evidences of being able to start new lines— the supernatural stories of her last stages are only inferior to the *Chronicles of Carlingford* themselves.   Yet, once more, we look for a masterpiece in vain: in fact in Mrs. Oliphant's case we ask, how could any human being, on such a system of production, be expected to produce masterpieces?   Scott, I think, once wrote four or nearly four novels in a year: and the process helped to kill him. Mrs. Oliphant did it over and over again, besides alternating the annual dose still more frequently with twos and threes. In her case the process only killed her novels.

Three remarkable novelists of the other sex may be mentioned, in the same way, together.   They were all acquaintances of the present writer, and one of them was his friend: moreover, he is quite certain that he could not write as good a novel as the worst of theirs, and only takes credit to himself for not having attempted to do so. These are James Payn, William Black, and Sir Walter Besant. Mr. Payn was an extremely agreeable person with a great talent for amusing, the measure of which he perhaps took pretty early—consoling himself for a total absence of high pretension by a perhaps not quite genuine affectation of good-natured but distinctly Philistine cynicism, and a half serious, half affected belief that other men's delight in their schools, their universities, the great classics of the past, etc., was *blague*. He never made this in the least offensive; he never made any one of his fifty or sixty novels anything but interesting and (when the subject required it) amusing. There never was any novelist less difficult to read a first time: I really do not know that it would be extremely difficult to read him a second; but also I have seldom come across a novelist with whom I was so little inclined to try it. It is a great thing, no doubt, as has been said, from a certain point of view—that of *pastime*—that the reading of a novel should be easy and pleasant. But perhaps this is not all that you are entitled to ask of it. And as Mr. Payn began with *Poems*, and some other suggestive books, I am inclined to think that perhaps he did *not* always regard literature as a thing of the kind of a superior railway sandwich.

It is quite certain that, in his beginning, Mr. William Black entertained no such idea; for his actual *débuts* were something like what long afterwards were called problem-novels, and *In Silk Attire* (1869), *Kilmeny* (1870), and the charming *Daughter of Heth* (1871) attempted a great deal besides mere amusement. It is true that no one of them—

not even the last—could be called an entire success: a
"little more powder" was wanted to send the shots home,
and such flight as they achieved did not even seem to be
aimed at any distinct and worthy object.   But fortunately
for his pocket, unfortunately for his fame, he hit the public
taste of the time with a sort of guidebook-novel in *The
Strange Adventures of a Phaeton* (1872) and *A Princess of
Thule* (1873), and was naturally tempted to continue it,
or to branch off only into not very strong stories of society.
Once he made an effort at combining tragic romance with
this latter kind in *Macleod of Dare* (1878), but, though this
was nearer to a success than some of his critics admitted,
it was not quite a success: and though he wrote fully a
score of novels after it, he never came nearer the actual
bull's eye.   In fact his later work was not up to a very
good average.

Neither of these writers, except, as has been said, perhaps
Black in his earliest stage, had taken novel-writing very
seriously: it was otherwise with the third of the trio.
Mr., afterwards Sir Walter, Besant did not begin early,
owing to the fact that, for nearly a decade after leaving
Cambridge, he was a schoolmaster in Mauritius.   But he
had, in this time, acquired a greater knowledge of literature
than either of the other two possessed: and when he came
home, and took to fiction, he accompanied it with, or rather
based it upon, not merely wide historical studies, which
are still bearing fruit in a series of posthumous dealings
with the history of London, but rather minute observation of the lower social life of the metropolis.   For some
ten years his novel production was carried on, in a rather
incomprehensible system of collaboration, with James Rice,
a Cambridge man like himself and a historian of the turf,
but one to whom no independent work in fiction is attri-

buted, except an incredibly feeble adaptation of *Mr. Verdant Green*, entitled *The Cambridge Freshman* and signed "Martin Legrand." During the seventies, and for a year or two later, till Rice's death in 1882, the pair provided a long series of novels from *Ready-Money Mortiboy* (1871) to *The Chaplain of the Fleet* (1881), the most popular book between being, perhaps, *The Golden Butterfly* (1876). These belonged, loosely, to the school of Dickens, as that school had been carried on by Wilkie Collins (*v. inf.*), but with less grotesque than the original master, and less "sensation" than the head pupil; with a good deal of solid knowledge both of older and more modern life; with fairly substantial plots, good character-drawing of the more external kind, and a sufficient supply of interesting incident, dialogue, and description.

It was certain that people would affect to discover a "falling off" when the partnership was dissolved by Rice's death: but as a matter of fact there was nothing of the kind. Such books as the very good and original *Revolt of Man* (which certainly owed nothing to collaboration), as *All Sorts and Conditions of Men* (1882), the first of the kind apparently that Besant wrote alone, as *Dorothy Forster* (1884), and as the powerful if not exactly delightful *Children of Gibeon* (1886) were perhaps more vigorous than anything earlier, and certainly not less original. But the curse of the "machine-made" novel, which has been already dwelt upon, did not quite spare Besant: and in these later stories critics could point, without complete unfairness, to an increasing obsession of the "London" subject, especially in regard to the actual gloom and possible illumination of the East End, and on the other to a resort to historical subjects, less as suggestions or canvases than as giving the substance of the book.

T

The first class of work, however (which actually resulted in a "People's Palace" and was supposed to have obtained his knighthood for him), is distinctly remarkable, especially in the light of succeeding events.   Most of the unfavourable criticisms passed upon Besant's novel-work were in the main the utterances of raw reviewers, who thought it necessary to "down" established reputations.   But it would be impossible for any competent critic, however much he might be biassed off the bench by friendship, not to admit, on it, that he also shows the effect, which we have been illustrating from others, of the system of novel-production *à la douzaine*.   In such a case, and on the, in themselves, salutary conditions of the new novel, the experiences and interests of life may or must come to be regarded too regularly as supplying "grist for the mill"; nay, the whole of life and literature, which no doubt ought in all cases to furnish suggestion and help to art and inspiration, are too often set to a sort of *corvèe*, a day-task, a tale of bricks.   It is, one allows, hard to prevent this: and yet nothing is more certain that bricks so made are not the best material to be wrought into any really "star-y-pointing pyramid" that shall defy the operations of time.

A very curious and characteristic member of this group, Wilkie Collins, has not yet been mentioned except by glances.   He was a little older than most of them, and came pretty early under the influence of Dickens, whose melodramatic rather than his humorous side he set himself to work to develop.   In fact Collins was at least as much melodramatist as novelist: and while most of his novels are melodrama in narrative form, not a few of them were actually dramatised.   He began as early as 1850 — the dividing year—with *Antonina:* but his three great triumphs in the "sensation" novel (as it was rather stupidly called) were *The Dead Secret* (1857), *The Woman in White* (1860), and *No Name* (1862). Throughout the sixties and a little later, in *Armadale* (1866), *The Moonstone* (1870), perhaps *The New Magdalen* (1873), and even as late as 1875 in *The Law and the Lady,* his work continued to be eagerly read. But the taste for it waned: and its author's last fifteen years or so (he died in 1889), though fairly fruitful in quantity, certainly did not tend to keep it up in quality. Although Collins had a considerable amount of rather coarse vigour in·him (his brother Charles, who died young, had a much more delicate art) and great fecundity in a certain kind of stagy invention, it is hard to believe that his work will ever be put permanently high. It has a certain resemblance in method to Godwin and Mrs. Radcliffe, exciting situations being arranged, certainly with great cleverness, in an interminable sequence, and leading, sometimes at any rate, to a violent " revolution " (in the old dramatic sense) at the end. Perhaps the best example is the way in which Magdalen Vanstone's desperate and unscrupulous, though more than half justifiable, machinations, to reverse the cruel legal accident which leaves her and her sister with " No Name " and no fortune, are foiled by the course of events, though the family property is actually recovered for this sister who has been equally guiltless and inactive. Of its kind, the machinery is as cleverly built and worked as that of any novel in the world: but while the author has given us some Dickensish character-parts of no little attraction (such as the agreeable rascal Captain Wragge) and has nearly made us sympathise strongly with Magdalen herself, he only succeeds in this latter point so far as to make us angry with him for his prudish poetical or theatrical justice, which is not poetical and hardly even just.

`. The specialist or particularist novel was not likely to be without practitioners during this time: in fact it might be said, after a fashion, to be more rife than ever: but it can only be glanced at here. Its most remarkable representatives perhaps—men, however, of very different tastes and abilities—were Richard Jefferies and Joseph Henry Shorthouse. The latter, after attracting very wide attraction by a remarkable book—almost a kind to itself—*John Inglesant* (1880), a half historical, half ecclesiastical novel of seventeenth-century life, never did anything else that was any good at all, and indeed tried little. The former, a struggling country journalist, after long failing to make any way, wrote several three-volume novels of no merit, broke through at last in the *Pall Mall Gazette* with a series of studies of country life, *The Gamekeeper at Home* (1878), and afterwards turned these into a peculiar style of novel, with little story and hardly any character, but furnished with the backgrounds and the atmosphere of these same sketches. His health was weak, and he died in early middle age, leaving a problem of a character exactly opposed to the other. Would Mr. Shorthouse, if he had not been a well-to-do man of business, but obliged to write for his living, have done more and better work? Would Jefferies, if he had been more fortunate in education, occupation, and means, and furnished with better health, have co-ordinated and expanded his certainly rare powers into something more "important" than the few pictures, as of a Meissonier-*paysagiste*, which he has left us? These inquiries are no doubt idle: but, once more, one may draw attention to the way in which two men, so different in tastes and fortune, neither, it would seem, with a very strong bent towards prose fiction as the vehicle of his literary desires and accomplishments, appear to have been forced, by the overpowering attraction and popularity of the kind, to adopt the novel as their form of literature, and to give the public, not what they wanted in the form which they chose, but something at least made up in the form that the public wanted, and disguised in the wrappers which the public were accustomed to purchase.

The principal development of mid-nineteenth-century fiction had been, as we have seen, in the direction of the novel *proper* — the character - study of modern ordinary life. But, even as early as *Esmond* and *Hypatia*, signs were not wanting that the romance, historical or other, was not going to be content with the rather pale copies of Scott, and the rococo - sentimental style of Bulwer, which had mainly occupied it for the last quarter of a century. Still, though we have mentioned other examples of the fifties and sixties, and have left ever so many more unmentioned, it was certainly not as popular [1] as its rival till, towards the end of the latter decade, Mr. Blackmore's *Lorna Doone* gave it a fresh hold on the public taste. Some ten years later again there came to its aid a new recruit of very exceptional character, Mr. Robert Louis Stevenson. He was a member of the famous family of light-house engineers, and was educated for the Bar of Scotland, to which he was actually called. But law was as little to his taste as engineering, and he slowly gravitated towards literature—the slowness being due, not merely to family opposition or to any other of the usual causes (though some of these were at work), but to an intense and elaborate desire to work himself out a style of his own by the process of "sedulously aping" others. It may be

---

[1] Anthony Trollope, in one of the discursive passages in his early books, has left positive testimony to the distaste with which publishers regarded it.

very much doubted whether this process ever gave any one a style of perfect freedom: and it may be questioned further whether Stevenson ever attained such a style.

But there could be no question that he did attain very interesting and artistic effects, and there happened to be at the time a reaction against what was called " slovenliness " and a demand for careful preparation and planned effect in prose-writing. Even so, however, it was not at once that Stevenson took to fiction. He began with essays, literary and miscellaneous, and with personal accounts of travel: and certain critical friends of his strongly urged him to continue in this way. During the years 1878 and 1879, in a short-lived periodical called *London*, which came to be edited by his friend the late Mr. Henley and had a very small staff, he issued certain *New Arabian Nights* which caught the attention of one or two of his fellow-contributors very strongly, and made them certain that a new power in fiction-writing had arisen. It did not, however, at first much attract the public: and it was the kind of thing which never attracts publishers until the public forces their hands. For a time he had to wait, and to take what opportunity he could get of periodical publication, " boy's book "-writing, and the like. In fact *Treasure Island* (1883), with which he at last made his mark, is to this day classed as a boy's book by some people who are miserable if they cannot classify. It certainly deals with pirates, and pieces of eight, and adventures by land and sea; but the manner of dealing— the style and narrative and the delineation of the chief character, the engaging villain John Silver—is about as little puerile as anything that can be imagined. From that time Stevenson's reputation was assured. Ill health, a somewhat restless disposition, and an early death prevented him from accomplishing any great bulk of work: and the merit of what he did varied.   Latterly he took to a teasing process of collaboration, which his sincerest admirers could have willingly spared.   But his last completed book, *Catriona* (1893), seemed to some judges of at least considerable experience the best thing he had yet done, especially in one all-important respect—that he here conquered either an unwillingness to attempt or an inability to achieve the portraiture of feminine character, which his books had previously displayed.   The general opinion, too, was that the unfinished *Weir of Hermiston* (1897), which he left a fragment at his death, was the best and strongest thing he had done, while it showed in particular a distinct relinquishment, for something freer and more spontaneous, of the effective but also rather affected and decidedly laboured style in which he had hitherto written. For us, however, his style is of less importance than the fact that he applied it almost wholly to the carrying out of that rejuvenescence of romance of which we have been speaking, and which may be taken, as anybody pleases, either for a mere alterative to the domestic novel or as a definite revolt against it.   It was speedily taken up by writers mostly still living, and so not to be dwelt on now.

Very late in the century the genius of Mr. William Morris turned from verse to prose tale-telling in a series of romances which caught the fancy neither of the public nor of the critics as a whole, but which seem to some whom the gods have made not quite uncritical to be, if rightly taken, of much accomplishment, and of almost more promise and suggestion.   These, seven or eight in number, from *The House of the Wulfings* (1889) to *The Sundering Flood*, published after the author's death in 1898, were actual romances—written in a kind of modernised fifteenth-century English, and dealing, some with far back incidents of the conflict between Romans and "Barbarians," most with the frank no-time and no-place of Romance itself. They came at an unfortunate moment, when the younger generation of readers were thinking it proper to be besotted with crude realism or story-less impressionism, and when some at least of those who might have welcomed them earlier had left their first faith in poetry or poetic prose. There was, moreover, perhaps some genuine dislike, and certainly a good deal of precisian condemnation, of the "Wardour Street" dialect. Yet there was no sham in them: it was impossible for Mr. Morris to have anything to do with shams—even his socialism was not that—and they were in reality a revival, however Rip van Winklish it might seem, of the pure old romance itself, at the hands of a nineteenth-century sorcerer, who no doubt put a little of the nineteenth century into them. The best—probably the best of all is *The Well at the World's End* (1896)—have an extraordinary charm for any one who can taste romance: and are by no means unlikely to awake the taste for it in generations to come. But for the present the thing lay out of the way of its generation, and was not comprehended or enjoyed thereby. For it is no doubt nearly as annoying to have bread given to you when you want thistles as to have thistles given to you when you want bread. But just as the ballad is the appointed reviver of poetry, so is romance the appointed reviver of prose-fiction: and in one form or another it will surely do its work, sooner or later.

Here it may be best to stop the actual current of critical comment on individuals. Something has been hinted as to the general present condition of the novel, but there is no need to emphasise it or to enter into particulars about it:

indeed, even if such a proceeding were convenient in one way it would be very inconvenient in another. One might, for instance, have to consider, rather curiously, a remarkable statement recently attributed to a popular novelist that "the general standard of excellence in fiction is higher *to-day* than ever it was before." But we can take higher ground. Far be it from me to bow to the Baal of " up-to-dateness," for even if I had any such hankering, I think I should remember that the surest way of being out-of-date to-morrow is the endeavour to be up-to-date to-day. Only by keeping perspective can you hope to confirm and steady your view : only by relinquishing the impossible attempt to be complete can you achieve a relative completeness.

Yet it is well to remember that Lockhart, one of the best critics who ever lived (when he let himself be so), a novelist too, and not likely to lose an opportunity of magnifying his office if he could, took occasion, in noticing the novels of his friend Theodore Hook at poor " Mr. Wagg's" death, gravely to deplore the decadence of the novel generally : and not much later, in reprinting the article, had the wisdom to recognise, and the courage to record, the fact that Thackeray had disappointed his prognostications. Literature, it has been said, is the incalculable of incalculables : and not only may a new novelist arise to-morrow, but some novelist who has been writing for almost any number of years may change his style, strike the vein, and begin the exploitation of a new gold-field in novel-production.

But this does not affect the retrospect of the past. There we are on perfectly firm ground—ground which we have traversed carefully already, and which we may survey in surety now.

We have seen, then, that the prose novel—a late growth both in ancient and in modern times in all countries—was a specially late and slow-yielding one in English. Although Thoms's *Early English Prose Romances* is by no means an exhaustive collection, and for this reason was not specially referred to in the first chapter, it is impossible not to recognise that its three rather small volumes, of matter for the most part exceeding poor and beggarly, contrast in the most pitiful fashion with the scores and almost hundreds containing Early English Romances in verse. Malory of course brings the prose-scale down very considerably from its uncomfortably *meteoric* position, and some other things help: but the total of prose and verse before 1500 can be brought level by no possible sleight of weighing. Still, as we have seen, this did not matter very much: for the verse got " transprosed " sooner or later, and the romances and tales of other countries were greedily admitted *ad eundem* in sixteenth and seventeenth century English.

Yet the novel proper lingered: and, except in the single and eccentric masterpiece of Bunyan, the seventeenth century ended without having seen one real specimen of prose fiction that was thoroughly satisfactory. Nearly half the eighteenth had gone too, with nothing but the less isolated but still not perfect performances of Defoe, and the once more still eccentric masterpiece of *Gulliver*, before the novel-period really opened. It is literally not more than two long lifetimes ago—it is quite certain that there are now living hundreds, perhaps thousands, of persons born when others were still living who drew their first breaths in or before the year when Pamela made her modest, but very distinctly self-conscious, curtsey to the world. How soon it grew to a popular form of literature, and how steadily that popularity has continued and increased, there is not much need to say or to repeat. Statistical persons every year give us the hundreds of novels that appear from the presses, and the thousands of readers who take them out of, or read them in, public libraries. I do not know whether there exists anywhere a record of the total number published since 1740, but I dare say it does. I should not at all wonder if this total ran into scores of thousands: if you were to bring in short stories it would certainly do so. People have almost left off shaking their heads over the preponderant or exclusive attention to fiction in these public libraries themselves: in fact the tendency seems to be rather to make out that it is decreasing. It may be so; or it may not. But what remains certain is that there is a very large number of educated people to whom " reading " simply means reading novels; who never think of taking up a book that is not a novel; for whom the novel exhausts even the very meaning of the word " literature." We know that the romance was originally so called simply because it was the commonest book in " Romance " language. We are less unsophisticated now: but there are certainly large numbers of His Majesty's subjects by whom a novel on this principle ought to be called " an english " though it might have to share that appellation with the newspaper.

Yet, as we have seen, for this or that reason, the *average* novel did not come to anything like perfection for a very long time. In a single example, or set of examples, it reached something like perfection almost at once. Fielding, Scott, Miss Austen, and Thackeray are the Four Masters of the whole subject, giving the lady the same degree as the others by courtesy of letters. But in the first (as for the matter of that in the last) of the four the success was rather a matter of individual and inimitable genius than of systematic discovery of method practicable by others. Nobody, except Thackeray himself, has ever followed Fielding successfully, and that only in parts and touches; as Fielding had (unfortunately) no opportunity of following Thackeray, no one has ever followed Thackeray satisfactorily at all. Such reasons as presented themselves have been given for the fact that nearly half of the whole period passed before the two systems—of the pure novel and the novel-romance—were discovered: and even then they were not at once put to work. But the present writer would be the very first to confess that these explanations leave a great deal unexplained.

Yet whatever faults there might be in the supply there could be no doubt about the demand when it was once started. It was indeed almost entirely independent of the goodness or badness of the average supply itself. Allowing for the smaller population and the much smaller proportion of that population who were likely to— who indeed could—read, and for the inferior means of distribution, it may be doubted whether the largest sales of novels recorded in the last half century have surpassed those of the most trumpery trash of the " Minerva Press " period—the last decade of the eighteenth and the first of the nineteenth century. For the main novel-public is quite omnivorous, and almost absolutely uncritical of what it devours. The admirable though certainly fortunate Scot who "could never remember drinking bad whisky" might be echoed, if they had the wit, by not a few persons who never seem to read a bad novel, or at least to be aware that they are reading one.

At the same time, the failure of the quest for novel-recipes was compensated by an absence of that working of those recipes to death which the last century—or the last three-quarters of it—has seen. The average work of any one of a dozen nineteenth-century producers of novels by the dozen and the score, whom at this place it is not necessary to name, is probably on the whole a much better turned out thing—one better observing its own purposes, and open to less criticism in detail—than even the best of the works of the earlier division outside of Fielding. But the eighteenth - century books — faulty, only partially satisfying as they may be in comparison, say, with a well-succeeded Trollope or one of the better Blackmores—very often have a certain idiosyncrasy, a freedom from machine-work, which supplies something not altogether unlike the contrast between the furniture of the two periods. Stress and dwelling have been purposely given, to some minor books of this period, for this very reason.

But at the same time the limitations, outside the greatest, are certainly peculiar. It seems wonderful that a man like Cumberland, for instance, who had not a little literary talent, should not have been able to make *Henry* into a story of real interest that might hold the reader as even second-class Trollope—say a book like *Orley Farm*—does. We have ungraciously recognised that some of our lady novelists, who wrote by forties and by fifties, did not always sustain the interest of their novels. Miss Burney wrote four in all, and could hardly keep up the interest of hers right through the second. Above all, there is the difficulty of their failure with conversation and, in fact, with any diction proper for conversation. If Horace Walpole, a contemporary of the eighteenth-century novel from its actual start to practically its finish, could give us thousands and all but tens of thousands of phrases that want but a little of being novel-conversation ready made, why could not the other people make it for their own purposes? But we have got no answer to these questions: and probably there is none.

The way in which Scott and Miss Austen themselves simultaneously found out the secrets of the two kinds of novel is no doubt, as such ways always are, in the larger part mysterious: but to a certain extent it can be explained and analysed, independently of the direct literary genius of each. One of the greatest gifts of Scott—one with which the non-historical novelist can dispense as little as his brother the historical—was that " genius of history " with which Lord Morley—a critic not likely to be misled by sympathy in some respects at any rate—has justly credited him. For unless you have this " historic sense," as it has been more generally and perhaps better termed (though to the intense disgust of some professed historians), it is not only impossible for you to delineate scene and character at a distance from your time, but you become really disqualified for depicting your own time itself. You fail to distinguish the temporary from the permanent; you achieve perhaps a fairly faithful copy of actual manners and fashions, but you do nothing more, and as the subject dies so does the picture. Contrast Hook, say, with Thackeray, and the difference will emerge at once.

Secondly, Scott had, besides this historic sense and the relish for humanity which must accompany it, a knowledge of literature with which he has been too seldom credited to the full. When he published *Waverley* he had been reading all sorts and conditions of books for some five-and-thirty years, and assimilating them if, as the pedants will have it, with a distressing inaccuracy in particulars, with a general and genial fidelity of which the pedants do not even dream and could not comprehend, or they would not be pedants. He was thus furnished with infinite stores of illustrative matter, never to overpower, but always to accompany and season, his knowledge of life. In a few instances this felicity of adoption has been recognised, but not a tenth part of it has ever been systematically put on record. The more widely and the longer a man reads, the more constantly will he find that Scott has been before him, and has "lifted " just the touch that he wanted at the time and in the place.

But perhaps a greater gift (there were still others which it would be long to perscribe—descriptive faculty, humour, pathos, half a dozen other things of the highest importance in themselves, but of less special application) was that which enabled him to discover and apply something like a universal novel *language*. He did this, not as Shakespeare did (and as nobody but Shakespeare, except perhaps Dante to some extent, ever has done or apparently could do), by making a really universal language which fits all times and persons because it is universal like its creator's soul. Still less did he do it by adopting the method which Spenser did consummately, but which almost everybody else has justified Ben Jonson by doing very badly:—that is to say by constructing a mosaic of his own. But his own method was nearer to this latter. For historical creations (the most important of his non-historic, *Guy Mannering* and the *Antiquary*, were so near his own time that he had no difficulty) he threw back with remarkable cunning to a period somewhat earlier, and coloured this up to the required tint by actual suggestions from contemporary, or nearly contemporary, literature, where he could get it. He has done this so consummately that perhaps the only novel of his where the language strikes us as artificial is the single one in which he actually endeavoured to be " up-to-date "—*St. Ronan's Well*.

This question of " Lingo," on the other hand, was Miss Austen's weakest point: and we have seen and shall see that it continued to be a weak point with others. Some admirers have defended her even here: but proud as I am to be an Austen Friar, a knight (or at least squire) of the order of St. Jane, I cannot go to this length. She very nearly succeeded, and sometimes she did quite: but not always. The easy dialogue and phrase that we find as early as Horace Walpole, even as Chesterfield and Lady Mary, in letters; which, in her own early days, appears in Fanny Burney's diaries but not in the novels, does not seem always within Miss Austen's grasp. But her advance in this respect is enormous: she is, for instance, far beyond Scott himself in *St. Ronan's Well:* and when she is thoroughly interested in a character, and engaged in un-folding it and gently satirising it at the same time, she rarely goes even a hair's-breadth wrong. In almost every other respect she does not go wrong to the extent of the minutest section of a hair. The story is the least part with her: but her stories are always miraculously *adequate :* neither desultory and pillar-to-post, nor elaborated with the minuteness which seems to please some people, but which is quite indifferent to the majority, and is certainly a positive nuisance to a few who are not quite of negligible judgment. But the reason of this adequacy in story contains in itself her greatest triumph. Not being a poet, she cannot reach the Shakespearian consummateness of poetic phrase: though she sometimes comes not so far short of this in the prose variety. But in the other great province of character, though hers is but a Rutland to his Yorkshire—or rather to his England or his world—she is almost equally supreme. And by her manipu-

lation of it she showed, once for all, how the most ordinary set
of circumstances, and even the most ordinary characters in
a certain sense, can be made to supply the material of prose
fiction to an absolutely illimitable extent. Her philo-
sopher's stone (to take up the old parable again) does not
lose its powers even when all the metal in the house is
exhausted—if indeed the metal, or anything else, in the
House of Humanity were exhaustible. The chairs and
tables, the beds and the basins — everything — can be
made into novel-gold: and, when it has been made, it
remains as useful for future conversion, by the same or any
other magician of the same class, as ever. One of the most
curious things about Miss Austen is the entire absence of
self-repetition in her. Even her young men—certainly
not her greatest successes—are by no means doubles of each
other: and nature herself could not turn out half a dozen
girls more subtly and yet more sufficiently differentiated
than Catherine and Elizabeth, Marianne and Fanny,
Elinor and Emma, and finally the three sisters of *Persuasion*, the other (quite other) Elizabeth, Mary, and Anne.
The " ruts of the brain " in novelists are a by-word. There
are none here.

In these two great writers of English novel there is,
really for the first time, the complementary antithesis after
which people have often gone (I fear it must be said)
wool-gathering elsewhere. The amateurs of cosmopolitan
literature, I believe, like to find it in Stendhal and Michelet.
They praise the former for his delicate and pitiless psychological analysis. It had been anticipated a dozen years,
nay, nearly twenty years, before he saw the Beresina: and
was being given out in print at about the very moment
of that uncomfortable experience, and before he himself
published anything, by a young English lady—a lady if

U

ever there was one and English if any person ever was—
in a country parsonage in Hampshire or in hired houses,
quite humdrum and commonplace to the commonplace
and humdrum imagination, at Bath and Southampton.
They praise Michelet for his enthusiastic and multiform
apprehension of the plastic reality of the past, his re-
creation of it, his putting of it, live and active, before the
present. The thing had been done, twenty years earlier
again, by a Scotch advocate who had deliberately turned
from poetic form, though he retained poetic imagination,
and who did not disdain not to make a fool of himself, as
Michelet, with all his genius, did again and again. Of all
the essentials of the two manners of fictitious creation—
Michelet's was not fictitious, but he almost made it so,
and Stendhal's was not historical, but he almost made it
so likewise—Scott and Miss Austen had set the types,
given the methods, arranged the processes as definitely as
Fust, or Coster, or Gutenberg, or Fust's friend Mephis-
topheles—who perhaps, on the whole, has the best title to
the invention—did in another matter three hundred years
before.

That Scott's variety should be taken up first, and should
for a time have the great popularity, the greater number
of disciples, the greater acceptance as a mode of pleasing—
was, as has been pointed out, natural enough; it is not a
little significant that (to avert our eyes from England) the
next practitioner of the psychological style in European
literature, Balzac, went through a long and mostly un-
successful probation in the other kind, and never wholly
deserted it, or at least always kept looking back to it. But
the general shortcomings (as they have been admitted to
be) in the whole of the second quarter of the century (or a
little less) with us, were but natural results of the inevitable

expatiation, unsystematic and irresolute, over the newly
discovered provinces. And they gave admirable work of
various kinds—work especially admirable if we remember
that there was no general literary uprising with us as there
was, in France and elsewhere, about 1830. If it were in
any way possible—similar supposings have been admitted in
literature very often—it would be extremely interesting to
take a person *ex hypothesi* fairly acquainted with the rest
of literature—English, foreign, European, and classical—but
who knew nothing and had heard nothing of Bulwer,
Disraeli, Peacock, Marryat, even Ainsworth and James
and others between Scott and the accomplished work of
Thackeray (Dickens's is, as has been said, mainly a sport of
genius), and to turn him loose on this work. I do him the
justice to suppose that he would find not a few faults: I
shall also do him the justice to think it likely that he
(being, as said, *ex hypothesi* furnished with the miscellaneous knowledge necessary to enjoy them) would enjoy
them very keenly and thoroughly. If you added the
minorities of the time, such as that very clever Miss Robinson
(I think her name was Emma) who wrote *Whitefriars* and
other historical romances in the forties; such as Charles
Macfarlane, who died, like Colonel Newcome, a poor brother
of the Charterhouse after writing capital things like *The
Dutch in the Medway* and *The Camp of Refuge*—if, I say, you
gave him these things and he was a good man, but lazy,
like Gray, I think he would vote for a continuance of
his life of novels and sofas without sighing for anything
further. But undoubtedly it might be contended that
something further was needed: and it came. This was
verisimilitude—the holding of the true mirror to actual
society.

This verisimilitude, it should be observed, is not only

difficult to attain: it seems not to be easy even to recognise. I have seen it said that the reason which makes it " hopeless for many people even to try to get through *Pickwick* " (their state itself must be " hopeless " enough, and it is to be hoped there are not " many " of them) is that it " describes states of society unimaginable to many people of to-day." Again, these many people must be somewhat unimaginative. But that is not the point of the matter. The point is that Dickens depicts no " state of society " that ever existed, except in the *Dickensium Sidus*. What he gives is full of intensely real touches which help to create its charm. But it is difficult to say that there is even a single person in it who is real as a whole, in the sense of having possibly existed in this world: and the larger whole of the book generally is pure fantasy—as much so as one of the author's own favourite goblin-dream stories.

With Thackeray the case is exactly the opposite. It is a testimony no doubt to Dickens's real power—though perhaps not to his readers' perspicacity—that he made them believe that he intended a " state of society " when, whether he intended it or not, he certainly has not given it. But Thackeray intended it and gave it. His is a " state of society " always—whether in late seventeenth century, early or late eighteenth, early or middle nineteenth—which existed or might have existed; his persons are persons who lived or might have lived. And it is the discovery of this art of creation by him and its parallel diffusion among his contemporaries that I am endeavouring to make clear here. Fielding, Scott to some extent, Miss Austen had had it. Dickens, till *Great Expectations* at least, never achieved and I believe never attempted it. Bulwer, having failed in it for twenty years, struck it at last about this time, and so did, even before him, Mrs. Marsh, and perhaps others, falteringly and incompletely. But as a general gift—a characteristic—it never distinguished novelists till after the middle of the century.

It is, I think, impossible to find a better meeting and over-lapping place of the old and the new novel, than that very remarkable book *Emilia Wyndham*, which has been already more than once referred to. It was written in 1845 and appeared next year—the year of *Vanity Fair*. But the author was twenty years older than Thackeray, though she survived him by nearly a dozen; she had not begun early; and she was fifty-five when she wrote *Emilia*. The not unnatural consequence is that there is a great deal of inconsistency in the general texture of the book: and that any clever cub, in the 'prentice stage of reviewing, could make columns of fun out of it. The general theme is age-old, being not different from the themes of most other novels in that respect. A half-idiotic spendthrift (he ends as very nearly an actual idiot) not merely wastes his own pro-perty but practically embezzles that of his wife and daughter; the wife dies and the daughter is left alone with an extravagant establishment, a father practically *non compos*, not a penny in her pocket after she has paid his doctor, and a selfish baronet-uncle who will do less than nothing to help her. She has loved half unconsciously, and been half consciously loved by, a soldier cousin or quasi-cousin: but he is in the Peninsular War. Absolutely no help presents itself but that of a Mr. Danby, a convey-ancer, who, in some way not very consonant with the usual etiquette of his profession, has been mixed up with her father's affairs—a man middle-aged, apparently dry as his own parchments, and quite unversed in society. He helps her clumsily but lavishly: and her uncle forces her to accept his hand as the only means of saving her father from jail first and an asylum afterwards. The inevitable disunion, brought about largely by Danby's mother (an awful old middle-class harridan), follows; and the desk-and-head incident mentioned above is brought about by her seeing the (false) announcement of her old lover's death in the paper. But she herself is consistently, perhaps excessively, but it is fair to say not ridiculously, angelic; Danby is a gentleman and a good fellow at heart; and of course, after highly tragical possibilities, these good gifts triumph. The greatest danger is threatened, and the actual happy ending brought about, by an auxiliary plot, in which the actors are the old lover (two old lovers indeed), his wife (a beautiful featherhead, who has been Emilia's school-fellow and dearest friend), and a wicked " Duke of C."

Even from this sketch the tolerably expert reader of novels may discover where the weak points are likely to lie; he will be a real expert if he anticipates the strong ones without knowing the book. As was formerly noticed, the dialogue is ill supplied with diction. The date of the story is 1809: and the author had for that period a fairly safe pattern in Miss Austen: but she does not use it at all, nor does she make the lingo frankly that of her own day. There are gross improbabilities—Mr. Danby, for instance (who is represented as wrapped up in his business, and exclusively occupied with the legal side of money matters and the money side of the law), actually discharges, or thinks he is discharging, hundreds and thousands of Mr. Wyndham's liabilities by handing his own open cheques, not to the creditors, not to any one representing them, but to a country attorney who has succeeded him in the charge of the debts and affairs, and whom he knows to be a sharp practitioner and suspects to be a scoundrel. The inhuman

uncle and the licentious duke are mere cardboard characters:
and the featherheaded Lisa talks and behaves like a
mixture of the sprightly heroines of Richardson (for
whom Lady Mary most righteously prescribed a sound
whipping) and the gushing heroines of Lady Morgan.
There is too much chaise-and-four and laudanum-bottle;
too much moralising; too much of a good many other
things.   And yet, somehow or other, there are also things
very rarely to be found in any novel—even taking in
Bulwer and the serious part of Dickens—up to the date.
The scene between Danby and his mother, in the poky
house in Charlotte Street, when she discovers that he has
been giving a hundred-pound cheque to a young lady is
impressingly good: it is not absolutely unsuggestive of
what Thackeray was just doing, and really not far from
what Trollope was not for some years to do.   There are
other passages which make one think of George Eliot, who
indeed might have been writing at the very time; there
are even faint and faltering suggestions of Ibsenic " duty
to ourselves."   Mr. Danby (the characters regularly call
each other " Mr.," " Mrs.," and " Miss," even when they
are husbands and wives, daughters or nieces, and uncles or
fathers) is a miss, and not quite a miss, of a very striking,
original, possible, and even probable character.   His
mother, with something more of the Dickensian type-
character, can stand by her unpleasant self, and came ten
years before " the Campaigner."   Susan, her pleasanter
servant, is equally self-sufficing, and came five years before
Peggotty, to whom she is not without resemblances.[1]

But it is not so much the merits on the one hand, or the
defects on the other, of the book that deserve attention

---

[1] Another novel of Mrs. Marsh-Caldwell's, *Norman's Bridge*, has
strong suggestions of *John Halifax*, and is ten years older.

here and justify the place given to it: it is the general " chip-the-shell " character. The shell is only being chipped: large patches of it still hamper the chicken, which is thus a half developed and half disfigured little animal. All sorts of didactics, of Byronic-Bulwerish sentiment, of conventionalities of various kinds, still hold their place; the language, as we have said, is traditional and hardly even that; and the characters are partly drawn from Noah's Arks of various dates, partly from the stock company of the toy theatre.   On the other hand, besides the touches of modernity already mentioned, and assisting them, there is a great attention to·" interiors."   The writer has, for her time, a more than promising sense of the incongruity between Empire dress and furniture and the style of George II.: and the shabbiness or actual squalor of Charlotte Street and Chancery Lane show that she had either been a very early and forward scholar of Dickens, or had discovered the thing on her own account.   Her age may excuse some of the weak points, but it makes the presence of the strong ones all the more remarkable: and it shows all the more forcibly how the general influences which were to produce the great central growth of Victorian novel were at work, and at work almost violently, in the business of pulling down the old as well as of building up the new.

Of that new novel it is not necessary to say much more. In the last fifty or sixty years of the nineteenth century it did, as it seems to me, very great things—so great that, putting poetry, which is supreme, aside, there is no division of the world's literature within a time at all comparable to its own which can much, if at all, excel it.   It did these great things because partly of the inscrutable laws which determined that a certain number of men and women of

unusual power should exist, and should devote themselves
to it, partly of the less heroic-sounding fact that the
general appetite of other men and womenkind could make
it worth while for these persons of genius and talent not to
do something else.   But even so, the examination, rightly
conducted, discovers more than a sufficient dose of nobility.
For the novel appeal is not, after all, to a mere blind animal
thirst for something that will pass and kill time, for something that will drug or flutter or amuse.   Beyond and
above these things there is something else.   The very
central cause and essence of it—most definitely and most
keenly felt by nobler spirits and cultivated intelligences,
but also dimly and unconsciously animating very ordinary
people—is the human delight in humanity—the pleasure
of seeing the men and women of long past ages living,
acting, and speaking as they might have done, those of
the present living, acting, speaking as they do—but in each
case with the portrayal not as a mere copy of particulars,
but influenced with that spirit of the universal which is the
secret and the charm of art.   It is because the novels of
these years recognised and provided this pleasure in a
greater degree than those of the former period (except the
productions of a few masters) that they deserve the higher
position which has been here assigned them.   If the novels
of any period, before or since or to come, have deserved,
may or shall deserve, a lower place—it is, and will be,
because of their comparative or positive neglect of the
combination of these conditions.   Perhaps it is not easy
to see what new country there is for the novel to conquer.
But, as with other kinds of literature, there is practically
no limit to its powers of working its actual domains.   In
the finest of its already existing examples it hardly
yields in accomplishment even to poetry; in that great

secondary (if secondary) office of all Art—to redress the apparent injustice, and console for the apparent unkindness, of Nature—to serve as rest and refreshment between those exactions of life which, though neither unjust nor unkind, are burdensome, it has no equal among all the kinds of Art itself.

INDEX

LETCHWORTH
THE TEMPLE PRESS
PRINTERS